Andrew Linn

Cambridge 1994

Introducing Phonology

Peter Hawkins

London

First published in 1984 by
Hutchinson & Co. (Publishers) Ltd

Reprinted in 1992 by
Routledge
11 New Fetter Lane, London EC4P 4EE

© Peter Hawkins 1984

Set in Times Roman

Printed and bound in Great Britain by
Biddles Ltd, Guildford and King's Lynn

British Library Cataloguing in Publication Data

Hawkins, Peter
 Introducing phonology.
 1. English language—Phonology
 I. Title
 421'.5   PE1133

Library of Congress Cataloging in Publication Data

Hawkins, Peter
 Introducing phonology.
 Bibliography: p.
 Includes index
 1. Grammar, Comparative and general—Phonology.
 2. English language—Phonology. I. Title.
 P217.H34   1984   414   84–3826

ISBN 0–415–08397–4

Contents

Preface

Phonology is the study of sound patterns in language. It stands alongside syntax, morphology, and semantics as one of the major branches of linguistics. While closely linked to phonetics, it emphasizes the *patterns* of sounds to be found in any particular language (and in languages generally), and the *relationships* between those sounds, rather than the *description* of the sounds in articulatory or auditory terms (which is the subject-matter of phonetics). Phonology is also a major component of several 'applied' fields such as variation between (and within) speakers of the same language ('dialects'), historical change, children's learning of their first language ('language acquisition'), and the teaching and learning of foreign languages.

Phonology is itself divided into two major components; *segmental* phonology, which is concerned with individual sounds (i.e. 'segments' of speech) and their patterns, and *suprasegmental* (or *non*-segmental, as it is sometimes called) phonology whose domain is the larger units of connected speech: words, phrases and sentences. The plan of this book is organized accordingly. Chapters 1 to 5 are concerned with segmental phonology; Chapters 6 and 7 discuss suprasegmental aspects, including stress, rhythm and intonation. The last three chapters are devoted to different fields of 'applied' phonology: Chapter 8 to dialects; Chapter 9 to historical change, i.e. the sound changes which take place within a language over a period of time; and Chapter 10 to language acquisition, with a focus on both 'normal' and 'delayed', or abnormal, development – the latter field being one which is now rapidly establishing itself, under the title of 'clinical phonology'. The last three chapters are included not just because they discuss practical and applied aspects of phonology, but also because these areas provide much of the raw material which informs (or should inform) theoretical phonology.

The book is intended as an introductory course for first or second year university students or the equivalent. It is not, however, intended for those who have done no phonetics at all. Readers should be at least familiar with the basic terms of articulatory phonetics – terms such as *bilabial, fricative, lateral, voiceless, aspirated,* etc. – and with the *symbols* which denote these classes of sounds (for example, [k g ŋ x] as instances of the category *velar,* etc.). As there are already a number of good introductory textbooks available I decided that it would not be advisable to include chapters on articulatory phonetics, even in an introductory text. I have, however, included a *glossary* of basic terms for reference purposes, and some exercises for practising the notation used in this book for the transcription of English.

Each chapter includes a number of exercises, which readers are recommended to work through. In some cases the exercises have been incorporated within the chapter as an essential part of it: the exercise is followed by a 'discussion' section which uses the data as its raw material. The aim is to encourage readers to *do* the exercises – if they are grouped at the end of a chapter it is all too easy to ignore them!

Every author should declare his theoretical bias – particularly in linguistics which has seen, in recent years, a number of significant theoretical changes and the proliferation of various 'schools'. It is undeniable that the dominant model has been, until recently, the 'orthodox generative' phonology of the 1960s. While sympathetic towards this model, I have tried to avoid both its more dogmatic aspects and the excessive formalism it has given rise to. There is thus virtually nothing on such topics as rule ordering and the interrelationships between different phonological rules, topics which provoked endless, but essentially unproductive, theoretical argument during the 1970s. I have also avoided the excessively abstract analyses favoured by orthodox generative phonology, preferring instead a 'near-the-surface' approach which respects 'phonetic facts' (for discussion, see Chapter 5). I believe it is important to be guided not only by the phonetic data, but also by the views of ordinary native speakers of the language, as reflected where possible in their (linguistic) behaviour.

The first two chapters are (I hope) theoretically uncontroversial. Chapter 3 traces the development of distinctive features and Chapter 4 the concepts of neutralization and language universals, all of which are an accepted part of current phonology. In Chapter 5 I have faced up to the theoretical issues, looking first at the problems of 'classical' phonemics, then at the generative 'solution', and finally offering a critique of the generative view.

Theoretical phonology can (and, in my view, should) be concerned with the description and validation of the fundamental phonological processes of language – processes which are found over and over again in different languages and at different periods of time, and which often apply in several different fields, such as dialectal variation, language acquisition, etc. These phonological processes will be the main concern of the last two chapters, but they are introduced in several earlier chapters (including Chapters 2, 4 and 6), and they form what is perhaps the work's main theoretical 'theme'.

Examples and data in the book are taken from a variety of languages, but mainly from English for two reasons: first, because more linguistic/phonological analysis is available for English than for any other single language; and second, because the readership is aimed at native and non-native English speakers. In gathering data from other languages I have confined myself to languages of which I have first-hand experience or a very reliable source. Illustrations are thus mainly from European languages, which again are those likely to be most familiar to the readers themselves, who can thus verify the accuracy (or otherwise!) of the data.

I am indebted, in particular, to my students. Not only have they tried out most of the exercises, but their transcriptions (particularly the errors) have provided a valuable resource for observing 'native speaker intuitions', i.e. for establishing just how much a native speaker 'knows' (or does not know) of his language. I owe also a debt of gratitude to those who taught me phonetics and phonology at the University of Manchester and at University College London: in particular to Edward Carney, Professors Fry and Gimson, Messrs O'Connor and Arnold, and Dr John Wells.

Transcription symbols for English

Given below is the notation used in this book to transcribe the phonemes of English.

The transcription is based on the standard accent of English known as Received Pronunciation (RP). As a notation it will therefore be more appropriate for English (as opposed to Scottish or Irish) accents, and for RP-related accents in other parts of the English-speaking world. For Scottish, Irish and American accents, some modifications will be necessary; for example most of them would not require /iə, eə, uə/, and for most American accents the vowel of *pot* would be /ɑ/ rather than /ɒ/. Differences between the various accents of English are discussed in Chapter 8.

Apart from exceptions just mentioned (/iə, eə, uə, ɒ/), the phonemes in the list below are the 'basic' phonemes which will be recognized by virtually all speakers of English – they are in a sense, the 'universal' phonemes of English.

The notation we use corresponds very closely to that of Ladefoged (1975). It differs in minor details from other popular notations such as:

1   the one used by Gimson in his *Introduction to the Pronunciation of English* (3rd edn 1980)* and in the *English Pronouncing Dictionary* from the 14th Edition (1977) onwards;
2   the notation used by J. Windsor Lewis in his *Concise Pronouncing Dictionary* (1972) and in the *Oxford Advanced Learner's Dictionary* from the 3rd Edition (1974) onwards;
3   the notation of Longman's *Dictionary of Contemporary English*.

---

*Full references quoted in the text are contained in the Bibliography beginning on p. 309.

Vowels

1   *Simple*

/ɪ/	pit		/ʌ/	putt
/e/	pet		/ɒ/	pot
/æ/	pat		/ʊ/	put
			/ə/	potato

2   *Long vowels and diphthongs*

/i/	beat		/iə/	beer
/eɪ/	bait		/eə/	bear
/aɪ/	bite		/uə/	tour
/ɔɪ/	boy			
/u/	boot		/ɜ/	Bert
/oʊ/	boat		/ɔ/	bought
/aʊ/	bout		/ɑ/	bart

Consonants

Plosives	/p/	pin	Fricatives	/f/	fin
	/b/	bin		/v/	vine
	/t/	tin		/θ/	thin
	/d/	din		/ð/	then
	/k/	kin		/s/	sin
	/g/	gain		/z/	zinc
				/ʃ/	shin
Affricates	/ʧ/	chin		/ʒ/	measure /'meʒə/
	/ʤ/	gin			
Nasals	/m/	ram	Approximants	/l/	lime
	/n/	ran		/r/	rhyme
	/ŋ/	rang		/j/	yet
				/w/	wet
				/h/	hen

Reading and transcription practice

Exercise 1

Read the following texts, given in the notation used in this book.

/wʌn mɔnɪŋ ə bæŋk mænədʒə ɒn ɪz weɪ tə wɜk ɪn nju jɔks wɔl
strit wəz stændɪŋ niə ði oʊpən dɔz əv ðə sʌbweɪ kærɪdʒ. sʌdn̩li ə
kɜli heəd jʌŋ mæn dʒʌmpt ɪntə ðə kærɪdʒ, brʌʃt əgenst ɪm, ənd
lept aʊt əgen. ðə bæŋkər ɪnstɪŋktɪvli felt fər ɪz wɒlət ænd,
faɪndɪŋ ɪt mɪsɪŋ, hi rɪtʃt aʊt ən græbd ðə jʌŋ mæn baɪ ɪz koʊt
kɒlə. ðə sʌbweɪ dɔz kloʊzd wɪð ðeə rʌbər edʒəz raʊnd ðə
mænədʒəz ɑmz bʌt i held ɒn ivən wen ðə kærɪdʒ stɑtəd muvɪŋ,
ən i drægd ði ʌðə mæn sevrəl fit əlɒŋ ðə steɪʃn̩ plætfɔm. faɪnəli
ðə kɒlə tɔr ɒf, livɪŋ hɪm wɪð ə fju ɪntʃəz əv tætəd klɒθ ɪn ɪz
hænd. stɪl æŋgri, hi mɑtʃt ɪntu ɪz ɒfɪs. ðə foʊn ræŋ. ɪt wəz ɪz
waɪf. baɪ ðə weɪ, diə, ʃi sed, dɪd jə noʊ jə left jɔ wɒlət ət hoʊm./

Exercise 2

Transcribe the following into the notation given. Begin and end with
a slant line to denote 'phonemic transcription'.

I take it you already know
Of though and bough and cough and dough?
Others may stumble, but not you
On hiccough, thorough, rough and through
Well done! And now you wish, perhaps,
To learn of less familiar traps?
Beware of heard, a dreadful word
That looks like beard and sounds like bird,
And dead: it's said like bed, not bead.
For goodness sake don't call it 'deed'!
Watch out for meat and great and threat,
(They rhyme with suite and straight and debt);
A moth is not as 'moth' in mother,
Nor both in bother, broth in brother.
And here is not a match for there,
Nor dear and fear for bear and pear,
And then there's dose and rose and lose –
Just look these up – and goose and choose.

And cork and work, and card and ward,
And font and front and word and sword,
And do and go, and thwart and cart,
Come, come I've hardly made a start!
A dreadful language? Man alive,
I'd mastered it when I was five!

1 Phonemic and phonetic

Phoneme, allophone

When we talk about the sounds of a language, the term 'sound' can be interpreted in two rather different ways. In the first place, we can say that [p] and [b] are two different sounds in English, and we can illustrate this by showing how they contrast with each other to make a difference of meaning in a large number of pairs, such as *pit* vs *bit*, *rip* vs *rib*, etc. But on the other hand, if we listen carefully to the [k] of *key* and compare it with the [k] of *car*, or if we compare the vowel of *chew* with the vowel of *coo*, we can hear that the two sounds are not the same; the [k] of *key* is more 'fronted' ('palatalized') in its articulation and has a higher pitch, while the [k] of *car* is articulated further back and has a lower pitch. Similarly, the vowel [u] is fronted when it follows the palato-alveolar [ʧ], but retracted after the velar [k]. In each case we have two different 'sounds', one fronted and the other retracted. Yet it is clear that this sense of 'sound' differs from the first sense, for we could also say that fronted and retracted [k] are both variants of the one 'sound' k (and likewise, both forms of [u] are variants of the 'same' vowel). To avoid this ambiguity, the linguist uses two separate terms: *phoneme* is used to mean 'sound' in the former (i.e. the contrastive) sense, and *allophone* is used for sounds which are variants of a phoneme: sounds which differ, but which do not contrast. We would thus say that fronted [k] and retracted [k] are *allophones* (i.e. variants) of the *phoneme* k, and to make the distinction quite clear in writing, we enclose allophones in square brackets, [ ], and phonemes in slants, / /. Using this notation we can now write [k̟] (fronted k) and [k̠] (retracted k) as allophones of /k/.

Further examples of phonemes/allophones are readily available.

1   The [n] of *tenth* differs from the [n] of *ten*; in *tenth* the sound is dental, [n̪], while in *ten* it is the 'ordinary' English alveolar [n] (compare the two sounds by looking into a mirror as you pronounce

them). [n̪] and [n] are allophones of the phoneme /n/; the dental allophone is found whenever another dental ([θ, ð]) immediately follows.

2   The [l] of *lip* differs, in many accents, from the [l] of *pill*. In *pill*, the [l] is accompanied by a raising of the back of the tongue: it is *velarized*. This sound, known as 'dark l', and written [ɫ], differs from the 'clear l' of *lip*, usually written simply as [l]. These two sounds are allophones of the phoneme /l/. There is a corresponding difference of distribution: [l] occurs *before* a vowel, [ɫ] *after* one.

3   The [s] of *seep* and the [s] of *soup* are not identical. The phoneme /s/ has a plain, unrounded allophone, [s], in *seep*, and a rounded, or *labialized*, allophone [s̫] in *soup*. As we might expect, the rounded allophone is used when a rounded vowel follows, and the unrounded allophone elsewhere.

Contrastive function

The native speaker[1]* is quite readily aware of the phonemes of his language but much less aware of the allophones: it is possible, in fact, that he will not hear the difference between two allophones like [k̟] and [k̠] even when a distinction is pointed out; a certain amount of ear-training may be needed. The reason is that the phonemes have an important function in the language: they differentiate words like *pit* and *bit* from each other, and to be able to hear and produce phonemic differences is part of what it means to be a competent speaker of the language. Allophones, on the other hand, have no such function: they usually occur in different positions in the word (i.e. in different *environments*) and hence cannot contrast with each other, nor be used to make meaningful distinctions.

For example, as noted above [ɫ] ('dark l') occurs *following* a vowel as in *pill*, *cold*, *school*, but is not found before a vowel, whereas [l] ('clear l') only occurs *before* a vowel, as in *lip*, *late*, *like*. These two sounds therefore cannot contrast with each other in the way that /l/ contrasts with /r/ in *lip* vs *rip* or *lake* vs *rake*; there are no pairs of words which differ only in that one has [l], the other [ɫ].

Predictability

The difference between phoneme and allophone can be seen in terms

---

* Superior figures refer to the Notes beginning on p. 301.

of predictability. Allophones are predictable in that we can say: in environment P we find allophone A; in environment Q, allophone B; in environment R, allophone C, etc. Thus, given the sequence -Vl# or -VlC, where V stands for (any) vowel, C for (any) consonant, and # for word-boundary, we can predict that the allophone of /l/ occurring here will be [ɫ] and not [l].

Phonemic contrasts are not predictable in this way. Given the environment /–ip/, we have a choice between /p/ (*peep*) vs /l, w, s/, etc. From the phonetic environment there is no way of predicting which phoneme will occur. We shall see below that the predictability of the allophones can be expressed more formally by means of rules.

Most of the examples given so far have involved consonants. A well-known case of allophonic variation in vowels is the length difference, which is determined by the type of consonant following. Vowels are shorter in duration before voiceless consonants such as p, t, k, s, f, and longer before voiced sounds, such as b, d, g, z, v. The vowel of *lock* is shorter than that of *log*, and the vowel of *rice* shorter than that of *rise*. Using the length mark [ː], we can show two allophones for each vowel: [ɒ, aɪ], short, and [ɒː, aɪː], long (for details of relative durations, cf. Umeda and Coker (1975: 552)). This example illustrates the points we made above; first, that the native speaker is not normally aware of allophonic differences (it requires careful listening to detect the difference between the shorter vowel of *lock* and the longer vowel of *log*), and second, that the allophones are predictable in terms of their phonetic environment: short before voiceless sounds, long before voiced ones.

Perception of allophones

We are, as noted, not normally aware of allophonic variation in our own language; in listening to or learning another language, however, we may be able to perceive allophones which native speakers of that language are themselves unaware of, particularly if the allophones correspond to a *phonemic* distinction in our own language. An example is the relationship between voiced plosives ([b, d, g]) and voiced fricatives ([β, ð, ɣ]) in English and Spanish respectively. In Spanish there are three pairs of allophones, [b, β], [d, ð] and [g, ɣ], distributed as illustrated:

[b]	[beso]	'kiss'	[β]	[aβa]	'bean'
	[bala]	'ball'		[deβer]	'owe'
	[bomba]	'bomb'			

[d]	[dama]	'lady'	[ð]	[boða]	'wedding'
	[duro]	'hard'		[toðo]	'all'
	[donde]	'where'		[θjuðað]	'city'
[g]	[gato]	'cat'	[ɣ]	[aɣosto]	'August'
	[gaŋga]	'bargain'		[laɣo]	'lake'
	[grande]	'big'			

For a Spaniard, [b] and [β] are 'the same sound', as are [d] and [ð], [g] and [ɣ]; each pair are allophones of a single phoneme, the distribution being determined by the phonetic environment, namely:

> *plosives* occur word-initially and after nasals (and laterals)
> *fricatives* occur between vowels ('intervocalic') and (for [ð] only) finally

The English speaker has little difficulty in distinguishing [d] and [ð] since the difference is *phonemic* in English: compare *breathe* and *breed*, *riding* and *writhing*. Similarly, [b, β] are readily distinguished, since although [β] is not an English sound, it is sufficiently similar to [v] to be heard as such; and /b, v/ is a phonemic distinction in English, like /d ð/. But [g, ɣ] are different; English has no /ɣ/, nor anything acoustically similar to it. In fact, [ɣ] is sometimes an allophone of /g/ in English: it is often found as a 'reduced' or casual pronunciation of /g/ between vowels, as in *again*, *Agatha*, *eagle*. Since [g, ɣ] are allophones in English as well as in Spanish, the perceptions of speakers in both languages tend to be similar: they are not normally aware of a difference.

In German, the 'ch' sound has two allophones; a velar fricative [x] after back vowels, and a palatal fricative [ç] after front vowels. English speakers are more aware of this difference than Germans, because they associate [x] with k-like sounds (i.e. with other velars), and [ç] with the acoustically similar [ʃ], which is a different phoneme. Germans perceive [x, ç] as 'the same' sound, since they constitute a single phoneme.

Often, therefore, we become aware of allophonic variation in our own language as a result of observations from speakers of other languages. Sapir, for example, found that his Haida (an American-Indian language) informants could readily distinguish the [tʰ] of English *top* from the unaspirated [t] of *stop*, a difference noted only with difficulty by English speakers themselves. The reason is that, in Haida, [st–] contrasts phonemically with [stʰ–], i.e. the sound-difference is used to make differences of meaning. On the other hand these informants could hardly distinguish [t] from [d] (as in *steer* and *dear*), because Haida has no voiced–voiceless contrast (Sapir 1970 (1921): 55).

Similarly, Jones (1950: 37) reports the case of the speaker of Syriac, who noticed a difference between the [tʰ] of English *ten* and the [t] of *letter*, a difference which is phonemic in Syriac but only allophonic in English. In Kikuyu, [d ð θ] are all allophones of one phoneme. When a writing system (an *orthography*) was provided for that language, it was devised by English speakers, who, hearing a difference between [d] and [θ, ð], allocated two separate symbols, 'd' for [d] and 'th' for [θ, ð]. They did not realize that, as far as the Kikuyu is concerned, all three are for him the 'same' sound, for which a single symbol would be appropriate.

The phonetician is trained to listen carefully for all possible differences of sound regardless of the particular language they occur in. But even phoneticians are native speakers of some language, and may be more familiar with, say, European languages in general than with any others. This tends to colour their interpretation of the sounds they hear in unfamiliar languages, and acts as a bias, however unconscious. As Bloomfield says, the phonetician's equipment is 'personal and accidental: he hears those features which are discriminated in the languages he has observed' (1933: 84). For this reason, the phonetician does not rely too heavily on his own phonetic transcription of what he hears: he consults native speakers of the language as early as possible, to ascertain the distinctions they are readily aware of, and to make use of their intuitions and insights for interpreting the data.

Methods of phonemic analysis

It is obviously important to have some means of determining, for an unfamiliar language, which differences of sound are phonemic and which are allophonic. A number of principles have been established for ascertaining the phonemic structure of a language, and to illustrate how these work we can take some hypothetical examples involving the sounds [s] and [z]. Let us assume that a field-worker has collected a list of words, with their meanings, in a hitherto unfamiliar language, X. This language contains the following words:

[s]	[z]
[sak]	[zapi]

[setu]	[zen]
[suni]	[zudok]

It has been established that each word has a different meaning, and the sounds have been transcribed according to the IPA conventions: thus [s] represents a voiceless (and [z] a voiced) alveolar fricative. This is a *phonetic* transcription: we do not yet know whether the [s] and [z] are contrastive in this language, or whether they are merely variants of one phoneme. Hence square brackets are used, and the notation gives as much detail as possible. Since we do not know yet whether [s] and [z] are allophones or phonemes, we must call them simply *phones*. A phone is hence 'a sound whose status in the language is hitherto undetermined'.[2]

From this small set of words we cannot definitely decide whether [s] and [z] are separate phonemes, but we can hazard a guess: both sounds appear before the vowel [e] (setu, zen), before [a] (sak, zapi), and before [u] (suni, zudok); both sounds occur at the beginning of the word (*word-initially*, to use the technical term). Since they occur in similar environments like this, it is most probable that they are contrastive, and hence separate phonemes. If they were allophones, we would have to find differences in their environments, which in this case would be difficult. We might propose that [z] occurs only in one-syllable words (as in *zen*) and [s] only in polysyllabic words (for example, *setu*) but this is contradicted immediately by the examples *zapi* and *sak*. On the existing evidence, therefore, [s] and [z] are separate phonemes.

To strengthen this conclusion, we might be lucky enough to find what is called a 'minimal pair': two words with different meanings which differ *only* in that one word has [s], the other [z], such as [sed] vs [zed]. This would be strong evidence that [s] and [z] are contrastive in this language and hence can be regarded as two phonemes, /s/ and /z/. Minimal pairs are useful for establishing quickly and simply the phonemes of a language; for English, the frame /–ɪp/ immediately gives us /p, t, k, d, s, z, ʃ, l, n, r, h, w/ as separate phonemes. But not all languages afford examples of minimal pairs as readily as English.

Let us now suppose that in another unfamiliar language, Y, the following set of words occurs:

[s]	[z]
[sato]	[bazo]
[sip]	[okezi]

[nis]   [lozak]
[pos]   [retizen]

From this small amount of data, it appears that the two sounds occur in different environments: [s] is found word-initially (*sato*, *sip*) and word-finally (*nis*, *pos*), while [z] occurs between vowels. This distribution of [s] and [z] makes good phonetic sense, for we find the voiced sound between other voiced sounds (vowels), while voiceless [s] is either preceded or followed by silence, i.e. by a state of voicelessness.

The data suggests, then that [s] and [z] here are not separate phonemes: they are allophones of one phoneme, and we could expect that further data would show, analogously, that [s] is found only in a 'voiceless' environment (for example, before a voiceless consonant) and [z] only in a 'voiced' one. The *distributions* of [s] and [z] are different; and they complement each other, for [z] is not found in [s]-type environments, nor [s] in [z]-type. When this happens, the two sounds are said to be in *complementary distribution*. In English [l] and [ł] are in complementary distribution, because their environments are always different.

Since [s] and [z] are allophones of one phoneme in this language, we shall most probably find that native speakers of it are not normally aware of a difference between these two sounds, and that the difference would only be appreciated with difficulty, if at all. This would come as a surprise to native speakers of English, who find it hard to imagine that anyone could fail to hear the difference between [s] and [z]. It is a good illustration of the fact that, where languages are concerned, everything is relative. English speakers hear the difference because it has an important function in the language, distinguishing many pairs of words. Speakers of language Y do not hear the difference because it is of no importance in the communication process; the allophones are entirely predictable according to the phonetic environment, and thus carry no useful information.

Symbols

If [s] and [z] are allophones of one phoneme, what symbol are we to use for the phoneme? Is it to be represented as /s/, or as /z/? Clearly, either symbol could be used: the choice is arbitrary. But whichever we choose, we must be consistent; we shall transcribe *all* the words above with the same symbol. If we choose /s/, then [bazo] and [okezi] will be phonemically transcribed as /baso/ and /okesi/. This seems wrong to us as speakers of English, but it will be entirely in accord with the feelings of a native speaker of Y, for whom [s] and [z] are 'the same sound'. If *sato* is transcribed with /s/, he will want to use /s/ for *bazo* and *okezi* as well, just as in English we are happy to use the same symbol, /l/ for both the [l] of *leap* and the [ł] of *peel*; cf. also the Kikuyu example, mentioned above.

Native speaker knowledge

Let us digress for a moment to consider an important theoretical point.

The fact that this analysis of [s] and [z] accounts for the intuitions of the native speaker is the real reason why we adopt it, for one of the aims of a grammar is to explain and take account of native speaker feelings about his language, as far as this is possible, and this applies to the phonological part of the grammar just as much as to the area of syntax. That [s] and [z] are in complementary distribution is a fact about the language, but it would be of little interest in itself and this is not the real reason why we treat these two sounds as one phoneme; the real reason is that the native speaker *feels* they are one phoneme. This shift of emphasis parallels, to some extent, changes which have taken place in linguistic theory, for the 'structuralist' model of languages which flourished from the 1930s to the 1950s emphasized the 'facts about the language' approach and regarded the phoneme as something to be justified in terms of complementary distribution and the other principles we are presenting in this chapter. Thus the fact that [s] and [z] were similar phonetically and were found to be in complementary distribution would have been sufficient justification, for the structuralists, to treat them as one phoneme.

The 'generative' model of language, which appeared during the 1960s, put greater emphasis on the need for a linguistic analysis to have explanatory power, that is, to explain adequately what the native speaker intuitively 'knows' about his language. Hence the phonemes of a language are 'discovered' in consultation with native speakers and not by the rigid application of the methods outlined here.[3] These methods are still useful, however, because they point to the reasons why the native speaker feels as he does; thus, [s] and [z] are felt to be one phoneme because their distribution is complementary, and because they are never used to make meaningful contrasts in the language.

Realization rules

To return to the main argument: we showed above that the choice of symbol for the s/z phoneme was partly arbitrary; we could write it either as /s/ or as /z/. Alternatively, we could invent a new symbol, such as /s̲/, or we could take a completely abstract symbol like the number /10/. All we would need is some specification to state that phoneme number 10 is pronounced [s] in some environments and [z] in others, but – and this is our next major observation – such a specification is needed anyway, *whatever* symbol we choose. For even if we represent the phoneme.as /s/, we still need to know that it is pronounced [s] in some environments and [z] in others, if we are to have a full account of the language.

These specifications, then, will be our guide as to how exactly each phoneme in the language is actually pronounced. We shall call them *realization rules*,[4] because they describe how each phoneme is actually realized as physical sound. For the s/z phoneme, which we shall arbitrarily write as /s/ rather than as /s̲/, /10/, etc., we shall need a realization rule something like the following:

$$/s/ \rightarrow [s] \quad \text{word-initially, word-finally}$$
$$\rightarrow [z] \quad \text{between vowels}$$

The arrow here means 'is realized as', 'is pronounced as'. In recent years various notations have been developed for phonological rules of this kind; using some of the conventions that have been widely adopted, we could express the above rules as:

$$/s/ \rightarrow [s] \quad /\# \_\_, \_\_ \#$$
$$[z] \quad /V \_\_ V$$

The slant line here separates the operation of the rule (to the left of it) from the environment (to the right), and # represents a word boundary. The dash (__) represents the position of the sound itself in relation to its environment, so # __ means 'word-initially', V __ V means 'between two vowels', etc. Hence this rule can be read as: /s/ is pronounced [s] in two environments: first, immediately *after* a word-boundary (# __); and second, immediately *before* one (__ #). It is pronounced [z] when it occurs *between vowels* (V __ V).

Symbol values

Notice how the symbol *s* has two quite different 'values'; in square brackets it gives a fairly precise description of a physical sound: a voiceless alveolar fricative. In slant brackets it is much less precise: it stands for more than one sound, and we therefore cannot know how this /s/ is actually *pronounced* until we have looked at the realization rule. This means that if one is given a *phonemic* transcription of words or sentences in an unfamiliar language, they cannot be read aloud because there is no way of knowing what value each phoneme has in each environment. /s/ could be pronounced [s], but it might equally be [z], or [ʃ], or [ʂ], etc. Reading aloud can only be done from a *phonetic* transcription, or alternatively from a phonemic one with the aid of the realization rules, which amounts to the same thing. This is a point worth making, because often a language may be written with an alphabetic notation in which each symbol corresponds to one phoneme; one is tempted to believe that, even though the language is unfamiliar, the words can be pronounced simply by reading what is written. Only a native speaker of the language can do that, because he knows the realization rules intuitively. A foreigner requires the realization rules as well as the phonemic transcription.

A realization rule for English vowel length might be written as follows:

$$/V/ \rightarrow [V] \quad / \underline{\quad} \quad [- \text{ voice}]$$

$$[V{:}] \quad / \underline{\quad} \quad \left\{ \begin{array}{c} [+ \text{ voice}] \\ \# \end{array} \right\}$$

The first part of the rule means: a vowel (any vowel) is pronounced (relatively) short when followed by a *voiceless* ([− voice]) sound; the second part, that vowels are relatively long when preceding *either* a voiced sound *or* a word-boundary. The curly brackets denote the 'either–or' relationship.

Rules like this are only expressing, by a convenient notation, something that can equally be stated less formally. The advantage of the formal statement is a gain in economy; there may also be gains in precision, because sometimes facts are brought to light which might not have been noticed from the less formal statement alone.

Free variation

The data we have used so far has illustrated two possibilities: that [s] and [z] are separate phonemes (when their distribution is *contrastive*), and that [s] and [z] are allophones of one phoneme (when their distribution is *complementary*). There is, however, a third possibility; namely, that the sounds [s] and [z] both occur in the language but speakers are inconsistent in the way they use them. Let us suppose that the language has the words

     [silap]   [snud]   [dislik]   [ras]

but we find variants of these words: [zilap] has the same meaning as [silap]; [znud] occurs, but is regarded as 'the same word' as [snud], etc. Clearly [s] and [z] cannot be contrastive phonemes, but nor are they allophones in the usual sense, for their distribution is parallel. We must then take them as *free variants* of a single phoneme, but since the situation seems somewhat unusual we would take some trouble to find the *reason* for the variation: it is most unlikely that variation of this kind could be completely 'free', i.e. completely arbitrary. If the variation occurs *between* speakers, then we shall try to explain it on the basis of *dialect*: dialects can be regional (for example, speakers from town X might use [s], those from city Y might use [z]) or social (when usage will be defined according to social class, level of education, etc.). If the variation is found *within* individual speakers, then the language situation must be studied more closely: it could be that [z] is a 'prestige' form which the speaker uses when he is consciously 'monitoring' what he says, while [s] is the pronunciation found in casual or less formal speech. If all other explanations fail then we have truly 'free' variation, but this label is, in a sense, an admission that the critical factors at work have not yet been explained.

It is interesting to compare speakers' reactions to each of the three possibilities discussed so far.

1   If [s] and [z] are separate phonemes, the native speaker has no difficulty in perceiving the difference.
2   If they are allophones of one phoneme, it is most probable that he/she fails to perceive the difference until asked to listen carefully.
3   If they are 'free variants', two possibilities arise:
    a   The difference is clearly perceived ('that speaker said [zilap]

and [znud]: you can tell he comes from the North. We say [silap] and [snud] down here').

b   The speaker is aware of a difference, but cannot pinpoint it ('I can tell he comes from another part of the country; it's something about his speech').

In the latter case, the speaker may become aware of the difference once it is pointed out.

Phonetic similarity

We have indicated so far that the analysis of the sounds of a language is based on such notions as *parallel* (contrastive) *distribution*, *complementary distribution*, *minimal pairs* and *free variation*. To these we must add two more concepts, those of *phonetic similarity* and *phonemic pattern*.

To illustrate phonetic similarity we can use the data from the second imaginary language, Y, where we found [s] and [z] to be allophones of one phoneme. We came to this decision because their distribution seemed to be complementary: [s] in a voiceless environment, [z] in a voiced one. But before we can justifiably regard them as one phoneme, we must be sure that they have some similarity – that they share some features in common. In this particular case the answer is obvious: we know that [s] and [z] are similar, and to support our view we can point to the shared features: both are alveolar, both are fricative – i.e. they share the critical features of both *place* and *manner* of articulation. But there are cases where the similarity is not so great, and there is one example from English which shows how the procedures outlined so far could easily be abused: this is the case of [h] and [ŋ].

[h] in English is defective in its distribution: it is only found initially in a syllable, and apart from a few words like *ahead*, *behave*, it is normally initial in the *word* as well. [ŋ] is also defective in distribution: it occurs only finally (*sing* /sɪŋ/) or before the other velar sounds /k/ and /g/ (*sink* /sɪŋk/, *finger* /fɪŋgə(r)/). It can occur between vowels only if there is a morpheme[5] boundary (for example, *sing-er* /sɪŋə(r)/). One could argue that [ŋ] and [h] both occur between vowels, but it seems that [h] when intervocalic always follows an *unstressed* vowel (*ahead*, *behave*, etc.) while [ŋ] intervocalically always follows a *stressed* one (*ringer*, *singing*, etc.). Hence, not only are there no minimal pairs to contrast [h] and [ŋ], but there isn't even the *possibility* of such a pair. The two sounds appear to be truly in

complementary distribution and could, according to our procedures, be regarded as one phoneme. To follow this argument to its rather absurd conclusion: we could invent the symbol /ɧ/ to represent this phoneme, and transcribe *head* as /ɧed/, *bang* as /bæɧ/, etc. *Hung*, which has both sounds, will be transcribed as /ɧʌɧ/. The realization rules would present no difficulty: we could have

$$/ɧ/ \rightarrow [h] \ / \ \# \ \_\_ , \ \breve{V} \ \_\_ \ V \text{ (where V represents an unstressed vowel)}$$

$$[ŋ] \ / \ \_\_ \ \#, \ \_\_ \begin{Bmatrix} k \\ g \end{Bmatrix}, \ 'V \ \_\_ \ V \text{ (where 'V represents a stressed vowel)}$$

While many linguists have discussed the possibility, it would be unlikely for anyone, linguist or non-linguist alike, to accept an analysis which identifies [h] with [ŋ]. We could justify our rejection on the grounds that the two sounds differ both in *place* of articulation ([h] is usually regarded as 'glottal'; [ŋ] is velar) and in *manner* ([h] is fricative; [ŋ] is a nasal), as well as in *voicing* ([h] is voiceless; [ŋ] is voiced). The sounds have nothing in common except that they are both consonants, and this is too general a feature to be sufficient. So we reject the association of [h] and [ŋ] on the grounds of (lack of) phonetic similarity.

Criteria for 'similarity'

This answer to the problem of [h] and [ŋ] is not entirely satisfactory, for there is no obvious criterion for deciding whether two sounds are sufficiently 'similar' or not; how similar must they be, in order to qualify as a single phoneme? Alternatively, how different must they be before we say, 'sounds x and y cannot possibly be variants of one phoneme'? There is no straight answer to these questions, and we can find examples from various languages to show, first, that phones which on the face of it seem quite dissimilar are in fact members of one phoneme, and are felt by native speakers to be (variants of) 'a single sound'; and second, that phones which seem remarkably *similar* can nevertheless be regarded by the native speaker as separate phonemes. To take the latter possibility first, we can look at English plosives in final position. Of three possible pronunciations, [kæpʰ], [kæpº] and [kæbº], the bilabial plosive of the first is voiceless, released, and aspirated; that of the second is voiceless and unreleased, while that of the third is voiced and unreleased (the raised circle denotes an unreleased consonant). The voicing of the latter, however, may manifest itself only as a lengthening of the preceding vowel, the plosive itself being voiceless and hence identical to [p°]. Hence, the difference between [pʰ] and [p°] is greater, phonetically, than that between [p°] and [b°], yet the native speaker associates the former pair as variants of /p/ (/kæp/, *cap*), but distinguishes the latter pair as two phonemes /p/ vs /b/ (*cap* vs *cab*). Sometimes, therefore, a fine phonetic difference can have critical significance and serve to distinguish two phonemes, while a bigger phonetic difference (as between [pʰ] and [p°]) can be ignored as irrelevant.

The other possibility, which is more central to our argument, can be illustrated by a well-known example from Japanese, where a single phoneme has as its variants (allophones) a bilabial fricative [ɸ], a palatal fricative [ç], and a glottal fricative [h]. The distribution of these three phones is complementary: [ɸ] occurs before /u/, as in [ɸuku] 'luck', [ç] before /i/, as in [çito] 'man', and [h] before /e, a, o/, for example [hana] 'nose' (cf. Jones 1950: 20). From an articulatory point of view these allophones range across the whole spectrum of *place* of articulation, from bilabial at the front to glottal at the back. How can such dissimilar phones be members of a single phoneme?

To understand what is happening here we must briefly examine speech as a communication process, and we shall see that phonetic similarity, like the discipline of phonetics itself, can be viewed from two perspectives, one concerning the speaker, the other the listener. Phonetics, the discipline, is divided into three branches, each corresponding to a different stage in the communication process. Articulatory phonetics studies the movements made by the speaker, and the resulting sounds are described in articulatory terminology such as *labio-dental*, *fricative*, *voiceless*, etc. Acoustic phonetics studies, by instrumental methods, the disturbances of air particles resulting from the speaker's articulations: it studies the transmission stage between speaker and listener. Auditory phonetics studies what the listener perceives: the impressions made by the sounds on the listener's receptive mechanisms, and his interpretation of what he hears. Auditory phonetics is a study of perception, and has connections with psychology in the same way as studies of visual perception have.[6]

Until recently, articulatory phonetics has been the dominating branch, and most descriptive work has been done in articulatory terms. Furthermore, there has appeared to be no need to alter the balance (in favour of auditory description) in any substantial way, since in most cases there is a one-to-one correspondence between what happens at the speaker's end (articulation) and what the listener is aware of (perception): a difference in articulation (such as plosive vs fricative) has a corresponding acoustic effect and is hence perceived as different by the listener. Conversely, whatever the hearer perceives as different, requires a difference of articulation on the part of the speaker: one cannot use the same articulation to make two different sounds.

There are occasions, however, when this one-to-one correspondence breaks down, for it is possible in some cases for different articulations to result in rather similar acoustic effects, which may be perceived as identical by the listener. The Japanese example quoted above is an illustration of this, for the three sounds [φ], [ç], and [h], although articulated at widely differing points, nevertheless produce acoustic effects which are reasonably similar. We are, therefore, justified in assuming phonetic similarity for these sounds, in spite of the articulatory differences. Phonetic similarity in this instance is based on the auditory effect, and not on the articulation; it is listener- rather than speaker-oriented.

Examples of the same kind can also be found in English. For instance, [ʔ] ('glottal stop', used commonly in English dialects as a pronunciation of /t/ both finally, as in *wait*, and medially, as in *water*) and [t] are treated by native speakers as allophones of one phoneme, /t/. In word-final position [ʔ] is in free variation with [t°] (i.e. an unreleased [t]) or with a double articulation [ʔt] in which closures are made simultaneously at the alveolum and at the glottis. It is often difficult to hear whether the /t/ of a word like *bit*, pronounced without a release, has been realized by [ʔ], [t°], or [ʔt] (cf. Roach 1974). The auditory effect of these three sounds is almost identical for English-speakers, yet in articulatory terms their description differs greatly: one is alveolar, the other glottal, two points of articulation which could scarcely be further apart, and which are, moreover, separated by an intervening plosive, the velar [k].

These examples illustrate the point that phonetic similarity should not be thought of in purely articulatory terms. Sounds may differ greatly in place or manner of articulation, and yet share certain auditory properties which justify regarding them as similar. The traditional dominance of speaker-oriented description in phonetics has tended to make us think that sounds can only be similar if their articulation is similar. This is in fact often true, but not always.

Phonetic similarity can be determined *either* on an auditory *or* on an articulatory basis.

We have still not arrived at an objective answer to the question 'how similar is similar?', posed above, but we have at least widened the basis of phonetic similarity. In many cases, of course, the allophones of a phoneme resemble each other on both counts, but there are, as we have seen, some instances where a one-to-one correspondence does not hold. Looking again at the case of [h] and [ŋ] in English, we can now see that these sounds are dissimilar both in articulation *and* in perception, and therefore have no basis at all for being treated as phonetically similar. This makes it very unlikely that they could be members of a single phoneme, but the strongest argument in favour of their separateness (apart from the intuition of native speakers) rests on the concept of phonemic pattern, to which we now turn.

Phonemic pattern

A phonemic analysis needs to take account of the overall pattern of sounds, and their structural relationships, in the language concerned: phonemes are not isolated, unrelated phenomena.

To illustrate the principle in operation, take the example of [tʰ] (as in *ten*) and [t] (as in *letter*). The aspirated/unaspirated distinction here can be extended to the other voiceless plosives /p, k/ in the same environments; aspirated [pʰ, kʰ] occur initially in a stressed syllable, unaspirated [p, k] occur intervocalically. Without the principle of phonemic pattern, we would be faced with a problem, for we can see that unaspirated [t] is in complementary distribution not only with [tʰ] but also with [pʰ] and [kʰ], since [t] is found only intervocalically whereas [pʰ, tʰ, kʰ] never occur in that position. Why then should we take [t] with [tʰ], rather than with [pʰ] or [kʰ]? And similarly, why should [p] be associated with [pʰ] rather than with [tʰ] or [kʰ]? The answer is, of course, that since we have aspirated and unaspirated variants of all three plosives we must pair them off, [pʰ] with [p], etc. The problem has been raised only for the sake of demonstrating that the principle of complementary distribution, taken by itself at face value, is not enough; the overall pattern of the sounds must be taken into account.

We shall see more critical examples of the usefulness of this principle later on: note, however, that [h] and [ŋ] are not only phonetically dissimilar, but also pattern differently. [h] behaves (in some respects) like other voiceless fricatives such as /f, θ, s/; it can be followed by any vowel or by /j/ (and by /w/ in some dialects);[7] whereas [ŋ] behaves like other nasals: compare *im-possible* with [m]; *in-tolerable* with [n]; *in-calculable* with [ŋ] (before the /k/); [ŋ] is strongly associated with [n] in particular (notice that *incalculable* can also be pronounced with [n]): indeed, the question of whether [ŋ] is a phoneme, or only an allophone of /n/, will be raised later (see below, p. 261).

The reader may feel, in view of the example of aspirated/unaspirated plosives above, that phonemic pattern is merely phonetic similarity under another guise, since we could argue just as plausibly that [p] goes with [pʰ], [t] with [tʰ], etc., on the basis of phonetic similarity. It is true that the two principles are closely linked, and it may even be possible to suggest that the question 'how similar is similar' is partly answered on the basis of overall patterning: sounds which pattern in the same way have a strong reason for being regarded as similar. The example of [h] and [ŋ] is sufficient to show us, however, that phonetic similarity and phonemic pattern are two separate concepts, for we can establish the former by referring only to the internal properties (the features) of the two sounds concerned, while for the latter we have to consider the sounds in their wider relationship.

To summarize the main points so far:

1   A particular phoneme in a language is not always pronounced in exactly the same way but has variants according to the environment in which the phoneme occurs. These variants are known as allophones. The native speaker is well aware of the phonemic contrasts in his language and can usually be quite easily taught an alphabetic notation for writing them, whether he is a speaker of an unwritten language or whether he speaks a language in which, as in English, the existing writing system does not correspond one-for-one with the phonemes of the language. (Phonemic transcription is usually one of the first procedures to be taught in linguistics courses, because it can be based on something the native speaker is already aware of.)

2   The phonemes of the language are related to the allophones by means of realization rules, which give a precise guide as to how the phoneme is actually pronounced in particular environments. To distinguish phonemes from allophones in writing, slant brackets are used for the former and square brackets for the latter. Symbols in *slant* brackets are only a rough and approximate guide to the

pronunciation, and the symbol itself has been chosen on grounds which are partly arbitrary. A phoneme symbolized as /s/ in a particular language might be pronounced [s], or [z], or [ʃ] or [ʂ], etc.; we shall not know which until we have 'been through' the realization rules.[8] Symbols in *square* brackets, on the other hand, represent a more detailed and precise denotation of an actual pronunciation, a physical sound. The square-bracket symbols have absolute values which are constant and are (or should be) known by phoneticians the world over, so that when we write [ʂ] we know that this 'means' a voiceless, retroflex alveolar fricative. Square brackets send us to the IPA chart and its conventions, or to the absolute vowel-values denoted by Jones's cardinal vowel scheme. In sum, *phonemics* (slant brackets) is concerned with relationships between contrasting sounds in a language. *Phonetics* (square brackets) is concerned with a more precise description of physical sounds, regardless of any particular language.

3   In studying the relationships between the phonemes and allophones in a language, we can be guided by the principles and procedures we have already outlined such as complementary distribution, free variation, and so on. But it must be appreciated that these principles are useful only in so far as they explain what the native speaker already knows intuitively, the latter being the goal of our descriptive grammar of the language.

Co-articulation

Why does a language have allophonic variation? Why aren't sounds 'the same' wherever they occur? Linguists have often been content just to mention the variations they observe at the phonetic level, without asking *why* they occur. And the reason for this reticence is that it may be difficult to know why particular allophones are restricted to particular environments. But it is sometimes possible to suggest reasons: for example, the different k's of *key* and *car* are conditioned by the kind of vowel which follows them. The fronted [k̟] of *key* anticipates the front vowel /i/, and the [k̠] of *car* anticipates the back vowel /ɑ/. Similarly, *tenth* has a dental [n̪] because the following consonant is also dental, whereas the [n] of *ten* retains its 'ordinary' alveolar position. The rounded [s̫] of *soup* and *soot* is explained by the roundedness of the following vowels, /u/ and /ω/; and so on.

Variation of this kind has long been recognized, and has gone under various names. In the 1930s Harold Palmer wrote of 'contactual phonemes' (today we would call them contactual allophones); Ladefoged at one time used the term *intrinsic* allophones (1971); but the present more generally accepted term for this kind of variation is *co-articulation* (Daniloff *et al.* 1973).[9] Co-articulation can be seen as a facilitating device, from both the speaker's and the listener's point of view. From the speaker's (i.e. the articulatory) aspect, it is 'easier' to pronounce a sequence of sounds if some of the sounds are accommodated to the sounds which precede and follow them. From the listener's point of view, co-articulation helps the recognition and identification of the sounds, since some of their features may be anticipated in preceding segments. A labialized [s̫], for instance, indicates to the hearer that the next vowel will be rounded, and a nasalized vowel signals the likelihood of a nasal consonant in the immediate environment.

Phoneme as 'mental image'

Closely related to the concept of co-articulation in the explanation of allophonic variation is the idea of the phoneme as a 'target' or 'mental image', from which the allophones 'deviate' to a greater or lesser extent according to the phonetic environment. For example, the [s] of *soup* has /s/ as its target, but under the influence of the following rounded vowel, it is [s̫] which is actually pronounced. Similarly, in *tenth* the speaker 'aims for' /n/, but the dental [θ] which follows it makes the realization [n̪] instead of [n]. Fronted velars ([k̟]), nasalized vowels, and indeed most of what are generally called secondary articulations (the '-izations': labialization, palatalization, nasalization, etc.) would be explained in the same way.

The concept of the phoneme as 'target' is not new: Sommerfelt (cited in Twaddell 1935) described phonemes as 'models which speakers seek to reproduce', but the idea goes back at least to Baudouin de Courtenay (1895), who wrote of phonemes as 'mental images' and distinguished two areas of study, physiophonetics, which is concerned with the sounds actually uttered, and psychophonetics, which studies the mental images these sounds represent. The 'psychological' or 'mentalistic' view of the phoneme was brought back into favour by generative phonology, and the idea of the phoneme as a 'target' has recently been revived, albeit under a different terminology, by Tatham (1980).

Not all allophonic variation, however, can be explained so readily. Why, for instance, are vowels longer before voiced consonants (and when final) than before voiceless ones? Is the target a long vowel, from which the short one 'deviates', or is the target the short vowel, and the long one a deviation? Note, first, that this phenomenon is not confined to English: it is found in many languages, though not always quite so prominently as in English. It may possibly be explained on a physiological (i.e. a 'mechanical') basis; the explanation, though a little complicated, is worth pursuing.

1 Vocal cord vibration (the source of voicing) requires a moving column of air across the glottis, i.e. the air pressure below the glottis has to be greater than the pressure above it:

subglottal pressure > supraglottal pressure

If the air pressures are equal, or almost equal, there will be little or no vibration of the cords.

2 The voiceless sounds require greater energy of articulation, because they do not have the support of voicing to amplify the sound wave: so [f] for example is a more 'energetic' sound than [v], as is implied by the terms *fortis* (= 'strong') and *lenis* (= 'weak'), which are regularly correlated with *voiceless* and *voiced* sounds respectively.[10]

3 The fortis sounds thus require greater oral (i.e. supraglottal) air pressure to maintain audibility. This in turn reduces the pressure differential across the vocal cords, and the cords stop vibrating. Before a lenis sound, or finally, voicing continues for a longer period. There is, therefore, a 'mechanical' explanation for the difference of vowel length: it would be reasonable to conclude that vowels are 'naturally' longer (as evidenced by their length in final position) but deviate from this target (by being shortened) when they precede a fortis consonant (for further discussion, cf. Chen 1970; Halle and Stevens 1967).

Phonological space

Complementary to the concept of phonemic 'targets' is the concept of 'phonological space', the relative 'distance' between one phoneme and the next. If a phoneme is relatively 'distant' from, and independent of, its neighbours, it has greater latitude for variation than a relatively more restricted phoneme. English /r/ will serve as an example of the former; it has a wide range of variants, including: the alveolar flap [ɾ], found *a* in Scottish English (as in [gɾiːn] 'green'), and *b* in some varieties of RP,[11] intervocalically ([mæɾɪ] 'marry'); [ʁ] or [ʁ] (a uvular approximant or fricative), found on Tyneside; [ɹ] in RP and many other accents; [ɹ] after voiceless sounds; [ɻ] (a retroflex approximant) in West of England accents; [ʋ] (a labio-dental approximant, often known as 'defective' r); and others. It is acceptable for /r/ to have so many widely differing variants, because it is the only consonant phoneme of its kind: the only restrictions are that it must not overlap with the variants of /l/ (or of /w/). English /p/, by contrast, is more restricted: its basic features are all necessary to distinguish it from neighbouring phonemes; [bilabial] to distinguish it from /t/, [−voice] to contrast with /b/, [plosive] in opposition to /f/. Only the non-distinctive feature of aspiration is variable in degree. In Japanese, /h/ is the only non-strident fricative the language has: there is no /f, θ/, etc. So the widely differing variants [ɸ], [ç], [h] are possible, and they are 'mechanically' determined: [ɸ] before a high back vowel,[12] [ç] before a high front vowel, and [h] elsewhere. The extent of allophonic variation of a phoneme thus depends on its place in the overall pattern, the 'distance' which separates it from its neighbours.

Sometimes a phoneme has latitude in some of its features but not in others. For example, /u/ has the properties of being [high], [back], [rounded] and [long]. [high] distinguishes it from /oʊ/ and [long] from /ʊ/, while [back] and [round] work together to distinguish it from /i/. This means that, provided *one* of the latter is maintained, the other is free to vary. We thus encounter allophones of /u/ which are fronted, to [ü] or even [y]: so long as rounding is present, there is no risk of confusion with /i/. Fronted [ü] is found after 'front' (i.e. palatal) consonants, such as /tʃ, ʤ, j, kj-/, etc.: compare the different values of /u/ in *chew* and *coo*, *Jew* and *goo*, *queue* and *too*, *you* and *do*.

Other allophones

Much phonetic (allophonic) variation can be explained by appealing to the interlinked notions of co-articulation, of 'deviation' from 'targets', and of 'phonological space'. But not all such variation can be accounted for in this way. One exception is the occurrence of [l] and [ɫ] as allophones of English /l/. It is not clear why [ɫ], which involves an additional raising of the back of the tongue, should occur in the particular postvocalic environments in which it does occur. In other languages (as in French, and German, for instance), the sound which occurs postvocalically is [l], i.e. 'clear' l; furthermore, [ɫ] is found *before* (as well as after) a vowel in some dialects of English, and in other languages too. So there seem to be no articulatory reasons for the particular distribution of /l/ which is found in RP. In other words, allophonic variation cannot always be explained as co-articulation; on some occasions it is apparently arbitrary.

Phonetic notations

Square bracket representations are intended to be language-independent, i.e. universal. They are also supposed to be more accurate, in what they denote, than a phonemic representation. Since accuracy depends on the values given to the symbols, it is important to consider the basis of the notation, and some of the problems arising from it.

The International Phonetic Association (IPA) has given accepted values to an inventory of symbols, mainly alphabetic but with additions, and to a set of diacritics.[13] 'Agreed values' means, for example, that the symbol [g] represents a voiced velar plosive as in *gate* and not the orthographic g of *gin*, which is notated as [ʤ]. The system has proved extremely useful but there are a number of problems, largely arising from the fact that a symbol has to represent a bundle of simultaneous features, for example, [f] for a sound which is simultaneously *voiceless*, *labio-dental* and *fricative*. The main problems are as follows:

1 Some sounds have their own symbol, whereas others of similar status are presented as 'modifications' of a 'basic' sound by adding diacritics. It seems somewhat inconsistent, for instance, that a (voiceless) palato-alveolar fricative has its own symbol, [ʃ], whereas a (voiceless) retroflex alveolar fricative is represented as [ʂ], giving it the appearance of a 'modification' of [s].

2 A more serious problem is that there may be sounds which have no satisfactory notation because they have to be treated as a variant of one sound, X, or as a variant of another sound, Y, where in reality their status is midway between X and Y. An example is the voiceless unaspirated plosives, the sounds which occur for instance after /s–/ in *spin*, *steam*, and *school*. These sounds have to be represented either as versions of [p t k], namely as [p⁼ t⁼ k⁼],[14] or as versions of [b d g], namely [b̥ d̥ g̥]. The former gives preference to one feature (voiceless), the latter to the other (unaspirated). A notation intermediate between p, b, etc. would clearly be desirable, so as to show the intermediate 'neutral' status of these sounds, as well as to avoid a situation in which different symbols 'mean' the same sound, as with [p] = [p⁼] = [b̥].

3 A third problem with the symbols is that the same symbol may represent more than one sound. Sometimes this is a superficial

difficulty which could easily be cured by finding a new symbol (or diacritic). For example, it is just a nuisance that the same symbol, [j], is used for both the *palatal approximant* and the *voiced palatal fricative*. More serious is that, where diacritics are used, they permit no recognition of *degrees* of modification. For example, there is only one symbol for nasalization (the diacritic ˜), yet a nasalized vowel may be *a* nasalized during the first part only of its total length (as when it follows a nasal consonant, for example, the [æ] of *mat*); *b* nasalized during the latter part (as when it *precedes* a nasal, for example, the [æ] of *can*); or *c* nasalized throughout. In the latter case, degrees of nasality (heavy – moderate – light, etc.) may depend on i whether the language uses nasal vowels contrastively as phonemes, as French, for example, does (compare English and German, which do not); ii on the position of the vowel between two nasals, as in *mean* and *man*; or iii on dialect differences, such as the noted 'nasality' of Australian and American dialects of English. The one symbol [Ṽ] thus represents a wide range of different sounds.

A similar example is the diacritic of 'devoicing' as in [ɣ̥ ʐ̥], etc. 'Devoicing' means that the voicing (i.e. vibration of the vocal cords) is not maintained throughout the duration of the sound: but the voiceless part may be the initial stage (when the sound is in initial position, for example, [ɣ̥] in *vine*) or the final stage (when the sound occurs word-finally, for example, [ɣ̥] in *five*) or even the whole sound, if the symbol is used for the voiceless unaspirated plosives [b̥ d̥], etc. Furthermore, the devoicing symbol when applied to approximants may mean either that the sound is voiceless *and fricative*, as with the [ɹ̥] of *train*, the [l̥] of *plane* and the [w̥] of *twenty*, or merely partially voiceless, as with the [ɹ̥] of *drain* and the [l̥] of *blade*.

These examples show that a symbol in square brackets may often represent a range of similar, but nevertheless different and distinguishable sounds.

4 In some cases there may be more than one notation for what amounts to the 'same' sound. It is difficult to distinguish, for instance, even at the phonetic level, between a palatal nasal, [ɲ], a *palatalized* nasal [nʲ], and the sequence nasal + palatal glide [nj], particularly since in the latter case we would expect the nasal component to become palatal through assimilation to the following [j]. Similarly, palatal(ized) laterals pose the problem of distinguishing between [ʎ], [lʲ] and [lj]. Any one of these notations would be satisfactory (unlike the example of [p, p˭, b̥], etc. in 2 above, where *none* of the choices is satisfactory): the problem is an 'embarrassment of riches'.

Phonetic representation of vowels

Square brackets refer us, as we have said, to a (theoretically at least) language-independent, universally applicable, and 'absolute' set of sound values. The problem of describing and classifying vowels for these purposes is rather different than for consonants. Consonants can be adequately described in articulatory terms – in terms of *place* and *manner* of articulation, and vocal cord action (for example, voicing). Vowels, however, do not have a 'place' of articulation specifiable by division of the oral cavity, and their *manner* of articulation is identical for all of them. Articulatory parameters are therefore unsuitable, and vowels have to be described in auditory terms, i.e. on the basis of differences perceived.

Cardinal vowels

For many years, Daniel Jones's scheme of cardinal vowels was widely accepted as the basis of vowel description. The system is still popular; but not now so universally accepted, for reasons which will become clear. The cardinal vowels are anchored around two points which are in fact specified in articulatory terms, namely the close front vowel [i], in which 'the raising of the tongue is as far forward as possible and as high as possible consistently with its being a vowel [and not a palatal fricative]' (Jones 1960: 31), and the open back vowel [ɑ], for which the tongue is 'lowered . . . and retracted as far as possible' (Jones ibid.). The intermediate vowels between these points are determined so that 'the degrees of acoustic [i.e. auditory] separation between each vowel and the next are . . . as nearly equal as it is possible for a person with a well-trained ear to make them' (Jones 1960: 32). This yields a 'front' series:

Cardinal number:	1	2	3	4
Symbol	[i]	[e]	[ɛ]	[a]

and a 'back' series:

Cardinal number:	5	6	7	8
Symbol	[ɑ]	[ɔ]	[o]	[u]

Jones envisaged these vowels as corresponding, approximately at any rate, to tongue positions, specified as 'the highest point of the tongue'. These positions are shown in Figure 1:

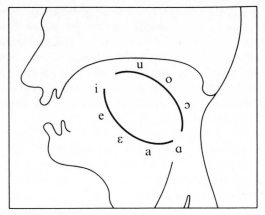

Figure 1 Approximate tongue positions of the eight primary cardinal vowels (cf. Jones 1960: 36)

The elliptical shape of the system was simplified 'for teaching purposes', originally to the shape of Figure 2:

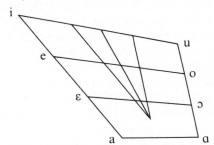

Figure 2 Original stylization of cardinal vowel diagram (Jones 1960)

and later to the shape now generally accepted (Figure 3):

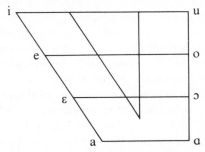

Figure 3 Widely used version of cardinal vowel diagram

Since the cardinal vowels are primarily based on auditory not articulatory criteria, their values 'cannot be learnt from written descriptions; they should be learnt by oral instruction from a teacher who knows them' (Jones 1960: 34). Jones does, however, give examples from specific languages, namely French and German 'as spoken . . . by the average educated inhabitant [of Paris and Berlin respectively]' and Scottish English as a guide to the values of these vowels:

Cardinal vowel	[i]	[e]	[ɛ]	[a]	[ɑ]	[ɔ]	[o]	[u]
French word	si	thé	même	la	pas	homme	rose	tous
German word	Biene					Sonne		gut
Scottish English		day					rose	

It was emphasized, even by Jones himself (1960), that these real-language illustrations must be viewed with caution, since 'it is the vowels of the key-words that should be described with reference to the Cardinal vowels' and not the other way round; and because 'most key-words are pronounced in different ways by different people'.

A set of *secondary* cardinal vowels is derived by changing the lip-rounding values of the primary set. In the primary set, vowels 1 to 5 ([i] to [ɑ]) are unrounded, while 6 to 8 ([ɔ, o, u]) are progressively more rounded. This arrangement reflects the fact that in most languages, front vowels are unrounded and back vowels rounded. Pronouncing a cardinal 1 [i] with rounded lips gives us the first vowel of the secondary set, cardinal 9 [y]; the other unrounded vowels can be treated similarly, though a rounded version of C4 [a] seems never to occur in any language. The *un*rounded equivalents of [ɔ, o, u] are [ʌ, ɤ, ɯ].

More recently, a few extra symbols have been added to the cardinal vowel scheme, to represent commonly-found vowels which are otherwise difficult to symbolize. [ɪ] and [ʊ] represent centralized and more open versions of [i, u] respectively; [ɨ, ʉ] are close *central* vowels (unrounded and rounded); [ə] is a mid-central vowel; [ɐ] is an open central vowel, and [æ] is a vowel midway between [ɛ] and [a]. The positions of these vowels are shown in Figure 4.

The vowel areas in between the 'cardinal' points are catered for by a set of diacritics, including [V̈] for centralization, [V̞] for 'more open than' and [V̝] for 'more close than'. In Figure 5, a vowel anywhere within the shaded area would be represented as [ë̞], namely a vowel whose quality is more open than, and more central than, cardinal [e].

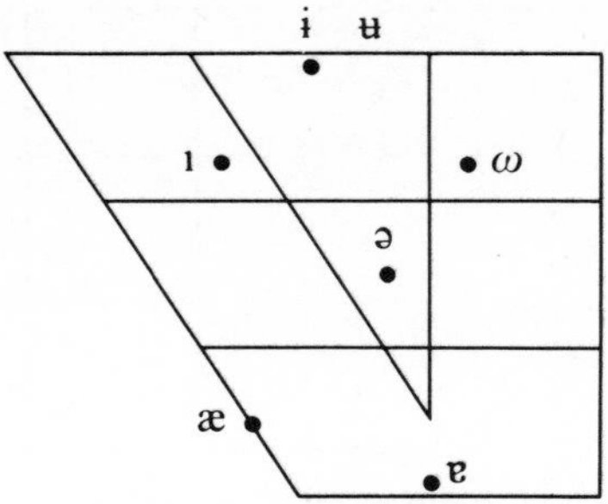

Figure 4 Additional cardinal symbols

Given the cardinals and the set of diacritics, we can now describe the vowels of any particular language, or dialect, or individual speaker, in terms of this system; thus an RP pronunciation of /eɪ/ in *day*, *plate* can be represented as [ɛ̝ɪ], indicating a diphthong starting from a raised (closer than) cardinal [ɛ] and gliding to [ɪ]. Needless to say, such a statement is highly generalized (individual speakers, and even the same speaker on different occasions, will vary) and not excessively precise (note the size of the shaded area in Figure 5). Once again, we must be careful not to imagine that a symbol appearing in slant brackets has the same value as that symbol in square brackets; /ʌ/, for example, means in an English context the vowel of *cup*, *run*, *hunt*, etc.; [ʌ] on the other hand means the unrounded, half-open, back cardinal vowel (see Figure 6). We could say that RP speakers realize /ʌ/ as [ʌ̈], or perhaps as [ə̞] or [ɐ̝], depending on which cardinal vowel we choose as the reference point. Not all examples are as awkward as this, of course; generally we try to give the phonemes a symbol which corresponds to the cardinal vowel(s) involved in the actual pronunciation, as with RP /eɪ/.

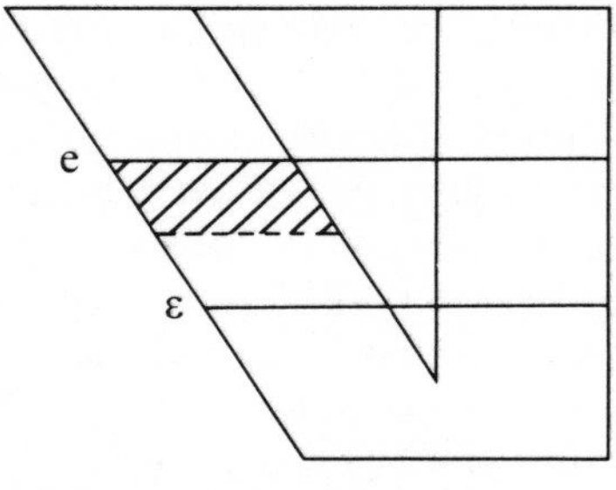

Figure 5 Shaded area shows range of [ɛ̝̈]

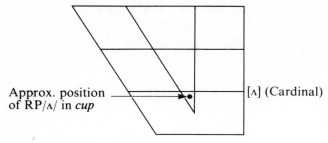

Figure 6   One symbol with different values: [ʌ] vs /ʌ/

There is no doubt that the cardinal vowel system has great advantages over a method of vowel description which relies only on reference to vowels in particular words in a particular language. To describe a vowel as being 'approximately the vowel of English *wet*, *ten*' is almost worse than useless, since different speakers will have greatly different pronunciations varying from, perhaps, [e] to [æ]. Describing the vowel as of C3 [ɛ] quality, or as midway between [e] and [ɛ], is more precise so long as all concerned know the cardinal vowel values.

Experimental evidence

The problems of learning the cardinal vowels have become more acute with the passing of the years. No longer is it possible to learn them from Jones himself, and although there are gramophone recordings of the vowels, with Jones pronouncing them, the quality leaves much to be desired. More seriously, doubt about the validity of the system was engendered by a series of classic experiments carried out by Ladefoged (1967: ch. 2). Using a sonograph, Ladefoged measured the cardinal vowel values in terms of their formant frequencies (on *formants*, see Chapter 3, p. 79). He found that, even with informants who had been trained in the system by Jones, and with sets of vowels (pronounced by the informants) chosen by Jones for accuracy, there was a great deal of overlapping of adjacent vowels across speakers, particularly among the back vowels where productions of [ɑ] overlapped with [ɔ], and [ɔ] with [o], but also among the front vowels ([i] and [e] showed a substantial overlap, though generally, the front vowels were quite well distinguished) (Ladefoged 1967: 93). Looking further at the pronunciations of individuals, there were again occasions where the back vowel [ɔ] was confused either with [ɑ] or [o] (Ladefoged 1967: 98–9). In a further experiment, eighteen trained phoneticians, fifteen of whom had trained in the British tradition and had extensive experience of the cardinal system, were asked to plot the vowels of ten (Gaelic) words from a recording. The fifteen who had been trained in the system showed much better agreement than the three who had not, but there was still substantial variation, particularly for three of the ten words. It is interesting to note that the seven words which produced good agreement among the judges all had vowels corresponding closely to a cardinal vowel, while the other three did not; the conclusion seems inescapable that the cardinal system works well for the description of an unknown language – provided it has vowels of cardinal quality!

The difficulties of learning the system accurately, and the fact that we cannot be confident that what is learnt is a universally applicable system of absolute vowel values, are the major drawbacks of the cardinal system. The system is, however, useful, provided we recognize that its vowel qualities are *relative* rather than absolute. This means that when we use, for example, the symbol [ɛ], we are not claiming that all phoneticians everywhere will agree on the quality of this vowel; we are saying that this symbol represents a vowel which is front, unrounded, and in openness about midway between [e] and [a]. Relative though such statements are, they are still more precise than a description based on particular words in particular languages.

'Broad' and 'narrow' transcription

Earlier in this chapter (p. 24), we suggested that a phonemic representation is always rather imprecise, whereas the phonetic representation (square brackets) aims to give a precise description of an actual pronunciation. We have seen from the foregoing sections, however, that the symbols given in square brackets, whether consonant or vowel, may be far from precise. They are more precise than the phonemic representation, but only relatively so. In earlier days, the term *broad transcription* was used for what we now call a *phonemic* representation, and *narrow transcription* for what is now an allophonic, or sub-phonemic, or phonetic, representation. These older terms have the advantage of implying that what we are really dealing with is a continuum; more or less broad, more or less narrow.

Wider implications

We have considered the phonemic–phonetic distinction at some length. To conclude, it is worthwhile to ask *why* the distinction is necessary, and what is its significance in a broader context. The question 'why' can be put in the form of a challenge: if phonemes alone distinguish meanings, why should we be even slightly interested in allophonic (sub-phonemic) variation? Of what use is it to point out that, for example, /k/ is pronounced [ḵ] before front vowels and [ḵ] before a back vowel? Are not co-articulations like this perfectly natural, totally expected, and hence completely uninteresting? And why should we bother to record that the vowels of *mat* and *tan* are partially nasalized, when we know that this is due to the preceding [m] or following [n]? We cannot quantify the nasality (our challenger might continue), and even if we could, it would be of no interest, since a different speaker on a different occasion might nasalize the vowel to a different degree. Surely all that matters is that *mat* is distinguished from *met* and *mart*, and *tan* from *ten* and *ton*? Only phonemes have any importance.

This challenge might be answered in two ways; first, by looking at the wider applications of phonology. In almost every area to which phonology makes a significant contribution, the phonemic–phonetic distinction has proved an important one; the learning and teaching of foreign languages; language acquisition; historical linguistics (the study of language change); clinical phonology; dialectology; all these disciplines regard the distinction as fundamental. We shall be considering some of these areas in later chapters, but for the present a single example, illustrating the value of the distinction, will suffice.

A child pronounces the following words with the pronunciation given (in square brackets) (data taken from N. V. Smith 1973):

[p]		[b]	
soup	[suːp]	band	[b̥ɛn]
bump	[b̥ʌp]	beetle	[b̥iːgu]
stamp	[d̥ɛp]	ball	[b̥ɔː]
escape	[ge̥ɪp]	bump	[b̥ʌp]

From this data, it looks as though the child has acquired both /p/ (as in *soup*, *stamp*, etc.) and /b/ (as in *band*, *ball*, etc.), since both [p] and [b] appear in the transcriptions, and since the child's [p] matches the adult /p/, and his [b] the adult /b/. But the child's [p] and [b] are in complementary distribution; [p] occurs word-finally (but not initially), and [b] occurs initially (but not finally). We must therefore consider the possibility that [p] and [b] are not two phonemes for the child, but two allophones of one phoneme. We can test this by seeing how the child pronounces the adult's initial /p/ and final /b/, as well as medial /p, b/: this is shown in the following data.

Initial /p/	Medial /p, b/	Final /b/
pudding [b̥ʊdɪn]	apple [ɛbu]	crib [ɡ̊ɪp][15]
please [b̥iː]	shopping [wɒbɪn]	
pedal [b̥ɛgu]	table [beɪbu]	

The distribution of the sounds, for the child, is now clear: word-initially, he has [b̥]; finally, he has [p]; and intervocalically, [b]. It is important to see that, although the child pronounces p and b, they are not phonemes in his system, but allophones in complementary distribution.

The second reason for emphasizing the importance of the phonetic–phonemic distinction is this; phonemes are important for distinguishing meanings; for knowing whether, for instance, the message was 'take it' or 'tape it'. But there is more to speaker–listener exchange than just the 'message' itself. The listener may pick up a variety of information about the speaker: his age; regional origin; level of education; emotional state (angry, tired, excited); physical factors (he has a cold); and much other information. Yet most of this other information comes not from *phonemic* distinctions, but from phonetic, or sub-phonemic, ones. Thus, while phonemic evidence is important for lexical (and grammatical) meaning, most other aspects of a communication are conveyed by more subtle differences, requiring more detailed description at the phonetic level. There is more to a speech act than just the meaning of the words.

Exercises 1–4   The distribution of allophones

In the following set of problems, the allophones are given in phonetic transcription, with an explanation of the symbols used. For each exercise (1–4) *a* work out the distribution of each allophone, i.e. the phonetic environment in which it is to be found, and *b* where possible, write a suitable realization rule. Here is an example:

Allophones of /j/:   [j] voiced approximant
                     [ç] voiceless, fricative

[j]		[ç]	
[jet]	'yet'	[kçu]	'queue'

[jɑn]	'yarn'	[pçuə]	'pure'
[jist]	'yeast'	[tçub]	'tube'
[njuz]	'news'	[ə'kçuz]	'accuse'
[vælju]	'value'	[ætɪtçud]	'attitude'
[mjuzɪk]	'music'	[pçænoɷ]	'piano'

Since the two sounds [j] and [ç] are allophones of one phoneme, we can expect their distributions to be complementary. [j] occurs *initially* and is apparently not affected by the kind of vowel which follows, since it precedes both front vowels (*yeast*) and back vowels (*yarn*); it also precedes close vowels (*yeast* again) and open vowels (*yarn*), rounded vowels (*news*) and unrounded vowels (*yet*). Nor is [j] affected by syllable stressing, since it occurs in both stressed (['mjuzɪk]) and unstressed (['vælju]) syllables. In addition to its occurrence word-initially, [j] is also found after /m, n, l/, all of which are *voiced* sounds.

[ç] is more restricted in its distribution; it is not influenced by the kind of vowel which follows (compare the back, close, rounded vowel of *pure* with the front, open, unrounded vowel of *piano*), but it occurs only after the sounds /p, t, k/, all of which are *voiceless plosives*. Since there are no instances of voiced [j] after a voiceless plosive, the distributions of [j] and [ç] are, in fact, complementary.

These distributions make good sense phonetically, since [ç], which is voiceless, occurs in the environment of voiceless sounds. The fricativeness of [ç] may be associated with the fact that the preceding sounds require a complete oral closure, which gives rise to friction when released.

We can now write a realization rule for /j/ as follows:

$$/j/ \rightarrow [j]/\# \underline{\quad} \qquad \text{(word initially)}$$
$$/[+\text{voice}]^{16} \underline{\quad} \quad \text{(after a voiced sound)}$$

$$\rightarrow [ç]/ \begin{bmatrix} -\text{voice} \\ \text{plosive} \end{bmatrix} \underline{\quad} \quad \text{(after a voiceless plosive)}$$

Realization rules can be simplified a little by using the 'elsewhere' formula; for example, the rule above could be given as:

$$/j/ \rightarrow [ç]/ \begin{bmatrix} -\text{voice} \\ \text{plosive} \end{bmatrix} \underline{\quad}$$

$$\rightarrow [j] \qquad \text{elsewhere}$$

The environments which are the shortest or easiest to state (in this case the environment for [ç]) are given first, and the longest, most awkward, or most general environments can then be assumed under 'elsewhere'. But this device should only be used when the data is adequate to cover all the possible allophones, since otherwise the 'elsewhere' label will be too general.

Now try the following. Remember to rearrange the data, if necessary, so that all examples of each allophone are together.

Exercise 1

The phoneme /oω/ in RP has two major allophones:

[əω] (the diphthong starts from [ə])
[ɒω] (the diphthong starts from [ɒ])

[kəɒt]	'coat'	[mɒɒl]	'mole'	[həɒz]	'hose'
[rəɒvə(r)]	'rover'	[ʃəɒ]	'show'	[pɒɒltrɪ]	'poultry'
[sɒɒld]	'sold'	[məɒd]	'mode'	[pəɒst]	'post'
[bəɒn]	'bone'	[ʃɒɒldə(r)]	'shoulder'	[ləɒð]	'loathe'

Exercise 2

The voiceless plosives /p, t, k/ have three major allophones:

1 released, aspirated, for example, [pʰ];
2 released, unaspirated, for example, [p];
3 unreleased, for example, [pº].

released, aspirated		*released, unaspirated*		*unreleased*	
tailor	['tʰeɪlə(r)]	spear	[spiə(r)]	locked	[lɒkºt]
powder	['pʰaɒdə(r)]	steam	[stim]	captain	['kæpºtɪn]
captain	['kʰæptɪn]	scales	[skeɪlz]	football	['fɒtºbɔl]
castle	['kʰɑsl]	askew	[ə'skju]	object	['ɒbdʒekºt]
repair	[rɪ'pʰeə(r)]	restore	[rɪ'stɔ(r)]	outpost	['aɒtºpoɒst]

Exercise 3

/t/ has the following allophones in many accents of English:

1 glottal stop [ʔ];
2 unreleased [tº];
3 alveolar flap [ɾ].

[ʔ]		[tᵒ]		[ɾ]	
late	[leɪʔ]	great	[greɪtᵒ]	quarter	['kwɔɾə(r)]
right	[raɪʔ]	tight	[taɪtᵒ]	British	['brɪɾɪʃ]
about	[ə'baʊʔ]	cricket	['krɪkɪtᵒ]	phonetics	[fə'neɾɪks]
kitten	['kɪʔn̩]	football	['fʊtᵒbɔl]	waiting	['weɪɾɪŋ]
certain	['sɜʔn̩]	outfit	['aʊtᵒfɪtᵒ]	thirty	['θɜɾɪ]
		(and see Exercise 2 above for further examples)		potato	[pə'teɪɾoʊ]

Exercise 4

The liquids /l, r/ have *devoiced* (i.e. partly voiceless) allophones, represented as [l̥, ɹ̥], and voiceless fricative allophones, represented as [ɬ, ɹ̥].

[l̥, ɹ̥]		[ɬ, ɹ̥]	
flat	[fl̥æt]	clear	[kɬɪə(r)]
slow	[sl̥oʊ]	plot	[pɬɒt]
freeze	[fɹ̥iz]	trees	[tɹ̥iz]
through	[θɹ̥u]	cry	[kɹ̥aɪ]
shrink	[ʃɹ̥ɪŋk]	proud	[pɹ̥aʊd]
afraid	[ə'fɹ̥eɪd]	approve	[ə'pɹ̥uv]

Exercise 5

The following rules are written in a fully explicit form. Convert them to a conventional notation.

1　Vowels are nasalized before and after nasal consonants.
2　Consonants are labialized before a rounded vowel.
3　/m/ is labio-dental before /f, v/ but bilabial elsewhere.
4　Voiced consonants are devoiced word-finally.

Exercise 6

The rules below are given in notation. Convert them to a fully explicit form.

1　/n/ → [n̪]/ ___ [dental]
　　　　[n] elsewhere

2　/u/ → [ʉ]/ __ l (C) #
3　/r/　→ [ɾ]/ V __ V
4　/w/ → [w]/# __
　　　　[w̥]/ C __

Exercise 7

The following English phrases are written in phonetic ('narrow') transcription. Convert them to a phonemic representation.

1　[çuːʤ tɹiːʐ fɛɫ d̪æ̃ɣn]
2　[ɛɪt̪θɪz ə lɒʔ b̥ɛɾə]
3　[tw̥aes kʰæpºt]
4　[spl̥iʔ pʰɪn tʰæxɫ̩]

Exercise 8

Convert the phrases below, phonemically transcribed, into a phonetic representation:

1　/fil ðə wɪdθ/
2　/greɪt brɪtɪʃ treɪnz/
3　/tɔl mjuzɪk stænd/
4　/ə lɪtl kɪtn/

2 Phonemes in sequence

We have so far been considering phonemes in isolation, as segments in the stream of speech. We shall now go on to consider phonological structure from the point of view of *combinations* of phonemes, i.e. in terms of permitted vs impossible sequences, and we begin by looking at possible combinations or 'clusters' of consonants.

Fortuitous vs structural omissions

It has often been remarked that, although there is no such word as /stɪn/ in English, there could well be such a word – indeed, we may have to resort to the dictionary to make quite sure that /stɪn/ does not exist before we can say with confidence that it does not. But there is not, and never could be, a word such as /btaɪŋt/. The reason is that the sequences and combinations of phonemes in /stɪn/ are all permissible: they are all part of English structure. /st–/ is found regularly, so is /stɪ–/ as in *still*, *stick*, etc., and /–ɪn, –tɪn/ are quite normal. The non-existence of /stɪn/ is thus an 'accidental' gap – it consists of a perfectly possible phonological sequence. /btaɪŋt/, however, is phonologically impossible on a number of grounds. The initial sequence /bt–/ never occurs; /aɪ/ is never followed by /ŋ/; and in word-final clusters of consonants, the sequence /–ŋt/ never occurs. It is thus no accident that /btaɪŋt/ does not exist as an English word. The likelihood that it would ever be introduced, say to name a new product, is nil.

We can thus recognize three possibilities:

1   Sequences which *actually occur* in a language (for example, *still*, *bring*, etc.).
2   Sequences which *could* occur, but do not (for example, *stin*, *fleg* in English).
3   Sequences which *could not* occur because they violate the phonological patterns of the language (for example, /btaɪŋt, pfaɒʃʃ/ in English).

In discussing the rules and restrictions for what is and what is not possible, we must be careful to preserve the distinction between pronunciation and spelling. The sequence pt-, for example, is found in the orthography, in a word like *ptarmigan*, but the phoneme sequence /pt–/ does not occur: *ptarmigan* is pronounced /t–/. Often, an unphonemic spelling reflects the actual pronunciation in the language from which the word comes (for example, *pterodactyl* from (Ancient) Greek *pteron*, 'wing'). In what follows we shall of course be interested in pronunciation rather than orthography.

Word-initial consonant clusters

The reader is now recommended to work out the rules for combining consonants word-initially, by doing Exercise 1.

Exercise 1   Initial consonant clusters[1]

Make a phonemic transcription of the following words (which are listed alphabetically). Then use this as data to work out which consonants can occur in each position before the vowel, 1 in clusters with two consonants (/pl–, kr–/, etc.), and 2 in clusters with three or more (/spr–/, etc.). The positions can be numbered outwards from the vowel, for example,

$$\frac{21}{pl–}\, \frac{321}{spr–}, \text{etc.}$$

Two-consonant clusters beginning with /s/ behave differently from the rest, so it is advisable to treat these separately. Aim to look for any possible regularities and generalizations (such as 'only voiceless fricatives are found in position X').

Note: Rare or unfamiliar words should be looked up in a dictionary.

beautiful	fright	piano	skewer	stupor
blue	glass	plural	sloth	suave
broad	gnaw	pneumatic	smooth	suit
chlorine	great	prize	sneeze	swamp
choir	guano	pseudo	special	thrifty
close	Gwent	puritan	spew	thwart
crew	huge	queue	sphinx	truth

cute	lurid	quiet	split	tulip
deuce	mnemonic	scholar	spring	twist
drift	mule	sclerosis	squib	view
dwelling	neuter	scrape	stave	where
flock	phlegm	shrink	strong	xerox
				Zeus

Discussion

Two-consonant (CC) clusters

Certain regularities emerge from this data, which can be generalized for many other items in the language. In clusters of two consonants, apart from those beginning with /s/, we find four possible sounds in position 1: /l, r, j, w/. The first two constitute the class of *liquids*, the latter two the class of semi-vowels or *glides*. Together, these four consonants are known as *approximants*. Position 1 in these clusters is thus restricted to the class of approximants.

Position 2 contains a wider range of possibilities; all the plosives and a number of fricatives; the nasals /m, n/ (/ŋ/ never occurs word-initially, even on its own); and /h/. But the approximants are found marginally, if at all (perhaps /lj–/ in *lewd*, *lurid*, etc., but many speakers have simple /l/ here). There is thus a kind of complementary distribution between the two positions: the sounds which are found in position 1 do not appear in position 2, and vice versa.

These generalizations may be stated as follows: for CC clusters not containing /s/

Rule 1   the C in position 1 will be an approximant;
Rule 2   the C in position 2 may be a plosive, a fricative or a nasal.

The combinations allowed by Rules 1 and 2 do not all occur with the same degree of probability:

1   Some clusters, such as /pr–/ and /fl–/, are found in many words, including commonly-used words.
2   Others, such as /gw–/, /dw–/, /ʃr–/, /θw–/ occur in only a very few words, some of which may be loan-words or proper names; /gw–/, for instance, occurs in *Gwent*, *Gwen*, *guava*, etc., but is not found in any truly 'native' words.
3   Some clusters are found only in rare words, used very occasionally by specialists, for example /θj–/ in *Thule*, /gj–/ in *gules*, *gubernatorial*.

4 Certain combinations are restricted to particular dialects or particular groups of speakers (though the words might be quite common). Initial /hw–/ is used by many Scottish and certain American speakers in the 'wh' words, *which*, *white*, etc. Some speakers (mainly older) retain /sj–/ in *suit*, *sue*, *superior*, etc., and /lj–/ in *lurid*, *lute*, etc. /tl–/ and /dl–/ do not occur in RP but are common in Midland and Northern dialects as pronunciations for /kl–/ and /gl–/ respectively. The *Survey of English Dialects* (Orton 1962) records [tl–] in *clothes*, *clumsy*, and *clouds* for locations in nearly all the Midlands counties, as far south as Warwickshire and Norfolk, and for most Northern counties as far north as Cumberland and Durham. The distribution of [dl–] in *gloves* is similar.[2] Thus, statements about the permitted clusters of English consonants depend on how one defines 'English'. Do we include rare words like *gules*, non-native (but common) words like *Gwent*, and dialectal pronunciations like [tl–]? Such questions also raise wider issues, to which we return later (pp. 56–72).

5 Finally, there are combinations such as /pw–, bw–, fw–, vw–, ʃj–, sr–/ which are permitted by the 'rules' above, but which do not seem to occur at all. Is their non-occurrence accidental? Or should the rules be modified so as to exclude them?

One way to answer this is to observe what happens to loan-words containing the clusters in question. If loan-words are accepted without change, this suggests that the clusters conform to potential (but non-existent) English patterns. If, however, the clusters are simplified or altered in some way, we would conclude that these sequences violate the rules of English and have to be 'Anglicized'. Loan-words with /pw–, bw–/, etc. come from Spanish and French, for example:

/pw–/	Puerto Rico, pueblo, (petit) pois
/bw–/	Buenos Aires
/fw–/	Fuego, (pate de) foie
/vw–/	(bon) voyage, voyeur

/vr–, vl–/ occur in some Russian names: *Vladimir*, *Vronsky*
/ʃl–, ʃw–/ are borrowed in some Hebrew and Yiddish words: *Schlomo*, *schwa* (the name of the vowel [ə]), *Schweppes*.

The evidence is not entirely conclusive. Educated speakers generally use pronunciations with the clusters given. 'Anglicized' versions, however, are sometimes found, especially with commonly-used names; Puerto (Rico) is often Anglicized to /pɔ(r)tə/, and I have heard /bjunɒs/ for *Buenos* from a (reputable!) travel agent. *Schweppes* too is often realized as /sw–/ rather than /ʃw–/. This suggests that, whereas some speakers are prepared to extend the 'actual' clusters of English to *potential* clusters of the same general type (i.e. plosive/fricative plus approximant), other speakers prefer to stay within existing confines.

Further evidence of a different kind points to similar conclusions.

1   Children's immature pronunciations, for example of /Cr–/ clusters (where C stands for (any) plosive or fricative) as [Cw–] are well known; they provide instances of [pw–] as in *prince*, [bw–] in *bridge* and [fw–] in *from*.
2   Mature speakers with 'defective r' actually use [ʋ], a *labio-dental* approximant; but *imitators* of this pronunciation (it is used by a number of prominant politicians) generally use [w], the *labio-velar* approximant; for example, [pʋɪns] 'prince' is imitated as [pwɪns].

Arguments based on children's behaviour must be treated with caution, however; immature pronunciations often include clusters which eventually die out, since they violate the English 'rules'. The authors of the Edinburgh Articulation Test, for example, record [βr–, bð–, bɣ–] as well as [bw–] among 'immature' pronunciations of /br–/ (*bridge*); they also record [ts–, tð–] and [tɬ–] as early forms of /tr–/ in *train* (Anthony, *et al.* 1971: 64). We would certainly not want to include clusters of this type within the rules for English.

CC clusters with /s/

A wider range of sounds is possible after /s/ than after other plosives and fricatives. We find /l, j, w/ as usual (/r/ follows /ʃ/ rather than /s/), but in addition /s/ combines with the (voiceless) plosives /p, t, k/, and the nasals /m, n/. The fricative /f/ occurs in a few words: *sphinx*, *sphere* and its derivatives, and loan-words such as the musical term *sforzando*.

Because /f/ is the only fricative that combines with /s/, and because few words are involved, not all phonologists interpret the data in the same way. In orthodox generative phonology (for example, Chomsky and Halle 1968), /sf–/ is regarded as being outside normal English patterns. The reason given is that if /sf–/ is ignored, a significant generalization about /s/ clusters can be made: /s–/ can be followed by all (and only) the sounds classed as *non-continuant*, namely, plosives and nasals.[3] This generalization, though attractive, is probably spurious. Speakers do not appear to feel that the /sf–/ words themselves are of 'foreign' origin or in some way 'un-English'; and there is no tendency to Anglicize these words (to /sp–/, or /s–/?), as there would be if /sf–/ was exceptional. A more realistic generalization, based on the data, is that /s–/ may be followed by a (voiceless) plosive or fricative – though we must exclude the *strident* fricatives /s, ʃ/, which are too similar to /s/ itself.

Rule 3   For CC clusters with initial /s/, the C in position 1 may be a (voiceless) plosive, a (voiceless) non-strident fricative, a nasal, or an approximant.

Clusters of three consonants

Three is the maximum permitted number of consonants in a word-initial cluster. The restrictions on co-occurrence are quite strict: in position 1, only the approximants /l, r, j, w/ can occur, as with two-consonant clusters. In position 2 we find only a voiceless plosive /p t k/, and in position 3 only /s/. The combinations can be diagrammed as follows:

3	2	1
s	p	l
	t	r
	k	j
		w

This should yield a total of $1 \times 3 \times 4 = 12$ combinations, but we do not find instances of /spw–/ or /stl–/, just as there is no /pw–, tl–/. The other gap is /stw–/, in spite of the existence of /tw–/. /stw–/ can only be found as an immature pronunciation of /str–/, but its absence seems to be fortuitous: it has the status of a potential, but non-existent English cluster.

Analysis of /tʃ, ʤ/

The affricate sounds occurring initially and finally as in *church*, *judge*, and medially as in *hatchet*, *rigid*, can be regarded either as unit phonemes (many American notations use the symbols /č, ǰ/ to emphasize this) or as sequences of /t + ʃ/, /d + ʒ/. Most phonologists prefer the unitary ('one phoneme') interpretation despite the greater economy of the two-phoneme alternative, and there are good reasons for this: /ʃ, ʒ/ do not belong in the class *approximant*, so that /tʃ–, dʒ–/ as *clusters* would be quite irregular and outside the normal pattern. This is perhaps the best argument for treating /tʃ, dʒ/ as units; another is the contrast between the pronunciation of /tʃ/ and the sequence /t + ʃ/ word-medially, though minimal pairs are hard to find; compare *hatchet* (with /tʃ/) and *hatshop* (with /t + ʃ/).

It has occasionally been suggested that /tʃ, dʒ/ could be regarded as palatal plosives, the affrication being an incidental feature commonly found with palatal plosives in other languages. English would then have a series of four plosives, /p t tʃ k/ (plus their voiced equivalents) instead of the commonly accepted three, /p t k/. The structure of consonant clusters suggests, however, that /tʃ, dʒ/ do not belong with the plosives, since all the plosives combine with /l, r, j, w/, whereas /tʃ, dʒ/ do not combine with any of them – they do not participate in clusters at all.

To summarize so far: permitted combinations of word-initial consonants in English can be described by the following five rules:

a   For two-consonant clusters:

Rule 1   the consonant in position 1 is an approximant.
Rule 2   the consonant in position 2 may be a plosive, a fricative or a nasal.

b   If /s/ is the first consonant:

Rule 3   the consonant in position 1 may be a (voiceless) plosive, a non-strident fricative, or a nasal (or an approximant, by rules 1 and 2).

c   For three-consonant clusters:

Rule 4   *a*   the consonant in position 3 is /s/;
       b   the consonant in position 2 is a (voiceless) plosive;
       c   the consonant in position 1 is an approximant.
Rule 5   CCC clusters presuppose the corresponding CC clusters (for example, /stj–/ presupposes /st–/ and /tj–/; /spw–/ is not possible because /pw–/ does not occur).

Loan-words

The strength of these 'rules' for English speakers can be tested by observing what happens when words borrowed from other languages (*loan-words*) contain clusters not permitted by the rules. Generally, the clusters are adjusted to make them conform to existing patterns, i.e. 'Anglicization' takes place. Thus German *Schnorkel* and *Schnapps* with [ʃn–] are changed to /sn–/, a sequence already permitted. The [ts–] of *tsetse* is changed either to /t/ or to /s/, since /ts–/ is not permitted. African names of people and places beginning with the 'impossible' sequences [mb–, nd–, ŋk–] are Anglicized in various ways; by putting a vowel before the nasal (for example, *Nkomo* /ʌŋˈkoɒmoɒ/) or with a vowel between the nasal and the plosive (/nəˈkrumə/ *Nkrumah*), or by making the nasal syllabic (/n̩doɒlə/ *Ndola*). The latter procedure is the least 'English' of the three, but the closest to the original. Anglicizations are particularly evident in the large collection of 'learned' words or word-elements borrowed from Greek, in which the original cluster is still evident from the spelling. *Mnemonic, pneumatic, pterodactyl* and *psycho*-all derive from Ancient Greek words which had the initial clusters [mn–, pn–, pt–, ps–] (and which are in most cases preserved in Modern Greek, cf. *mnimi* 'memory', *pnevma* 'spirit', *fteri* 'wing', *psixi* 'soul').

It would be wrong to imply that Anglicization of loan-words happens invariably. Speakers may well be aware of the foreign origin of the word, and make some attempt to pronounce it accordingly. Thus alongside /sn–/ in *Schnorkel*, /sw–/ in *Schweppes* and /sp–/ in *spiel* there exist pronunciations with [ʃn–, ʃw–, ʃp–], as in German. Learned words used mainly by well-educated speakers will tend to retain their original pronunciations, or a close approximation. Words which have become popular, or highly frequent in use, are more likely to be Anglicized.

If loan-words are not sufficiently frequent, evidence of pronunciation habits is also available by observing what speakers do when learning the sound patterns of other languages. Confronted with unfamiliar clusters such as German [pfl–] and [ts–], English speakers simplify ('Anglicize') them to /fl–/ and /s/ (or, in the case of [ts–], to /z–/, since German initial [ts–] is regularly spelt with a 'z'. Spelling exerts a strong influence on pronunciation – cf. below, p. 71). It should be noted that it is only when the clusters are *initial* that they are Anglicized; the medial [–ts–] of *Mozart* and the final [–ts] of *ersatz* are preserved as /ts/; final /–ts/ because it occurs already (*cats*), and medial /–ts–/ because it can be divided across the syllable boundary (for example, /moɒt.sɑ(r)t/).

Other languages

The cluster-patterns illustrated above are specific to English. Other languages, as implied by the discussion of loan-words, permit clusters of a type not found in English, while others again are more restricted than English in what can occur; indeed, there are languages which permit no clusters at all.

Familiar European languages offer many examples of clusters not found in English. French, for instance, has clusters with the approximant /ɥ/ (the rounded equivalent of [j]), as well as with /j/, as in:

pièce /pjɛs/ 'piece'	bien /bjɛ̃/ 'well'
puis /pɥi/ 'then'	buée /bɥe/ 'condensation'

It also has more complex clusters involving /w/, such as:

roi /rwa/ 'king'	loi /lwa/ 'law'
froid /frwa/ 'cold'	ploiement /plwamã/ 'folding'
trois /trwa/ 'three'	cloître /klwatr/ 'cloisters'

And similarly, clusters with /r, l/ followed by /j, ɥ/, as in:

pluie /plɥi/ 'rain'	lieu /ljø/ 'place'
bruine /brɥin/ 'drizzle'	rien /rjɛ̃/ 'nothing'

German has clusters with /ts–/ (*zehn*, 'ten'), /pf–/ (*Pferd*, 'horse'), /ʃp–/ (*Spanne*, 'span'), and more complex combinations such as /tsv–/ as in *zwei* 'two', /pfl–/ in *Pflaume* 'plum'. Italian, often considered relatively simple from a phonological point of view, nevertheless has clusters such as /dz–/ (*zonzo*, 'saunter'), /zv–/ (*svagare*, 'amuse'), /zn–/ (*snello*, 'nimble') and /zr–/ (*sradicare*, 'uproot'). Greek has a number of clusters involving sequences of plosive plus fricative or fricative plus plosive, such as /xt–/ (*xteni*, 'comb'), /ft–/ (*ftano*, 'arrive'), /ps–/ (*psilo*, 'thin'), /ks–/ (*ksero*, 'know'). There are also a number of fricative plus fricative clusters, for example /vɣ–/ (*vɣazo*, 'take off'), /sx–/ (*sxolio*, 'school'), /fθ–/ (*fθoŋgos*, 'sound').

Note that, although these languages have clusters which are complex and, from an English point of view, unusual, they also have the commoner, 'simpler' clusters of plosive (or fricative) plus approximant. Here are some examples of [pl–] and [br–] in each of the four languages:

	[pl–]		[br–]	
French	plage	'beach'	bref	'brief'
German	platz	'place'	brust	'breast'
Italian	placare	'appease'	brusco	'sharp'
Greek	platia	'square'	mbriki	'coffee pot'[4]

We have illustrated languages with a variety of clusters. At the other extreme, there are languages such as Maori and other Polynesian languages which permit no clusters at all: the only syllable type is CV and V. Maori has many borrowings from English: the words which have clusters in English have to be simplified, either by inserting a vowel between the consonants, or by deleting one of the consonants. Here are some examples of Maori loan-words from English:

Maori	*English original*
minita	minister
ranana	London (Maori has /r/ but no /l/)
kotimana	Scotsman
kura	school
tarai	try
piriti	bridge
pereki	brick

Universal constraints

The European-language illustrations show that there are not only many possible combinations of consonants, even within this relatively narrow range of languages, but also that there are combinations of a variety of types. Are there, then, any restrictions at all on what is possible, once we consider 'language' as a whole rather than specific languages? Can *any* combination of consonant be found to occur, somewhere? The answer seems to be, first, that there *are* restrictions on what may occur, and second (and more important), that the clusters found in any particular language are not random, but may be to some extent predictable.

1   There appear to be no languages which permit sequences such as [pb–], [dt–], or [rh–]: sequences which impose unrealistic demands on the articulatory mechanisms. This means that the restrictions governing sequences in any particular language can be divided into two categories: those which have a physiological basis, i.e. combinations which are *universally* excluded; and those which are specific to the language concerned (but do not necessarily apply to all languages). English for instance, disallows /lr–/ on universal grounds, but /ʃp–/ on a specific basis only – compare German, which allows /ʃp–/ but not /sp–/.

2   The type of sequence that can occur in a language is governed by certain 'universal' principles. It has been found, from observations of a wide range of different languages, that some sequences are more frequent, i.e. more 'likely', or 'natural', than others; and, furthermore, that if any particular language possesses an 'unlikely' sequence, it will also usually possess the more 'likely' ones as well: in other words the cluster-types form a 'hierarchy of implication', in which the presence of type X implies the presence of type Y, implies the presence of type Z, etc.

At the top of the hierarchy is the sequence CV, i.e. the most likely and expected sound to follow a consonant is a vowel. All languages have CV sequences, no matter what other types they possess. Of the languages with (initial) clusters, the most 'natural' is a sequence of a 'true' consonant (i.e. a plosive or fricative) and a liquid or glide, for example, [pl–, fr–, dj–, kw–], etc. – the type we have already found to be common in English. The naturalness of this sequence can be partly explained by the fact that liquids and glides (approximants) are the most vowel-like of all the consonants – glides are simply consonantal versions of the corresponding vowel (cf. [j]–[i], [w]–[u]), while liquids require the minimal degree of obstruction to the airstream. A sequence of true consonant plus nasal, such as [bn–, kn–, tm–], etc. is not only less common (than C plus approximant sequences) among languages of the world, but it also appears that languages possessing such sequences must also have consonant-plus-approximant sequences. Old English, for example, had /kn–/ and /gn–/ sequences (still reflected in the spelling of words such as *knee*, *knight* and *gnat*) but it possessed at the same time the more 'natural' sequences /pl–, fr–/, etc. Sequences of true consonant plus nasal are therefore 'lower' in the hierarchy than consonant plus approximant sequences. Further examples of the implicational hierarchy are:

1 The sequence 'nasal plus approximant' ([ml–, nr–, nw–], etc.) is less natural than, and implies the presence of, true consonant plus approximant clusters.

2 If a language has sequences of two or more 'true' consonants, then 'dissimilar' sequences of plosive plus fricative or fricative plus plosive ([ps–, ts–, pf–, sp–, ʃk–], etc.) are more likely than 'similar' sequences of plosive plus plosive ([pt–, kp–], etc.) or fricative plus fricative ([sθ–, fs–], etc.). English, for example, has one fricative plus fricative sequence, /sf–/, but its presence implies the existence of the 'dissimilar' clusters /sp–, st–/, etc.

3 Languages do not have three-consonant clusters unless they also have two-consonant clusters; and the CCC combinations usually imply CC combinations of a similar type. Thus English could not have /spr–/ unless it also had either /sp–/ or /pr–/, preferably both. Since English has no /tl–/, it could not (and does not) permit /stl–/. Similarly, French has /frw–/ and /trw–/, but it also has /fr–, tr–/ and /rw–/.

For further discussion of implicational hierarchies of clusters, see Cairns (1969).

Morphemes and syllables

The study of sequences of sounds in combination is generally known as *phonotactics*. In orthodox generative phonology the term *morpheme structure rules* was used, since the aim is to provide *rules* (such as Rules 1–4 above) to describe the permissible patterns of morphemes in a language. Later, following an article by Stanley (1967), the term morpheme structure *conditions* (MSCs) was adopted. We have illustrated the possibilities, for English, on the basis of *words*, in particular the sequences of *word-initial* clusters, though the analysis could easily be extended to *word-final* structures which, like the initial combinations, show certain regularities. The term morpheme can be preferred to *word* as being slightly more precise. A morpheme is a 'minimal unit of meaning': *playing* consists of the morphemes *play* and *ing*; *recycle* is made up of *re* and *cycle*; *denationalize* is *de, nation, -al, ize*. *Cycle, play* and *rule* are morphemes which also happen to be words. Generally, rules which apply to *words* in a language will also apply to *morphemes*, though the converse is not true; it is thus preferable to speak of *morpheme* structure conditions (or rules) rather than *word* structure conditions.

The question is, however, whether the kind of patterns we have been considering are really based on the morpheme, or on some other unit. Hooper (1973) has proposed that the unit involved is really the *syllable* rather than the morpheme. There are a number of arguments in favour of this; first, the patterns we have observed are phonological patterns, and the syllable is a phonological unit, whereas the morpheme is not a unit of phonology, but a unit of meaning (or grammar). Second, morphemes often have more than one syllable: examples are *finger*, *remember*, *hospital*, *plasticine* and *extra*. These morphemes have the medial clusters /–ŋg–, –mb–, –sp–, –st–, –kstr–/, etc. If the permitted combinations of medial clusters were stated on the basis of *morphemes*, there could be a vast number of possibilities, and it would be difficult to generalize the patterns simply and concisely. But stated in terms of syllables, the patterns are quite simple, since medial clusters can be regarded as sequences of syllable-final and syllable-initial clusters. Taking a rather complex example like *extra*, we find that the cluster /–kstr–/ can be divided syllabically either as /k.str/ or as /ks.tr/. Both /–k/ and /–ks/ are possible syllable-final patterns (cf. *sick*, *six*) and /str–, tr–/ are possible initial patterns (cf. *strain*, *train*). The medial /–kstr–/ sequence can thus be accounted for, on the basis of a syllable division, in terms of what already occurs initially and finally. A sequence such as the /–ŋg–/ of *finger* is difficult to explain on a morpheme basis, because /–ŋg/ is not possible finally (in RP at any rate), nor is /ŋg–/ a permissible initial cluster. But when /–ŋg–/ is divided across the syllable boundary, as /fiŋ.gə/, the sequence is seen simply as a combination of final /–ŋ/ (compare *ring*, *sing*) and initial /g/ (cf. *give*).

With the syllable as the appropriate unit, sequences which were earlier considered rare, but none the less potential, such as /gj–, gw–, θj–/ in English, begin to be found more frequently. /θj–/, unknown initially, occurs in *enthuse*, *enthusiasm*; /gw–/ in *language*, *distinguish*; /gj–/ in *argue*, *singular*. This is further confirmation of the value of the syllable as the basic unit of structure.

Exercise 2

Divide the following words into syllables. Consider whether each syllable consists of permissible initial and final sequences:

hungry	consequence
children	exclude

regular	assumption
umbrella	Atlantic
restrict	virulent

Exercise 3

Look at the morpheme-final clusters in the following data. What is predictable about the place of articulation of the nasals?

/læmp/	'lamp'	/hɪnt/	'hint'
/stʌmp/	'stump'	/flɔnt/	'flaunt'
/sænd/	'sand'	/bæŋk/	'bank'
/faɪnd/	'find'	/lɪŋk/	'link'

Exercise 4

The following loan-words and borrowed roots have all undergone Anglicization. What is the *pattern* of change in these words?

Item	Original		English
psychic	ps–	→	s
tsetse	ts–	→	s
bdellium	bd–	→	d
Dvorak	dv–	→	v
pterygium	pt–	→	t
pneumonia	pn–	→	n
xerox[5]	ks–	→ s →	z
ctenoid	kt–	→	t

We have suggested that phonotactic patterns are best described in terms of syllables, rather than in terms of words or morphemes. But it must be noted that the restrictions which apply to syllables are not always the same as the restrictions which apply to *morphemes*. For example, from Exercise 3 it will be clear that there is a restriction on the type of nasal which can precede certain plosives. A labial plosive (/p/) is always (and only) preceded by a labial nasal, an alveolar plosive by an alveolar nasal, and a velar plosive by a velar nasal. The locus (place-of-articulation) of the nasal is *governed by* the locus of the plosive, or, to put it another way, the nasal *assimilates to* the following plosive. Sequences such as /–np, –ŋt, –mk/, etc. do not exist: there are no English morphemes with final sequences of this sort. But when we look at what happens in syllables, a different picture emerges, because of words like *sums, rings, dimmed, wronged* and *strength*, with the sequences /–mz, –ŋz, –md, –ŋd, –ŋθ/. Each of these words has a morpheme boundary between the nasal and the following consonant: *sum-s, ring-s*, etc. (*strength* is from *strong*, plus *-th*). Thus the morpheme patterns, which permit only homorganic (same locus) nasals, are more restricted than the syllable patterns, which permit dissimilar loci (/–mz/, etc.) *as well as* homorganic ones. Which of the two is truly phonological? Surely it is the syllable-based pattern, since this reflects what an English speaker is capable of pronouncing.

The difference between the two patterns reflects historical developments in the language. Until about the fourteenth century, plurals and past tenses were pronounced as separate syllables, /əz/ (or /əs/) and /əd/. Gradually, the /ə/ vowel dropped out, giving rise to sequences like /–mz/, /–ŋd/ which had previously not been permissible.

In Modern English, the syllable patterns *could* become productive, i.e. new morphemes could be formed on the basis of patterns like /–mz, –ŋz/. An invented word like *clumse* (/klʌmz/), 'a clumsy person', could give rise to a new morpheme with a hitherto non-occurrent morpheme-final cluster. This productiveness would be further evidence for taking the syllable, rather than the morpheme, as the appropriate unit for discussing phonological sequences.

Language acquisition

Adult speakers adapt loan-word clusters to the patterns of pronunciation long established by habit; children acquiring the language for the first time also make adaptations, in this case of the adult pronunciations they hear, to conform to what they are able to pronounce at their own particular stage of development. Initial clusters are reduced from two (or three) consonants to one, but the pattern of simplification contrasts quite strikingly with the loan-word changes illustrated in Exercise 4 above. Look at the following data (adapted from Smith 1973: [b̥], [d̥], etc. represent plosives which are voiceless (like [p]) and unaspirated (like [b])):

Adult word	Cluster	Child
broken	/br–/	[b̥ugu:]
brush	/br–/	[b̥ʌt]

drum	/dr–/	[d̥ʌm]
crumb	/kr–/	[g̊ʌm]
cloth	/kl–/	[g̊ɔk]
glasses	/gl–/	[g̊aːgiː]
please	/pl–/	[b̥iː]
twice	/tw–/	[d̥aɪf]
queen	/kw–/	[g̊iːm]

Children typically simplify plosive-plus-approximant clusters by deleting the approximant and retaining the plosive (though the plosive may also 'lose' some of its distinguishing features, for example, voicing in the data above). Note that the approximant is lost (and the plosive retained), despite the fact that the approximant is nearer in sequence to the vowel. In the loan-words, by contrast, it is the consonant *nearest to the vowel* which is retained (for example, [ps–] simplifies to /s–/, not to /p–/).

A second category of clusters, those in which /s/ is followed by a plosive (/sp–, st–, sk–/) are regularly simplified by young children with the loss of the initial /s/:

Word	*Adult cluster*	*Child*
spoon	/sp–/	[buːn]
skin	/sk–/	[g̊ɪn]
stamp	/st–/	[d̥ɛp]
stop	/st–/	[d̥ɔp]

The simplification pattern for *three*-consonant clusters (of which the first must be /s/) is now predictable on the basis of what has already been observed: the initial /s/ is lost; the approximant is lost; the plosive is retained. Thus:

squeeze	/skw–/	[g̊iːb̥]
squat	/skw–/	[g̊ɔp]
scream	/skr–/	[g̊iːm]
stroke	/str–/	[g̊oːk]

Consonant 'strength'

We have observed that the process of simplification (or reduction) of clusters in loan-words is a regular process, in which the consonant nearer to the vowel in sequence is favoured (retained) at the expense of the more distant plosive; while the process of reduction in language acquisition is also quite regular, but in this case the plosive is favoured whether it is nearer to the vowel (as in /sp–, st–/, etc.) or more distant (as in /pl–, kr–, etc.). At one time, phonologists would have been content to report such observations as 'facts about the language'. Nowadays, however, we go further: we would like to find explanations for the facts and processes we observe. If we are correct in assuming that the two situations (loan-words, and language acquisition) are comparable, (i.e. we are assuming that both processes result from some general property of human language and that they are not 'isolated facts'), our aim is to find, if possible, explanations for the contrary tendencies of the two processes.

The notion of consonant 'strength' provides an explanation for some of the observations. The explanation proceeds along the following lines:

1   Consonant sounds belong to a hierarchy from 'most-consonant-like' ('strongest') to 'most-vowel-like' ('weakest'). Generally, the greater the obstruction to the airstream in articulation, the stronger the consonant.

2   The hierarchy is approximately as follows (strongest first):

> plosive   .
> fricative
> nasal
> liquid
> glide

3   When clusters are reduced, *weaker* consonants yield to *stronger* ones.

Since plosives are 'stronger' than approximants, the sequence plosive (or fricative)-plus-approximant reduces to plosive (or fricative), for example /pl/→[p], /fl/→[f]; similarly the sequence fricative-plus-plosive reduces to the plosive, for example, /sp–/→[p]; and in three-consonant clusters, the strongest consonant (the plosive) is retained in favour of the fricative and the approximant, which are lost.

This explanation fits the acquisition data well, but has difficulty in accounting for the treatment of loan-words, such as the reduction of [pn–] to /n–/ (rather than to /p–/) and of [ps–, ts–], etc. to /s–/, since in each case the weaker consonant (nasal or fricative) should yield to the plosive.

An alternative explanation to account for this, though admittedly tentative, could be based on perception. When a consonant cluster is pronounced, we can assume that one sound will be perceptually more *salient* to the listener than the other; when simplification takes place, we can propose that the more salient sound is the one to be retained. Generally speaking, stronger consonants are more salient than weaker; but when a plosive (or fricative) precedes anything stronger than a liquid in the hierarchy (i.e. anything from nasals 'upwards') the second consonant has the effect of 'masking' the properties of the first consonant. The reason is that the most salient element of the syllable as a whole is the peak, namely the vowel. There is a gradual increase of salience as the vowel is approached (and a gradual *loss* of salience in post-vowel clusters). Thus, the [k] of [kn–] or the [p] of [ps–] loses much of its prominence 'behind' the relatively strong sound ([n, s], etc.) which lies next to the syllable peak.

Such explanations, in terms of consonant 'strength' and 'perceptual prominence' are at present tentative. They must be tested against further data from observations of historical change, language acquisition, and borrowing. There seems, at any rate, to be a major distinction to be drawn between clusters with an approximant as second element, and clusters with nasals or 'strong' consonants in that position.

Exercise 5

None of the following forms are English words. Which ones are not *possible* words, and why?

[kneft]	[sræfɪd]
[splɒθ]	[ʃtɔɪp]
[tlaɪn]	[gjumi]
[θwil]	[ʤlest]
[hroɷ]	[stwɪŋ]

Exercise 6

None of the following are actual English words. However, some are more *likely*, as possible words, than others. Which words do you think would be more acceptable, and which less?

    [zɪlp]   [zilp]

[trelk]   [treɪlk]
[fɒmp]   [foɷmp]
[gæŋk]   [gɑŋk]
[prʌsk]   [prusk]
[jesp]   [jaɪsp]
[grʌŋ]   [graɷŋ]

Vowel length

Hitherto, we have considered one particular type of phoneme sequence – the consonant cluster. There are, however, other ways in which particular languages may impose restrictions on the types of sequence permitted. Often, certain types of consonant may follow, or precede, only certain types of vowel, and vice versa. Sometimes the restrictions can be stated in quite general terms; for example, in English, the consonants /j, w, h/ (and /r/ in 'non-rhotic' accents)[6] can only occur prevocalically (they must be followed by a vowel). At other times the restrictions are more particular. For example, in English, long vowels (including diphthongs) are never followed by clusters, unless the second consonant of the cluster is alveolar. English has no words like /aɪlk/, /eɪmp/, /aɷŋk/, despite the existence of the clusters themselves, as in *silk, bump, wink*, etc. The possible (i.e. existing) combinations are as follows:

1   short vowel plus (non-alveolar) cluster,[7] for example

   help, bulb, sump, shelf, shelve (labial)
   bulk, sink (velar)

2   long vowel plus (non-alveolar) single C, for example

   ape, strike, tube, rogue, pouch, leaf, etc.

3   long vowel plus *alveolar* cluster, for example

   a   *paint, count, field, sound, spoilt*, etc.
   b   *aches, ached, plagues, plagued, robes, robed*, etc.

The restrictions (i.e. the combinations which do *not* occur) are thus confined to sequences of long vowel followed by the clusters listed under 1 above, i.e. /–lp, –lb, etc./. In Exercise 6, the column on the left contains potential (but non-existent) English words; the items in the column on the right are much less acceptable (less 'English') since they violate the restriction on non-alveolar clusters after long vowels.

The reason for the restriction appears to be largely historical; at a certain stage during the Middle English period (eleventh to fifteenth centuries) long vowels became short when a cluster followed. But there were certain exceptions to this change, all of them involving alveolar clusters. In Modern English we therefore find a number of words like *paint*, *sound*, etc. which constitute exceptions to the general rule.

Note that the restriction extends to /–ŋ/, i.e. there are no words in which /–ŋ/ follows a long vowel, though /–ŋ/ may follow short vowels, as in *bring*, *hang*, *song*, etc. The reason is again historical; /–ŋ/ was originally /–ŋg/, as the spelling suggests (and indeed as it still is in many Midlands dialects). The restriction prohibiting non-alveolar clusters after long vowels thus included /–ŋg/, so it now applies likewise to /–ŋ/.

Note too that there are certain phonetic exceptions to the restriction. Some onomatapaeic words, such as *oink*, or /bədɔiŋ/, include a non-alveolar cluster (or /–ŋ/) after a long vowel. In casual speech, too, sequences of long vowels followed by the -ing morpheme may coalesce into long vowel plus /ŋ/, thus:

seeing	/si + ɪŋ/	pronounced [siŋ]
playing	/pleɪ + ɪŋ/	pronounced [pleiŋ]
drawing	/drɔ + ɪŋ/	pronounced [drɔiŋ]
flying	/flaɪ + ɪŋ/	pronounced [flaiŋ]

There is, then, a distinction to be drawn between what speakers actually *do*, and what appears 'possible' in terms of the language generally. As far as the vocabulary of English is concerned, sequences of long vowel plus non-alveolar clusters are not permitted; in actual fact, however, speakers may produce such sequences. *Oink* and [bədɔiŋ] are not 'possible' English words, yet, paradoxically, speakers may use them; [flaiŋ], etc. are also not 'permitted', but may nevertheless occur, as pronunciations of /flaɪ-ɪŋ/, etc. We have shown the difference by giving a phonemic representation (slant brackets) to the former, and a phonetic representation (square brackets) to the latter. This reflects the distinction, discussed in Chapter 1, between phonemic = 'what the speaker knows about his language', and phonetic = 'what the speaker actually does'. In the section on fast speech, below, we shall see further illustration of this distinction.

Loan-word sequences

Our pronunciation of words borrowed from other languages provides, as indicated in an earlier section, excellent evidence of our own
phonetic habits. Previously we have considered the pronunciation of
loan-word clusters: we can now broaden the discussion to observe
other types of sequence.

The simplest form of loan-word adaptation is the replacement of
the sounds in the original (lending) language with the corresponding
sounds in the receiver (borrowing) language, on the basis of an
approximate phonetic equivalent (APE). For example, the French word
coup is borrowed into English, with the pronunciation /ku/. In French,
the word would also be transcribed /ku/, but the sounds are not the
same: French initial [k] is less aspirated than English initial [kʰ], and
French [u] is short and 'pure' (i.e. there is no glide) whereas English [oᵘ]
is long and diphthongal. English /ku/ is thus the APE of French /ku/,
but there are phonetic differences of realization. Likewise, in the
borrowed word *crochet*, English speakers adapt the French uvular 'r'
([ʁ]) to the APE English /r/, namely [ɹ], and the French final vowel [e],
which is tense, is converted to the *long* English diphthong /eɪ/ (there are
other adaptations too, such as the stress pattern).

If there is no exact APE in the borrowing language, speakers may
make efforts to preserve the critical or distinctive features of the
original sound in whatever ways are possible. One method is to 'split'
the original into a sequence of two sounds, one of which preserves
some of the original features, and the other the remainder. For
example, French has a set of nasalized vowels, /ɔ̃, ɛ̃/, etc. When
English borrows words containing them, they are usually interpreted
as a sequence of vowel plus nasal consonant. Thus French 'bon', /bɔ̃/
becomes English /bɒn/; 'detente', /detɑ̃t/ becomes English /deɪtɑnt/.
All the significant features of the French sound (the vowel quality,
and the nasality) are preserved in English, but are split into a
sequence instead of being represented in a single phoneme. High
front rounded vowels, which are found in both French and German
but not in English, are treated similarly: /y/ is split into the sequence
/ju/, which is not only permissible in English but also preserves the
critical features of /y/: the features *high* and *front* are transferred to
/j/, while the feature *rounded*, which accompanies only *back* vowels in
English, is given to the high *back* vowel /u/. Thus the APE of French
'deja vu' is, in English, /deɪʒə vju/, and the German painter Dürer,
/dyrər/ in the original, is copied as /djurə/.

The pronunciation of loan-words is, it should be noted, often mediated through the spelling. Thus, instead of an APE, a loan-word is often pronounced by simply transferring the letter-values to those of the receiver language. An example is the borrowing into English of the Spanish word *junta*. The pronunciation /ʤʌntə/ is based on our orthographic conventions, in which letter j represents /ʤ/, letter u /ʌ/, and so on. In Spanish, letter j represents /h/, and letter u, [u] or [ʊ]. The APE of *junta* in English would therefore be /hʊntə/. Some speakers (notably those with Spanish contact, for example the 'Anglos' of California) do use this pronunciation, but the majority prefer the spelling-based version. The two are sometimes distinguished as *ear-borrowings*, in which the pronunciation is based on an APE, vs *eye-borrowings*, in which the pronunciation depends on the spelling. In a highly literate society, eye-borrowings tend to predominate.

Fast or 'casual' speech

The restrictions we have designated for the initial clusters of English syllables are applicable only so long as we are concerned with what we can call 'citation' forms, that is, with *individual* words, spoken in isolation at a reasonable speed and with a 'careful' rather than a 'casual' articulation. Beyond the limits imposed by these conditions, we find that speakers are capable of pronouncing all sorts of sequences which would otherwise be called 'unacceptable', 'un-English', etc. In fast speech, syllables may be 'telescoped' and vowels, especially unstressed vowels, elided, which brings together some unusual sequences of consonants. We are familiar with 'fast' or 'casual' pronunciations like *s'pose* for *suppose* and *p'lice* for *police*, which produce the clusters /sp–/ and /pl–/, found also in citation forms like *spoke* and *please*; but in a fast pronunciation of *potato* and *tomato* the loss of the /ə/ vowel (/pət–, təm–/) results in the clusters [pt–] and [tm–]. The possibilities for 'unusual' combinations are very large indeed; once the limitation of 'citation' forms is removed, almost anything is possible, within the limits of what is pronounceable in general, universal terms (i.e. in terms which would apply to 'language' as a whole, rather than to any *specific* language). Thus we will still not find sequences which impose unrealistic articulatory demands, such as [pb–, dt–, rh–]; we would want to exclude such sequences on universal, i.e. 'general phonetic' grounds. But apart from that type of sequence, a very wide range of possibilities becomes available. In a sense, therefore, the phonology of a particular language comes, once we go beyond citation forms, into the domain of the laws of general phonetics, i.e. of what is universally possible.

As mentioned in an earlier section, we can distinguish the citation forms, the 'ideal' forms which are part of the speaker's knowledge, from what the speaker 'actually does'. The former belongs at the phonemic level, the latter at the phonetic. For example, *potato* is phonemically /pəteɪtoɑ/, but may be pronounced in fact as ['pteɪtoɑ] (with, of course, other changes such as [ɾ] for the intervocalic /t/, yielding ['pteɪɾoɑ]). There is a useful and necessary distinction between items like *suppose* and items like *spoke*, even though both might be pronounced [sp–] in casual speech. The difference is that *suppose* can *also* be pronounced with /ə/ (/səpoɑz/), whereas *spoke* can *only* be /sp–/. The *difference* between them can be shown at the phonemic level:

> /səpoɑz/   'suppose'
> /spoɑk/   'spoke'

and the *similarity* at the phonetic level:

> [spoɑz]
> [spoɑk}

For *suppose* (but not for *spoke*), a rule of [ə]-deletion will be needed in order to link the phonemic representation to the actual pronunciation. The application of the rule will be optional; whether it operates or not can be related to 'external' factors such as 'careful' vs 'casual' or 'fast' speech. We return to this in Chapter 6.

Exercise 7

Loan-words

1   What is the source language of each of the following loan-words?
2   How are they pronounced in English?
3   What adaptations from the original have taken place?
4   Are they an *ear-borrowing* or an *eye-borrowing*?

apartheid	Don Quixote	rapport
autobahn	foyer	seance
chapati	joie de vivre	Sheikh
Chopin	mirage	slalom
cul-de-sac	paella	yoghourt

3 Distinctive features

The theory of distinctive features is based on the premise that the phonemes of a language can be analysed or broken down into a small number of components or features, these being the minimal elements ('atoms') from which the phonemes (the 'molecules') are built up. The analysis of phonemes into 'features' has a long history, but the theory has recently developed and expanded enormously, particularly since the publication of Jakobson's *Preliminaries to Speech Analysis* in collaboration with Fant and Halle in 1952. These developments were foreshadowed by the phonologists of the Prague School (including Jakobson himself) in the 1930s.

Details of the Jakobson features were revised subsequently (in *Fundamentals* 1956; and again in Malmberg 1968). Another major development of the features was the incorporation of feature matrices into generative phonology, as in Chomsky and Halle (1968). The features proposed there were further revised by Halle and Stevens (1971). Although the Chomsky and Halle features are perhaps the best known and the most widely recognized, both the individual features and the principles on which they are based have been criticized. Ladefoged, in particular, has proposed alternative sets of features which have a number of advantages (1971, 1972). These too have been subject to revision (for example, Ladefoged 1980). Thus, the question of *how many* features, and *which*, is still very much open.

In this chapter we shall look briefly at the 'traditional' features and then in detail at the proposals of, first, Jakobson, and then of Chomsky and Halle. We shall also discuss the aims and principles of the theory; in particular, we must ask what are the *purposes* and *functions* of the features we establish, since the features which best fit one purpose may not be the best for others.

Traditional features

The traditional analysis of speech sounds has always had an

articulatory basis. Because the articulation of consonants differs so markedly from that of vowels, the terms used for each have usually been quite distinct. Consonants are described according to three basic dimensions:

1   voicing (voiced–voiceless);
2   *place* of articulation (labial, dental, velar, etc.);
3   *manner* of articulation (plosive, affricate, nasal, etc.).

Thus /ʃ/ would, for example, be described as a voiceless palato-alveolar fricative, and these labels represent, in a sense, the *distinctive* properties of /ʃ/ since they each serve to distinguish it from at least one other sound: from /ʒ/, which is voiced, from /s/, which is alveolar, and from /tʃ/, which is an affricate.

Vowels are described by four basic dimensions:

1   length (short–long);
2   the 'vertical' point of reference (close–open, or high–low);
3   the 'horizontal' point of reference (front–back);
4   rounding (unrounded–round).

Thus /e/, for example, would be described as a *short mid front unrounded* vowel and, again, these labels serve to distinguish /e/ from the other vowels and thus represent its 'criterial' properties.

The advantage of these traditional features, which are still used and which form the basis of many of the generative distinctive features, is that they are straightforwardly phonetic, i.e. they relate directly to the articulation of the sound (rather than holding an indirect or abstract relationship as some of the more recent features do), and because of this, when they are used in descriptions of processes, their 'naturalness' is self-evident. For instance, if an 'alveolar' phoneme has a 'dental' allophone, as when /n/ is pronounced [n̪] before /θ/ and /ð/, there is no difficulty in relating 'alveolar' to 'dental' because we know that these are adjacent points of articulation and are therefore quite 'naturally' interchangeable. Similarly, if a vowel becomes 'nasalized' before a nasal consonant, this is recognized as a simple transfer of the *manner* of articulation of the consonant on to the preceding vowel.

The disadvantages of these articulatory features are of several kinds, and it is instructive to look into them in order to see in what ways the more recent proposals have solved, or failed to solve, the problems.

Economy of description

First, the articulatory features are not always very economical in accounting for the phonemes as a system. The feature 'voicing' is well utilized in English because it can be applied to no fewer than eight pairs of consonants (/p/ vs /b/, /f/ vs /v/, etc.), but many of the 'place' and 'manner' features are poorly utilized. 'Labio-dental', for instance, applies only to /f/ and /v/, 'glottal' only to /h/; 'lateral' applies only to /l/, and 'retroflex' only to /r/. For the twenty-four consonant phonemes of English, we require a total of sixteen articulatory features, which is not much better than giving each phoneme an individual description.

Consonants vs vowels

As we have seen, the set of features which describe the vowels are quite different from those which describe the consonants. Yet there is sometimes a relationship between some of the vowels and some of the consonants. One obvious example is the relationship of the glides /j, w/ to the vowels /i, u/: the glides are nothing more than 'rapid' versions of the corresponding vowels. Yet /j/ is described as a (*voiced*) *palatal glide* (or semi-vowel) while /i/ is given the features *close, front* and *unrounded*. Several consonants have close relationships of this kind with a vowel. /h/, for instance, is sometimes described in articulatory terms as a consonant (usually as a voiceless glottal fricative), but at other times as a voiceless *vowel*. /r/ has a relationship with /ə/, as we see from a comparison of the 'r-pronouncing' (or 'rhotic') vs 'r-less' (or 'non-rhotic') accents of English: compare the pronunciations of *fear* as [fiːr] vs [fiːə] or of *dare* as [der] vs [deə]. (When the non-rhotic accents 'lost' their [r] it was replaced first with [ə].) /l/, or rather dark [ɫ], has a relationship with a back vowel [o], as illustrated by those English dialects (such as London) in which final [ɫ] has been 'replaced' by [o]. In both cases, the [r] and [ɫ] *sound* very similar to their corresponding vowels [ə] and [o], yet we are forced to *describe* them in completely different terms: /l/, for example, as a (voiced) alveolar lateral, but [o] as a short half-close back rounded vowel. Instances in which consonants have properties closely related to specific vowels make excellent test cases for any theory of features, since an adequate theory is one which can show the relationship satisfactorily.

Relationships between non-adjacent sounds

There are a number of cases where two or more sounds appear to be related to each other, yet the relationship cannot be explained on an articulatory basis because the points of articulation are not adjacent. When /k, g/ are 'palatalized' before front vowels such as /i, e/ we accept that 'velars' become 'palatal' because we know that the two points are adjacent; but how do we explain that [ʔ], a glottal stop, is an allophone of /t/, an alveolar stop, in English?[1] 'Glottal' is separated from 'alveolar' by the intervening points *palato-alveolar* and *velar*. Similarly, the non-adjacent sounds [f] (labio-dental) and [x] (velar) are related historically in English. The /f/ of *enough, trough, cough*, etc. was pronounced [x] at an earlier stage of the language, and the change was from [x] to [f] directly, not a gradual development via the intervening points of articulation. In both cases we are dealing with a relationship between sounds which cannot be satisfactorily 'explained' in purely articulatory terms.

Higher-order features

The traditional features allow us to make some generalizations: for example, we can talk about 'all voiceless sounds', or 'all nasals'; but the articulatory description leaves many sounds apparently isolated, unrelated to any other sound. /l/, for instance, is fully distinguished from the other phonemes of English by the feature 'lateral', but at the same time this feature isolates it. In English, as in many other languages, /l/ is closely related to /r/: both sounds behave very similarly. We thus need a term which will include /l, r/ (but no other sound). The term 'liquid' will serve this purpose, but it is hardly a 'manner' feature; its real function is to group /l, r/ as a class. Similarly, it is advantageous to have a term to cover the four sounds, /l, r, j, w/ in English, which share certain properties; the recently-coined *approximant* has quickly proved its usefulness. We must recognize, however, that *liquid* and *approximant* are not 'distinctive' terms as such – they identify higher-order, more general categories.

Having looked at some of the problems of the articulatory features, we can now consider more recent feature systems.

The distinctive features of Roman Jakobson

Jakobson's proposals were first presented in detail in *Preliminaries*

(1952). They departed from traditional classifications of sounds in a number of important respects. Jakobson argued:

1   That all features should be *binary*. The binary principle gives each feature two 'values', symbolized ' + ' and ' − '. Some phonetic features are 'naturally' binary, for example *nasal* (+) vs *oral* (−), voiced (+) vs voiceless (−). In other cases, however, such as place of articulation or vowel height, binary divisions can be awkward, unnatural, and arbitrary: the binary principle thus remains controversial (see below, p. 95).

2   That the basis of the distinctions should be *auditory* (or acoustic) rather than *articulatory*. The role of the listener in a speech event is just as important as that of the speaker; the signals received by the listener must therefore convey the necessary distinctions. As noted earlier, acoustic impression and articulation are usually in a one-to-one relationship, and features may therefore be defined in terms of either, or both; auditory definitions will, however, take preference, in cases where more than one articulation results in the same acoustic impression.

3   That phonetic features are *universal* rather than specific to a particular language. Languages may differ only in the way they *select* from the common 'pool' of features, and in the ways in which the features are *combined*. Jakobson proposed an inventory of fifteen universal features (of which three are non-segmental, relating to stress, tone, etc.).

4   That the same features, if carefully defined, can apply to both consonants and vowels. This innovation was made possible by advances in the acoustic analysis of sounds, as will become clear from consideration of the individual features (below, pp. 83 ff).

Acoustic definitions of the features

A full understanding of the definitions of Jakobson's features requires considerable background knowledge of acoustic phonetics. Since we are concerned here with phonology, we can only explain briefly, and perhaps inadequately, the principles involved.[2]

Sounds are distinguished basically in terms of three dimensions; their *amplitude*, or 'loudness', measured in decibels (dB); their *pitch*, or frequency, measured in hertz (Hz); and their *duration* or length, measured in milliseconds (msecs). The spectrogram gives a visual presentation of this information for a particular utterance, and by comparing the spectrograms of many utterances of a sound by many speakers, we can measure the energy patterns *typically* associated with that particular sound.

It may be simplest to begin with an illustration showing two of the three dimensions. Figure 7, below, shows a typical spectrum for the cardinal vowel [e].[3] On the vertical scale is shown the pitch in Hz, and the amplitude is shown horizontally.

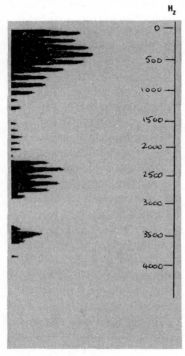

Figure 7   Spectrum of cardinal [e]

The spectrum shows peaks of energy at three different frequencies; a substantial peak at about 375 Hz, and lesser ones at about 2250 and 3350 Hz respectively. This distribution of energy is characteristic of [e]; other vowels show peaks at different frequencies.

The spectrogram gives the same information, but with the addition of the time dimension. Figure 8, opposite, is a spectrogram for the same vowel. The vertical scale now shows the frequency, and the horizontal shows time. The *intensity* (amplitude) is shown by the

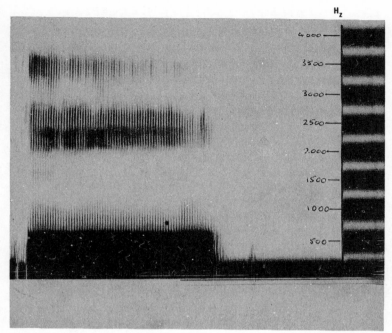

Figure 8 Spectrogram of cardinal [e]

darkness of the trace; notice that the band at 375 Hz is darker and heavier than the bands at around 2250 and 3350 Hz.

The peaks of energy characteristic of each vowel are created by the shape of the vocal tract. As the position of the tongue changes, the pattern of energy output changes and different spectra result.

The peaks of energy are known as formants, and are numbered from the bottom upwards. The spectrogram above shows three formants, F1 at around 375 Hz, F2 at 2250 Hz, and F3 at 3350 Hz. Most vowels are characterized by only two formants, F1 and F2, the third formant generally being rather weak. The frequencies do not have to be precise – their relative values are more important than their absolute values.

When the formant structures for a number of vowels are grouped together, a sort of pattern emerges. Table 1, p. 80, shows the major formants for most of the English vowels. We can see from Table 1 that the close vowels /i, u/ have a low value for F1. As the vowels become more open, the F1 value increases, reaching a peak with /ɑ/,

Table 1   *Formant values (F1, F2, F3) of English (RP) vowels (Data based on Ladefoged (1971: 73))*

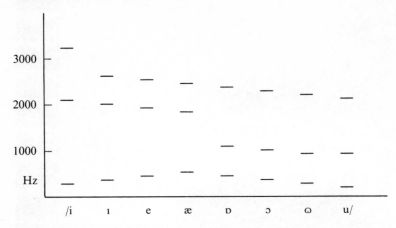

the most open vowel, and then declining again towards /u/. There seems to be a direct relationship between F1 values and the traditional vowel dimension, close–open.

The table also shows that the front vowels, /i, ɪ, e/, etc., have a high value for F2 and F3, whereas the back vowels have relatively low values for these two formants. This suggests another relationship, between the formants F2, F3 and the traditional dimension *front–back*. The distribution of energy in front vowels, however, is not quite like the distribution in the back vowels: the values of F2 and F3 are almost constant for all the back vowels, whereas the front vowels are sharply distinguished. This means that it is harder to discriminate between the various back vowels, because their F2/F3 is constant; we have to rely on the falling values of F1. Again, this corresponds to what we know about vowels in languages; we know that languages make more use of front vowels than of back vowels. There are often *more* front-vowel phonemes, and their frequency in use is greater.

In this section, we have digressed from our main theme to discuss acoustic vowel measurement. The significance of this will, I hope, become clear in the discussion of the features *compact/diffuse* and *grave/acute* in the following sections.

The distinctive feature matrix

Jakobson proposes a systematic differentiation of all the phonemes of

English by means of nine distinctive features, each with a binary value. The system can be represented in a matrix, with features for the rows and phonemes (segments) for the columns. The matrix (Figure 9) on p. 82 is adapted from the one given in *Preliminaries* (p. 43); I have rearranged the order of the vowels, and used the familiar symbols for /tʃ, dʒ/. In the matrix, the 'plus' symbol refers to the *first* value of the feature (i.e. the one on the left; *vocalic*, *consonantal*, etc.), and the 'minus' symbol refers to the second value, on the right of the pair (for example, *nonvocalic*, *diffuse*, etc.).

Following the matrix is the transcription of a 'famous test sentence', which shows how Jakobson proposes to use the six vowel phonemes to produce the long vowels (including diphthongs), which are treated as a sequence of two vowels. As short vowels, Jakobson's symbols correspond respectively to our /ɪ e æ ʌ ɒ ʊ/.

This analysis of English sounds is unsatisfactory in a number of ways: its treatment of the long vowels is inadequate; the representation of the glides /j, w/ as /i, u/ is odd; and there is no description of /r/ at all. But the analysis is successful in its broader aims:

1   In any feature system, a basic requirement is that each phoneme is given a specification which makes it distinct from each of the other phonemes. A quick check shows that the matrix above satisfies this requirement; no phoneme has exactly the same set of plusses and minuses as any other phoneme.

2   The number of features should be as small as possible to give the most economical analysis. To represent the thirty phonemes of English with only nine features is a significant achievement – compare the traditional analysis which requires sixteen. The theoretical minimum number of binary features required to distinguish thirty phonemes is five ($2^5 = 32$). But the features themselves must represent natural, realistic categories. It would be most unlikely for a language to make optimal use of every single natural feature.

3   The specifications should make 'good sense' when the phonemes are compared with each other. We would expect phonemes which we know to be closely related, to be distinguished by not more than one feature; and conversely, phonemes which we know are *not* related, should be distinguished by at least two or more features. This principle can also be tested by inspecting the matrix. For an obvious example, take the voiced–voiceless pairs, p/b, s/z, etc.; their specifications should be identical except for one feature, and they are: /p/ is identical to /b/ except for the feature *tense* (= voiceless) vs *lax*

	i	e	a	ə	o	u	p	b	f	v	m	t	d	θ	ð	s	z	n	ʃ	ʒ	tʃ	dʒ	k	g	ŋ	l	h	ø
Vocalic/nonvoc.	+	+	+	+	+	+	−	−	−	−	−	−	−	−	−	−	−	−	−	−	−	−	−	−	−	+	−	−
Constl./non-constl.	−	−	−	−	−	−	+	+	+	+	+	+	+	+	+	+	+	+	+	+	+	+	+	+	+	+	−	−
Compact/diffuse	−	+	+	+	+	+	−	−	−	−	−	−	−	−	−	−	−	−	+	+	+	+	+	+	+	+	+	
Grave/acute	−	−	+	+	+	+	+	+	+	+	+	−	−	−	−	−	−	−	−	−	−	−	+	+	+	−		
Flat/plain	−	−			+	+																						
Nasal/oral											+							+							+			
Tense/lax	+	−					+	−	+	−		+	−	+	−	+	−		+	−	+	−	+	−				
Contin./interrupted							−	−	+	+		−	−	+	+	+	+		+	+	−	−	−	−		+	+	
Strident/mellow							−	−	+	+		−	−	−	−	+	+		+	+	+	+	−	−			+	

Note: /h/ hil̥   /ø/ ill

ʤou tuk faəðəz ʃuu bentʃ aut ʃii uəz ueitiŋ ət mai lɔɒn
Joe took father's shoe bench out; She was waiting at my lawn

Figure 9 The distinctive features for English (RP) as proposed by Jakobson, Fant and Halle (1951)

(=voiced). For a rather less obvious example, try /m/ and /b/. We find identical specifications as far as *nasal/oral*, for which /m/ is + and /b/ −. /b/ is then further specified as *lax* (to distinguish it from /p/), and as *interrupted* (to distinguish it from /v/). /m/ does not need a specification for these features, because all nasals are lax (voiced), and continuant. For a third example, compare /f/ and /θ/. We know these sounds are closely related, because several English dialects (especially urban London) substitute /f/ for /θ/, as do children until a relatively late stage of language learning. Reliably, the matrix shows the difference as depending on only one feature, *grave/acute* (/f/ is grave, /θ/ is acute).

Explanation of the features

Several of the nine features are intelligible with a minimum of explanation. *Tense/lax*, for instance, obviously corresponds to the traditional feature of voicing. Tense (=voiceless) phonemes are defined acoustically as 'displaying a longer sound interval and a higher total amount of energy, with a greater spread of energy in the spectrum'. In articulatory terms, tense sounds require 'greater deformation of the vocal tract away from the rest position'. In other words, voiceless sounds require more energy because they do not have the voice (i.e. vibrations of the vocal cords) to 'support' them. Chomsky and Halle later (1968) used *tense/lax* to distinguish *long* vowels from *short* vowels: the acoustic definition involving a 'longer sound interval' and 'higher energy' was extended to the vowels. (For tense and lax *consonants*, however, they revert to the traditional feature, *voice*.)

The feature *continuant/interrupted* basically distinguishes between *stops* (interrupted) and *fricatives* (continuant). While an acoustic definition can be given, the basis of the distinction is just as much articulatory as acoustic. In the matrix, this feature distinguishes /p/ from /f/, /t/ from /θ/ and /s/, and /ʧ/ from /ʃ/, together with their voiced counterparts.

Strident distinguishes a set of six consonants, /ʧ ʤ, ʃ ʒ, s z/. Acoustically, strident sounds 'have irregular wave forms', with 'a random distribution of black areas in the spectrogram' (radio technicians refer to this as 'white noise'). In articulatory terms, stridents are 'rough-edged', because 'a supplementary obstruction creates greater turbulence at the point of articulation'. *Strident* is a useful feature, because we know that the six sounds which are

[+strident] behave as a group; for example, in the formation of regular plurals (and possessives) in English, words ending in any of these six sounds require insertion of [ə]: *buses, bushes, larches,* etc.

Vocalic/nonvocalic and *consonantal/nonconsonantal* broadly distinguish *vowels* (+ voc., −constl.) from *consonants* (−voc., +constl.). It seems uneconomic to establish *two* features to make this distinction, but the justification is the 'intermediate' group of vowel-like consonants, [l r] which are specified ' +' for both features, and [j, w, h, ʔ] which have ' −' for both. These specifications have proved unsatisfactory, and there are serious problems in defining these features in such a way that some sounds can be both 'vocalic' and 'consonantal' whereas other sounds can be neither. Some possible revisions are discussed below (pp. 96–8).

Compact/diffuse is an innovative feature which can be applied to both consonants and vowels, but in different ways. Among the consonants, it distinguishes 'front' (*diffuse*) from 'back' (*compact*). The dividing line lies between alveolar and palato-alveolar. Among vowels, this feature corresponds to the traditional *open–close* (or *high–low*); open vowels are *compact* and close vowels are *diffuse*. The acoustic basis for the distinction is that *diffuse* sounds have energy spread relatively widely (i.e. 'diffusely') across the spectrum, while *compact* sounds have energy concentrated in one area. This can be observed, for vowels at least, in Table 1 (p. 80): close vowels like [i, u] have their energy distributed widely, with F1 substantially separated from F2; open vowels by contrast have F1 and F2 concentrated into a small area.

A feature which distinguishes both consonants and vowels has the advantage of economy, but unless it can be demonstrated that there is some 'natural' relationship between, say, *front* consonants and *close* vowels (which are both 'diffuse') as against back consonants and open vowels, then the feature has little explanatory purpose. Since such evidence was lacking, Chomsky and Halle later redivided this feature; for consonants they proposed *anterior*, and for vowels *high* and *low*. It is important to realize, however, that the feature *anterior* has its origins in the acoustically-defined *compact/diffuse*, despite its articulatory definition.

Grave/acute is another innovative feature which spans both consonants and vowels. Among the vowels, it corresponds to the traditional *front/back* division. *Grave* sounds have relatively *low* pitch (i.e. frequency), *acute* relatively high. Table 1 (p. 80) shows that front vowels have high frequencies for F2 and F3 and are thus 'acute', while back vowels have a lower F2 and F3. The 'gravity' feature thus corresponds to the values of F2 and F3, while 'compactness' (see previous section) is largely determined by the value of F1.

Among consonants, the gravity feature distinguishes 'peripheral' consonants which are 'grave', from 'central' consonants which are 'acute'. Peripheral consonants are those which are articulated at the peripheries of the oral tract, namely labials and velars; central consonants include dentals, alveolars and palatals.

The advantage of this feature was, again, economy, but evidence for any natural association between, say, *back* vowels and *peripheral* consonants (both 'grave') was sparse. Chomsky and Halle thus redivided this feature just as they divided compactness; for vowels they use the traditional feature *back*, and for consonants a new feature, *coronal*. *Coronal* sounds involve a raising of the 'crown' (or centre) of the tongue, and thus correspond approximately (but not exactly – cf. Hyman 1975: 48) to Jakobson's *acute* consonants, while *SPE*'s *non-coronal* are approximately Jakobson's *grave* (i.e. peripheral) consonants. More recently, however, it has been claimed that there *is* substantial evidence supporting the earlier grave/acute distinction (Hyman 1973; Pagliuca and Mowrey 1980).

Exercises

Exercise 1

Without looking at the matrix on p. 82, classify each of the following sounds as either *compact* (+) or *diffuse* (−). Then check your answers against the matrix.

[d] [g] [m] [o] (= ɒ) [a] (= æ) [v] [ʧ] [ð]

Exercise 2

1 Again without looking at the matrix, classify each of the following sounds as either *grave* (+) or *acute* (−). Check your answers against the matrix:

[ð] [n] [f] [u] [b] [e] [m] [z]

2 [g] and [ŋ] are not specified for 'gravity' in the matrix.
   a Would they be *grave* or *acute*?
   b Why is it unnecessary to specify them?

Exercise 3

The matrix on p. 82 has many 'blanks' where particular features are left unspecified. Why is it unnecessary to specify vowels for the features *nasal/oral*, *tense/lax*, and *continuant/interrupted*? Why are [p, b] and [t, d] unspecified for *strident/mellow*?

Exercise 4

The sounds [p] and [ŋ] have no connection with each other phonologically. Which features distinguish them? Which features do they share? Is the difference between them reflected realistically by their feature specifications?

Flat/plain

Flat vs *plain* is a straightforward feature which distinguishes between *rounded* and *unrounded* vowels. *Flat* is defined acoustically in terms of pitch: as in music, a flat sound has a lower pitch (or frequency) than the corresponding 'plain' (in music the term is 'natural') sound. Rounded vowels are 'flat' because the rounding of the lips creates a larger, more 'hollow' oral cavity with a smaller aperture, and hence a lower note (cf. the 'peripheral' consonants). The feature *flat/plain* only applies distinctively to the back vowels in English, because all front vowels are unrounded ('plain'). The distinction is therefore as follows:

plain (unrounded)	*flat* (rounded)
ə	u
a	o

Many British phoneticians traditionally distinguish between *front*, *central*, and *back* vowels. In the Jakobson framework, *central* vowels are back, unrounded (i.e. *grave* and *plain*), whereas *back* vowels are back, rounded (*grave* and *flat*). The British three-way distinction is thus converted into two binary distinctions.

Chomsky and Halle take over the 'flatness' feature but relabel it with the traditional articulatory term, *round*.

The distinctive features of Chomsky and Halle (*SPE*)

It should be clear from the preceding account, that the features used by Chomsky and Halle derive in a quite direct way, but with certain changes and revisions, from the features proposed by Jakobson. To understand the basis of the later features, it is helpful, if not essential, to work through the features which preceded them and from which they derive. But it would be misleading to think that we can compare the *SPE* features with Jakobson directly, because there are three main areas of difference, two quite fundamental, the other more superficial. Let us take the latter first.

The articulatory basis

Chomsky and Halle abandon the idea of giving priority to acoustic descriptions of the features and revert to the articulatory basis. But this is not a return to the status quo – rather, it is an adaptation of Jakobson's fundamentally acoustic distinctions into an articulatory framework. Many of the features of course lend themselves to an acoustic or articulatory framework equally, and the transfer is merely one of labels: *flat/plain* becomes *round/non-round*, *tense/lax* corresponds to *voice*, *nasal/oral* becomes $+/-$ *nasal*. But the basically acoustic features *compact/diffuse* and *grave/acute* are now given *articulatory* definitions: *compact/diffuse* becomes *anterior*, *grave/acute* becomes *coronal*. Despite their articulatory labels, however, these features are acoustic in origin.

The abstractness of the segments

A second reason which makes any direct comparison difficult is the abstractness of Chomsky and Halle's segments. In their theoretical framework, a highly abstract set of phonological segments are converted to actual 'surface' pronunciations by a series of phonological rules. At the 'surface', the features are no longer necessarily binary (they can be multi-valued) and they may not even be 'distinctive'. At the 'deep' or abstract level of representation, the features are both distinctive and binary, but the inventory includes a considerable number of segments which never appear in any actual pronunciation, including total abstractions such as, for English, a vowel /œ/ (i.e. a front, open, rounded vowel), and the consonants /c, x, kʷ, gʷ and xʷ/. It may not be fair then, to compare Chomsky and Halle's matrix with

Table 2 *Distinctive feature specification for English consonants (adapted from SPE: 176–7)*

	i	e	æ	ɒ	ʌ	u	p	b	t	d	k	g	f	v	θ	ð	s	z	ʃ	ʒ	ʧ	ʤ	m	n	ŋ	l	r	j	w	h
voc.	+	+	+	+	+	+	−	−	−	−	−	−	−	−	−	−	−	−	−	−	−	−	−	−	−	+	+	−	−	−
constl.	−	−	−	−	−	−	+	+	+	+	+	+	+	+	+	+	+	+	+	+	+	+	+	+	+	+	+	−	−	−
high	+	−	−	−	−	+					+	+							+	+	+	+			+			+	+	−
back	−	−	−	+	+	+					+	+													+			−	+	
low	−	−	+	+	−	−																								+
ant.							+	+	+	+	−	−	+	+	+	+	+	+	−	−	−	−	+	+	−	+	+			
cor.							−	−	+	+	−	−	−	−	+	+	+	+	+	+	+	+	−	+	−	+	+			
round	−	−	−	+	−	+																						−	+	
tense	+	+	−	−	−	+																								
voice							−	+	−	+	−	+	−	+	−	+	−	+	−	+	−	+	+	+	+	+	+	+	+	−
contin.							−	−	−	−	−	−	+	+	+	+	+	+	+	+	−	−	−	−	−	+	+	+	+	+
nasal							−	−	−	−	−	−	−	−	−	−	−	−	−	−	−	−	+	+	+	−	−	−	−	−
strid.							−	−	−	−	−	−	+	+	−	−	+	+	+	+	+	+	−	−	−	−	−	−	−	−

Note: In the original matrix, the vowels are all specified 'minus' for [ant.] and [cor.]; all consonants (except /h/) are [−low]; and all consonants except the ones marked +, are [−high], [−back]. I have excluded this information in order to make the matrix clearer. I have, however, included the full specifications for /h/ since the treatment of this segment as vowel or consonant is unclear.

Jakobson's. But in spite of this, many consonants, and the short vowels, are roughly 'translatable' from one framework to the other. With these provisos, then, we present a matrix (Table 2) based on Chomsky and Halle (*SPE*: 176–7) which can be compared with Jakobson's earlier matrix. I have left out the controversial segments which never appear in actual pronunciations, and I have also left out the tense vowels, which appear at the 'deep' level in a form quite unrecognizable from their eventual pronunciation (and which are also controversial for that reason).

Specifications

The features in this matrix will be largely familiar from the preceding discussion. *Vocalic, consonantal, strident, nasal* and *continuant* are taken over directly, with minor revisions. /j, w/ are now included separately, with specifications identical to /i, u/ except that the glides are [− voc.], and the true vowels are [+ voc.]. /r/ has also been included; its specification is identical to /l/ except for the feature *anterior*. /f, v/ are specified as plus for 'strident', though this is unnecessary as they are already distinct from all other segments through other features. Nasals are now [− continuant] on the grounds that they require a complete *oral* closure. The features *voice, continuant, nasal* and *strident* are specified only for consonants, while *tense* and *round* apply only to vowels.

Exercise 5

Without consulting the *SPE* matrix, complete the table below for

	f	l	ɪ	p	s	æ	ŋ	k	r	ʌ	ʃ
voc.											
constl.											
high											
back											
low											
ant.											
cor.											
round											
tense											
voice											
contin.											
nasal											
strid.											

each segment by filling in the appropriate plus and minus values, or by leaving blanks where a feature need not be specified. High vowels are [+high, −low]; mid vowels are 'neither high nor low' ([−high, −low]); low vowels are [−high, +low]. Check your answers against the matrix.

Exercise 6

Compare the specifications in the matrix below with the *SPE* matrix and work out what each segment is. The first segment is /w/ and the whole answer makes a short English sentence.

	w									
voc.	−	+	−	−	+	−	−	+	+	−
constl.	−	−	+	+	−	+	+	−	+	+
high	+	−	+		−			+		
back	+	+			−			−		
low	−	+			+			−		
ant.			−	+		+	+		+	+
cor.			+	+		+			+	−
round	+	+			−			−		
tense	−	−			−			−		
voice			−	+		−	−		+	+
contin.			−	+		−	+		+	−
nasal			−	−		−	−		−	+
strid.			+	−		−	+		−	−

One important development is the fact that the consonants are specified for the features *high*, *back* and *low*,[4] which are basically features for distinguishing vowels. The specifications do not actually serve to *distinguish* any consonants (and could perhaps be better regarded as *redundant* features) but they provide a useful link between palatal consonants and high vowels (by specifying the palatals as [+high]) and between velar consonants and high, back vowels (velars are specified as [+high, +back]). One of the criticisms of the traditional features (cf. p. 75 above) was their inability to make connections between consonants and vowels.

Adequacy

Perhaps the most important difference between the *SPE* features and Jakobson's is the purpose for which they are designed. Jakobson's main aim was to provide a *maximally economic* set of features which would serve to distinguish each phoneme of English (and of any other language). Chomsky and Halle's main purpose, on the other hand, is to provide a set of features which will be most appropriate and suitable for the phonological rules by which they link abstract 'deep' representations to concrete 'surface' representations. They are not particularly concerned with the need for economy; note the increase in the number of features needed to specify the sounds of English, from nine to thirteen.

Since economy has been compromised, the *SPE* features must be judged on their ability to express, neatly and efficiently, a wide variety of phonological processes.[5] Chomsky and Halle are particularly interested in one type of process, namely, patterns of morphophonemic alternation, to which a substantial proportion of *SPE* is devoted. For English, they require features which will enable them to formulate rules to relate [k] to [s] as in 'criti*c*'–'criti*c*ize', or [d] to [ʒ] as in 'divi*d*e'–'divi*s*ion', or [aɪ] to [ɪ] as in 'div*i*ne'–'div*i*nity'. However, the adequacy of a set of features cannot be assessed in terms of such limited purposes alone; the features must be judged on their ability to describe a variety of processes, including processes of historical change, language acquisition, language pathology, dialectal variation, stylistic variation (such as 'casual' speech), as well as the structures internal to the language itself (such as the phonotactic patterns). The 'best' set of features for a language will be the set which can describe such processes in the most natural (and most economic) way.

With this in mind, we can look in detail at the two most significant innovative features of *SPE*, the features *anterior* and *coronal*.

Anterior

The feature *anterior* is a direct development of Jakobson's *compact–diffuse* as applied to consonants. It divides the continuous place-of-articulation sequence into two, down the middle, separating alveolars from palatals. In English, the division distinguishes /p/ and /t/ ([+ant.]) from /tʃ/ and /k/ ([−ant.]), and the fricatives /f, θ, s/

([+ant.]) from /ʃ/. It also separates /l/ ([+ant.]) from /r/, and /mn̩/ from /ŋ/, thus:

[+ anterior]	[− anterior]
p b t d	ʧ ʤ k g
f v θ ð s z	ʃ ʒ
l	r
m n .	ŋ

For binary purposes, of course, the continuous 'place' sequence has to be broken somewhere, and the question is, where is the most suitable point? Can we find good reasons for making a division between /p t/ and /ʧ k/, for example? Or would it be better to divide, say, /p/ from /t ʧ k/?

Taking the plosives first, the evidence favouring the 'anterior' division of /p t/ against /k/ is rather negative. Observable phonological processes do not offer much evidence (for English) of a relationship between /p/ and /t/. There are no dialects in which /p/ interchanges with /t/; no evidence of historical changes from /p/ to /t/ or vice versa; no evidence that young children pronounce p's as [t] or t's as [p]. Indeed the evidence from language acquisition suggests a profound separation of /p/ (and labials in general) from /t/ (and dental/alveolars in general); the earliest sounds acquired are equally labials [papa, baba, mama], and alveolars [tata, dada, nana], without any confusion or interrelationship between the two. On the other hand, when we compare /t/ and /k/, we find some evidence favouring an association between them: first, in language acquisition, /k/ words are regularly pronounced with [t] (and /g/ words with [d]) until the distinction is achieved; second, in speech pathology, children with language delay continue to pronounce velars as alveolars, a process known as 'fronting', which is really a prolongation (or delay) of the normal acquisition process; and third, in many dialects of English, the consonant sequences /kl–, gl–/ are pronounced as [tl–, dl–] (and listeners usually detect no difference – cf. Chapter 2, p. 53 above).

The evidence from nasals also associates velars with alveolars, and *fails* to link /m/ and /n/. In English, /ŋ/ is 'only just' a phoneme – in many respects, it behaves as an allophone of /n/. In many languages [ŋ] *is* an allophone of /n/, but it is extremely rare to find [n] as an allophone of /m/, or vice versa. The nasals clearly link [n] and [ŋ], to the exclusion of [m].

What about the fricatives? Does [anterior] reflect phonological processes here? It *links* /f θ s/, and *separates* /ʃ/. We can certainly find links between /f/ and /θ/ – several English dialects replace the rather 'difficult' and late-acquired sounds /θ, ð/ with /f, v/ respectively. We have mentioned earlier a link between /θ/ and /s/ ('lisping') and the pronunciation of /θ/ as [s] by foreign learners who lack /θ/ in their own language. But there are also links between /s/ and /ʃ/, i.e. 'across' the 'anterior' boundary: first, in many languages, [s] and [ʃ] are allophones of a single phoneme; second, the acquisition of /ʃ/ proceeds via an [s] stage, for example [fɪs] 'fish', [sɪp] 'ship', etc.; and third, German, with historical links to English and a similar consonantal pattern, has [ʃ–] word-initially in consonant clusters where English has /s–/ (compare *stahl* and *steel*). It is no accident that the IPA symbol for [ʃ] resembles an [s], and that /ʃ/ is represented as 'sh' in the spelling.

In sum, the feature [anterior] gets very little, if any, phonological support, and there is considerable evidence against it. One possibility, suggested by the links [t–k] and [n–ŋ], might be to draw the dividing line further forward, separating labials from anything further back. A feature called *lingual*, for example, could separate sounds made with the tongue ([+ling.]) from sounds made elsewhere ([–ling.]). This would be advantageous for the plosives and nasals, at least, but the fricatives encompass a series of links all the way along the continuum, /f–θ/, /θ–s/, and /s–ʃ/, which suggests that any division would be arbitrary and artificial.

Coronal

The feature *coronal* is a direct replacement, in articulatory terms, of Jakobson's *grave/acute* when applied to consonants. It makes the further division of the place-of-articulation continuum which a binary system requires in order to achieve a distinction between four separate points. The 'peripheral' consonants (the labials and velars) are [−coronal], and the 'central' ones (dentals, alveolars and palato-alveolars) are [+coronal]. Again, we need to ask whether this particular feature is justified by sound phonological evidence or whether it is just a convenient but arbitrary way of dividing up a continuum.

We require evidence for an association between /p/ and /k/ (and their voiced counterparts) and for a separation of these from /t/ and /tʃ/. For the fricatives, *coronal* links /θ, s, ʃ/ against /f/; and among the nasals, it links /m/ and /ŋ/ against /n/.

Jakobson himself provides very little evidence in favour of this feature. He mentions, almost in passing, the case of the consonant sequence [–pt] in Rumanian, in words which derive from Latin [–kt–], for example *drept* from Lat. *directum*. A change from [–kt] to [–pt] would be difficult to explain in articulatory terms, since it involves 'jumping' across several intervening points of articulation, for no apparent reason. However, if we can argue that /k/ and /p/ share certain *acoustic* properties, the change is easier to explain – speakers *hear* [p] instead of [k], particularly when the pronunciation is 'masked' by the following [t]. [p] and [k] are both 'low-pitched', i.e. both have energy at the lower end of the spectrum (hence the specification 'grave').

Another example involving 'gravity' is again a historical change, this time in English. English used to have a velar fricative, [x], which is still reflected by words with -gh- in the spelling. In a number of words this sound was replaced by /f/, for instance in *tough, enough, cough* and *laugh*. In German, the cognate ('related') words still retain their velar fricative; *laugh*, for example, is *lachen* ([laxən]) and *enough* is *genug* ([gənux]). How, on an articulatory basis, could a velar fricative become a *labio-dental* one? The change would be very difficult to explain. But since both sounds are *grave*, the change becomes explicable on an acoustic basis.

There are also 'gravity' links of a different kind. We observe that in many languages back vowels are normally rounded, and front vowels unrounded. Why should there be a link between the *backness* of the vowel, and lip-rounding? The answer is that in this way the acoustic properties of 'graveness' and 'acuteness' are maximized, producing the clearest distinctions. Back vowels become maximally low-pitched (grave), front vowels maximally high-pitched (acute). The opposite combination, of frontness with rounding, or backness with unrounding, produces 'muddy' vowels of indistinct character, which languages tend to avoid.

Similarly, it is not uncommon for languages to have other doubly-articulated sounds combining labiality with velarity – these are the *labio-velars*, such as [w], which are much more common in languages than *labio-palatals*, and are acquired easily and early by young children. Some languages have doubly-articulated plosives, [k͡p] and [g͡b], which also combine labial with velar.

The feature *grave* as applied to consonants thus has some phonological evidence to commend it. For further evidence, cf. Hyman (1973a), and Pagliuca and Mowrey (1980). Smith (1973) provides useful data on gravity assimilations at various stages of language acquisition. Whether *grave* can be satisfactorily relabelled as an *articulatory* feature, [coronal], is less certain, because the feature is obviously an *acoustic* one, and it only works because of the acoustic properties it distinguishes. In recognition of this, there is a good case for retaining the label *grave*.

Anterior, coronal in combination

Place of articulation is divided into four categories by the combination of the two binary features *anterior* and *coronal*. This means that some of the sounds along the continuum are distinguished by *two* features (i.e. have different values for two features), others by only one. Presumably, if the features are the right ones, the sounds distinguished by two features should be less closely linked phonologically than those distinguished by only one.

In the *SPE* system, *alveolars* are distinguished from *velars* by both features (alveolars are [+ ant., +cor.]; velars are [− ant., −cor.]) and likewise, *labials* from *palato-alveolars*. This is satisfactory in the case of labial and palato-alveolar since there is not much evidence to link them, though we do find front rounded vowels (i.e. *labial-palatal* vowels) in many languages (including French and German) and labio-palatal glides ([ɥ]) are also found, for example in French. For *alveolar* and *velar*, however, the specification is quite counter-intuitive, since as we have already seen, there are strong associations between these two both for plosives ([t–k]) and nasals ([n–ŋ]). On the other hand, the *SPE* system distinguishes *labial* from *alveolar* by only one feature, yet there is no evidence (apart from fricatives) of any phonological link between them; indeed, for plosives and nasals there is good evidence *against* any association.

In conclusion, the division of place-of-articulation into the binary features *anterior* and *coronal* is not satisfactory. *Anterior*, in particular, has little to recommend it, and much against it. *Coronal* is better justified, but the earlier title *grave* gives a better reflection of its acoustic basis.

One feature regularly used by Chomsky and Halle in their rules, but not included in the matrix because it is not *distinctive*, is the feature *sonorant*, with its opposite value *obstruent* (=[−sonorant]). This is a very useful 'cover' feature since it links the plosives, fricatives and affricates as *obstruent*, and the spontaneously-voiced sounds as *sonorant* – namely the nasals, liquids and glides. Obstruents as a class show a distinction for *voicing*; sonorants are the class of sounds for which voicing is predictable (and hence redundant). Although voiceless sonorants do occur in some languages, they always presuppose the presence of the corresponding voiced sonorants.

Assessment

Earlier in the chapter (pp. 74ff.) four reasons were given for why phonologists found the traditional articulatory features unsatisfactory. We can use these to assess Jakobson's and Chomsky and Halle's proposals. First, in terms of *economy*, Jakobson's matrix is very economical, but the advances were achieved largely at the expense of 'naturalness'. The *SPE* matrix by contrast is no more economical than the traditional one.

Second, *SPE* makes a little progress in linking *consonantal* properties to *vowel* properties: [j, w], for example, have specifications identical to [i, u] apart from one feature. But there is still no link between [l, r] and their corresponding vowels, and the specifications for the approximants, and [h, ʔ], are far from satisfactory: the use of *vocalic* and *consonantal* to distinguish [l, r] from [j, w] is inappropriate and (in view of the *definitions* of these features) unrealistic, and the specification of [h, ʔ] as [−constl.] unfortunate, because they behave as consonants in many languages.

Third, Jakobson's emphasis on the acoustic, in addition to the articulatory, basis of phonetic features has proved valuable in establishing links between hitherto unconnected sounds, such as labials and velars, which we know to be related phonologically for a variety of reasons. Both Jakobson and Chomsky and Halle are guilty, however, of establishing relationships for which there is little or no phonological justification (cf. for example, the discussion of *anterior*, above).

Fourth, and finally, a small number of useful *higher-order* features, such as *sonorant* and *strident*, have been established. In the following sections, we shall see what further developments have taken place since 1968 (i.e. since the publication of *SPE*), and suggest some possibly useful avenues for exploration.

Vocalic and consonantal

Recognizing the problems arising from the use of these two major classificatory features, Chomsky and Halle proposed, in an epilogue of *SPE*, to replace 'vocalic' with a feature 'syllabic', which would divide sounds into those occurring at the peak or centre of a syllable (normally vowels) and those occurring at the margins (consonants). The problem with a simple vowel–consonant division is, as we have seen, that sometimes vowels behave as 'consonants' and 'consonants' behave as vowels. The glides [j, w], for example, are phonetically vowels, yet they behave as consonants: they occur at the margin of a syllable and are interchangeable with, and combine with, other consonants. On the other hand, liquids and nasals can occur at the peak of the syllable, thus behaving as vowels, as in bott*l*e, butto*n*s, etc.; they are known as 'syllabic' [ḷ, ṇ], etc. One useful way of distinguishing between [j, w] and the corresponding vowels [i, u], then, would be to give them exactly the same specification except that [i, u] are [+syllabic] and [j, w] are [−syllabic]. Similarly, the liquids and nasals would be [−syllabic] except when they occur as 'syllabics' (when they would be [+syllabic]). Many years ago Pike (1943) made exactly the same observations. Noting the ambiguity of the terms *vowel* and *consonant*, he proposed to replace them with a twofold distinction, syllabic/non-syllabic, and contoid/vocoid.

'True' vowels ([i, e], etc.) are in this scheme *syllabic* and *vocoid*.
'Glides' ([j, w]) are *non-syllabic* and *vocoid* (i.e. they are 'vowel-like' in nature).
'True' consonants (all, except the glides) are *non-syllabic* and *contoid*.
Syllabic liquids/nasals are *syllabic* and *contoid*.

Thus all four combinations of the two distinctions are possible. Syllabic is a 'phonological' feature which classifies the sounds on the basis of their *function* (in the syllable); contoid/vocoid is a 'phonetic' feature, which classifies the sounds according to their physical (articulatory) properties.

In adopting the feature 'syllabic', Chomsky and Halle are making a radical departure from the principles of distinctive features in so far as these aim to provide a different specification for each phoneme of the language. The problem is that they are proposing *two* specifications for the same sound; the liquids and nasals will sometimes be [+syllabic], sometimes [−syllabic]. So the feature *syllabic* is not really a *distinctive* feature at all – it is, in fact, a way of showing how each segment is going to behave *in the sequence* of segments: will it be at the peak of the syllable, or at the margin? *Syllabic* is then a sequencing feature, not a distinctive feature: its role is *syntagmatic* (i.e. it is concerned with the *succession* of units or the 'horizontal' dimension) whereas distinctive features are fundamentally concerned with segmental contrasts and hence have a *paradigmatic* role. The feature *syllabic* may therefore be useful and valid, provided we recognize that it is not a distinctive feature. Examples of its use would be:

	p	l	i	z	d		r	e	d	i
[syllabic]	−	−	+	−	−		−	+	−	+

	k	e	t	l			j	u	n	aɪ	t
[syllabic]	−	+	−	+			−	+	−	+	−

Replacing *vocalic* with *syllabic* is thus an improvement, but it leaves a number of problems. The main one is that /l, r/ are no longer properly distinguished from the other consonants. The specification for /l/ (see matrix, Table 2) is in fact identical to that for /ð/. Chomsky and Halle offer no suggestions for a solution. A suitable specification for [l, r, h] and [ʔ] continues to elude us.

Sonority

Another recent development which is also a rediscovery of earlier observations (cf. Heffner 1950: 74) is the classification of sounds into a 'hierarchy of sonority', proposed by the followers of natural generative phonology (Hooper 1976: 196ff.; cf. also Sommerstein 1977: 99). 'Sonority' is defined in a number of overlapping ways: the more 'sonorous' sounds have greater carrying power and require less energy (acoustically), which corresponds in articulatory terms to the freedom of passage of air through the vocal tract (i.e. it corresponds to the notion of consonant 'strength' – cf. Chapter 2, p. 65, above). The hierarchy thus has the most 'vowel-like' sounds at one extreme, and the most 'consonant-like' at the other. The greater the sonority, the more likely the sounds are to form the peak of a syllable.

The least sonorous sounds are the plosives, for which the passage of air is completely interrupted and which also require the highest output of energy. Plosives cannot occur at all as the peak of a syllable. At the other extreme, vowels are the most 'sonorous' sounds, and thus the most likely to occur at syllable peaks. Open vowels are (as any singer appreciates) more sonorous than close vowels, predictably in view of the greater freedom of the passage of air through the vocal tract. A hierarchy of sonority can thus be established as follows (decreasing order of sonority):

> open vowels
> close vowels
> glides
> liquids
> nasals
> fricatives
> plosives and affricates

Clearly this hierarchy, being a continuum, could not easily be 'translated' into binary features. Its usefulness is in showing how there might be, in the middle, an overlap between 'vowels' and 'consonants'; it can thus help to explain certain phonological relationships such as the historical change of postvocalic [r] to [ə] (and the replacement of postvocalic [r] by [ə] during language acquisition), and to explain why some sounds (liquids and nasals) can appear as syllabics.

Non-binary features

The search for a definitive set of binary features is becoming more and more elusive. Ladefoged has proposed that features should be multi-valued, and in some cases numerical values can be applied, for example to vowel height (1975: 239):

4	i	u	w	j
3	e	ɪ	o	ɷ
2	ɛ	ɔ		
1	æ	ɑ		

In other cases, such as place of articulation, a numbered series makes no sense; Ladefoged thus uses the traditional terms, *labial*, *dental*, etc. (cf. the discussion in Ladefoged 1971: 43). He divides the sonority hierarchy for consonants into *stop*, *fricative* and *approximant*; otherwise, sounds are classified according to the traditional terms, *lateral*, *nasal*, *voice*, etc., with the addition of more recent features such as *syllabic* and *sonorant*. The introduction of *approximant* as a cover term for /l, r, j, w/ is a useful innovation. /r/ is classified only as an 'alveolar approximant', which is rather inadequate.

Distinctive and redundant features

The aim of a distinctive-feature specification for a sound is to distinguish it along several dimensions from all the other sounds of the language. However, alongside this a sound may possess other properties which are not needed to distinguish it, but which may be usefully specified for other purposes, such as for writing phonological rules, or explaining phonological relationships. Redundant features can often be added by general rules; for example, there is a rule in English that all nasal sounds are voiced. We therefore do not need to enter the predictable feature 'plus' for *voice* in specifying the nasals; the effect of the rule will be to add this specification at a later stage. Redundancy rules therefore serve to fill out some of the blanks in the matrix. The rule that 'all nasals are voiced' can be expressed in the form:

$$[+\text{nas.}] \quad \rightarrow \quad [+\text{voice}]$$

This notation means: to any segment specified with the feature (or features) to the left of the arrow, *add* whatever appears on the right. Thus, to any segment marked 'plus' for 'nasal', we will add the specification [+voice]. Sometimes several features can be predicted for a particular class of sounds. Thus, all (English) vowels are not only voiced, but also *continuant, non-nasal,* and *non-strident.* Using the *SPE* notation, the rule can be formulated as:

Rule 1
$$\begin{bmatrix} +\text{syll.} \\ -\text{constl.} \end{bmatrix} \longrightarrow \begin{bmatrix} +\text{voice} \\ +\text{continuant} \\ -\text{nasal} \\ -\text{strident} \end{bmatrix}$$

The effect of this rule is to add these values to the matrix. If desired, redundant values can be shown in brackets.

Exercise 7

1   Write a redundancy rule to show that (in English) all front vowels are unrounded.
2   What other properties are predictable (redundant) for nasals, apart from voice? Write an appropriate rule.

Redundancy in sequence

The kind of redundancy considered in the previous section applies to each segment individually. But a different kind of redundancy comes from observing sounds in sequence. In Chapter 2 we saw that, word-initially, only certain sequences of sounds are permitted: for instance English has /pl–/ but not /ps–/, /fj–/ but not /fm–/, etc. More generally, after a plosive or fricative, the only possible consonant is an approximant. These constraints can be expressed by using features, with redundancy 'rules' similar to those illustrated already. Assuming a feature 'approximant', the rule could be:

Rule 2   [– syll.] → [+ approxt.]/# [– syll.]__

i.e. after a non-syllabic first segment (a consonant), the next segment, if also non-syllabic, must be an approximant.

Exercise 8

Devise a sequence-redundancy rule to show that when a word begins with *three* consonants, the third must be an approximant.

Exercise 9

The traditional feature *affricate* could be expressed, in terms of *SPE* features, as

$$\begin{bmatrix} -\text{contin.} \\ +\text{strid.} \end{bmatrix}$$

because all (and only) the affricates share these two features. What combinations of features would be required to express the following?

1 plosive
2 velar
3 fricative
4 mid vowels
5 alveolar
6 central vowels

Conclusion

Developments in feature theory over the past thirty years have added new dimensions to the search for the minimal components of phonetic substance. Particularly welcome is the recognition that features may be established on acoustic grounds as well as on an articulatory basis. Also welcome is the recognition that features may serve different purposes – for example, either to achieve a highly economical classification of the sounds of a language; or to express the 'natural' relationship between sounds, observable as phonological processes.

Recent developments have added to our stock of features but no generally acceptable, adequate and complete feature analysis has yet been achieved, for English at any rate. Generative analyses of the phonology of other languages have used mainly the *SPE* features (which are supposed to be 'universal'); but these have proved as controversial as the *SPE* analysis of English (for Spanish, cf. Harris 1969; for French, Schane 1968; for Russian, Lightner 1965; and for critiques of these, see Derwing 1973; Linnell 1979; Hooper 1976). In view of the fact that adequate feature descriptions have yet to be produced for individual languages, the attempt to devise a universally-valid set seems premature.

Welcome additions to the traditional features include the acoustic feature *grave*, and the features which have proved valuable in describing phonological processes, such as *approximant*, *sonorant*, and *strident*. Other innovative features, such as Jakobson's *compact/ diffuse* and its *SPE* derivative (for consonants), *anterior*, have proved less successful. The use of two separate features, *vocalic* and *consonantal* to divide vowels from consonants (and the consequent difficulties in specifying the approximants) has proved unsatisfactory. The replacement of *vocalic* by *syllabic* is an improvement, but the role of *consonantal*, if equivalent to Pike's *contoid/vocoid*, remains undefined.

Apart from these innovations, many of the *SPE* features, such as *high*, *back*, *low*, *round*, etc. for vowels, and *voice*, *nasal*, etc. for consonants, are traditional terms grafted into a binary framework. The traditional place-of-articulation terms (*labial*, etc.) have not been adequately replaced, and still have a useful part to play.

The adequacy of particular features (or a set of them) must be judged by their ability to express the phonological relationships observable from speakers' behaviour, in language acquisition, dialectal variation, etc. These processes will be discussed in greater detail in later chapters. It would be more satisfactory from a theoretical point of view to establish features on the basis of these processes, rather than to produce a set of features beforehand and then attempt to make the processes fit into them. In establishing the features first, without reference to the processes, phonologists have been guilty of 'putting the cart before the horse'. The full set of relationships which sounds enter into must first be understood, before those sounds can be given a proper feature specification.

4 Neutralization, marking and language universals

Neutralization

The concept of neutralization, and the theory related to it, derives originally from the Prague School of phonology which flourished in the 1930s; it is particularly associated with Trubetskoy (1939 [1969]: 77ff.). Mainly through the influence of another member, Jakobson, neutralization and the ideas which developed along with it, such as marking, have been incorporated into generative phonology, and have played a prominent role in more recent developments, particularly in connection with language universals.

A neutralization is said to occur when two (or more) closely related phonemes, which are in contrast with each other in most positions, are found to be non-contrastive in certain other positions: i.e. there are some environments where the two phonemes do not contrast with each other, even though they normally do so. When this happens, the 'opposition' between the two phonemes is said to be 'neutralized'.

A well-known example of neutralization is the voicing contrast in German. The voiceless consonants /p, t, k, f, s/ contrast with their voiced counterparts /b, d, g, v, z/ in all positions of the syllable, except finally, where only the *voiceless* sounds occur. For example, /t, d/ contrast initially, as in *Teich* 'pond' vs *Deich* 'dike'; they contrast medially, as in *leiten* 'lead' vs *leiden* 'suffer'. But in final position, only [t] is found; *Grat* 'edge', and *Grad* 'grade', are both pronounced [gʁaːt]; *bunt* 'coloured', and *Bund* 'band' are both [bɔnt]. The other oppositions behave similarly; in final position, therefore, the voiced–voiceless contrast is neutralized. A similar neutralization is found also in Russian; here, however, the voicing contrast is neutralized more extensively, since there is a rule in Russian that all obstruents are *voiced* when they precede another *voiced* obstruent, but *voiceless* when they precede a *voiceless* obstruent; there are thus sequences such as [–db–], [–vz–], [–tp–], [–fs–], but no sequences such as [–tb–], [–vs–], etc. The voicing opposition is thus neutralized before obstruents, as well as word-finally.

In English, the voicing contrast is neutralized after initial /s– /. /t, d/, for example contrast in most environments:

initially	(*tip – dip*)
finally	(*cat – cad*)
after /l/	(*colt – cold*)
after nasals	(*shunt – shunned*)

But after /s–/, no contrast between /t, d/ is possible, nor, similarly, is there a contrast between /p, b/ and /k, g/ in this environment. The voicing opposition is neutralized after initial /s–/.

A further neutralization can be observed in the formation of English plurals. Compare:

[–ps]	'ropes'	[–bz]	'robes'
[–ts]	'bits'	[–dz]	'bids'
[–ks]	'docks'	[–gz]	'dogs'
[–fs]	'waifs'	[–vz]	'waves'
[–θs]	'breaths'	[–ðz]	'lathes'

After voiceless sounds, only [s] occurs, and after voiced sounds, only [z]. *Wherever* /s, z/ occur in such environments (for example, in verb-endings, as in *laughs*, *waits*, *waves*, etc.; and in possessives: *Jack's*, *Doug's*, etc.), no contrast between them is permitted. The environment, in this case, is restricted to obstruents, since /s, z/ may still contrast after a sonorant, as in *pence/pens*, *since/sins*, *else/sells*.

In many dialects of English which retain postvocalic /r/, such as the Middle and Western dialects of the United States, the opposition between short and long vowels is neutralized before a following /r/. In these accents, /i/ contrasts with /ɪ/ in all other environments (*heat* vs *hit*, *least* vs *list*, etc.), but before /r/ the contrast ceases to exist. The vowel of *near*, *pier*, *fear*, etc., is not clearly identifiable as either /i/ or /ɪ/, but is 'something in between'. *Mirror* has the same vowel as *nearer*, *spirit* has the same vowel as *period*, and likewise *Sirius* and *serious* (data from Wells 1982: 153ff.; 242ff.). This neutralization before /r/ is not confined to /i, ɪ/, however; it applies throughout the vowel system. The list on p. 106 shows the contrasts which are available (cf. Twaddell 1935).

pit }	pier	boat }	bore
peat }		bought }	

$$\left.\begin{array}{l}\text{pet}\\\text{pate}\\\text{pat}\end{array}\right\}\quad\text{pair}\qquad\left.\begin{array}{l}\text{put}\\\text{boot}\end{array}\right\}\quad\text{poor}$$

pet ⎫		put ⎫	
pate ⎬ pair		boot ⎭ poor	
pat ⎭		pout	power
pike	pyre	pert ⎫	
pot	par	putt ⎭ purr	

The fourteen vowel contrasts of general American which occur in all other environments, are reduced to eight in the 'pre-r' environment. In this accent, *Mary* and *fairy* have the same vowels as *merry* and *ferry*, and for most speakers, *Mary* is also not distinguished from *marry* nor *hairy* from *Harry*. The vowels /e, æ, eɪ/ are thus neutralized before a following /r/. The vowel of *square*, *fair*, *pear*, etc. is not clearly identifiable as either /e, æ/ or /eɪ/; it seems, to the speakers, to be somewhere in between all of them. Similar observations can be made about the vowels of *poor* and *tour*, which are intermediate between /ɷ, u/: the contrast between them, available in other environments (for example, *look* vs *Luke*), is neutralized before /r/.

The effect of a neutralization, then, is the *narrowing* of a set of contrasts in a particular environment. The contrast of voiced and voiceless consonants, or of long and short vowels, is readily observed in a wide range of contexts; but where neutralization occurs, the contrast is reduced to a single dimension.

Exercise 1

What neutralization is illustrated in the following data? What is the environment in which it occurs?

/–pt/	tapped	/–bd/	probed
/–kt/	attacked	/–gd/	lagged
/–ft/	laughed	/–vd/	behaved
/–θt/	earthed	/–ðd/	smoothed
/–st/	released	/–zd/	seized
/–ʃt/	crushed	/–ʒd/	sabotaged
/–ʧt/	watched	/–ʤd/	charged
/–lt/	kilt	/–ld/	killed
/–lt/	spoilt	/–ld/	foiled
/–nt/	faint	/–nd/	feigned
/–nt/	meant	/–nd/	mend

Exercise 2

Transcribe the following words. Is there a possible neutralization? Which two vowels are involved, and what is the environment?

cold	colt	golf
fold	bolt	Rolf
rolled	salt	involve
tolled	fault	dissolve
shoulder	poultry	solvent

Exercise 3

In New Zealand English, the first vowel in each of the following pairs of words is the same vowel (i.e. the vowels are not distinguished). What neutralization has occurred, and in which environment?

telly	:	tally
belly	:	ballet
elementary	:	alimentary
fellow	:	fallow
Val	:	well

Exercise 4

Many speakers, especially in North America, Australia, New Zealand and younger speakers in Britain, neutralize the /t, d/ contrast in words such as the following. What is the environment of neutralization? (Further data may be adduced if necessary.)

betting	:	bedding
latter	:	ladder
kitty	:	kiddy
waiter	:	wader
petal	:	pedal
writing	:.	riding
atom	:	Adam
parity	:	parody

Archiphonemes

In English, as noted earlier, the opposition between /p, t, k/ and /b, d, g/ is neutralized after initial /s–/. The sound which actually occurs in this environment (i.e. in words like *speak*, *steer*, *school*) does not correspond exactly to either the voiced or voiceless sounds, but shares the features of both of them. If we represent the /p/ of *peak*, as [pʰ], the /b/ of *beak*, as [b], and the sound of *speak* as [p⁼], the distribution of features is as follows:

[pʰ]	[p⁼]	[b]
bilabial	bilabial	bilabial
plosive	plosive	plosive
voiceless	voiceless	voiced
aspirated	unaspirated	unaspirated

This distribution of features shows that [p⁼] is truly intermediate between [pʰ] and [b]; it shares their common properties, *bilabial* and *plosive*; but then it shares one feature (*voicelessness*) with [pʰ], and the other (*unaspirated*) with [b]. Does it belong, then, with the phoneme /p/, or with /b/? Usually, phonologists have assigned it to /p/, on the grounds that voicing is more 'important' in English than aspiration, or for other similar reasons. There is a good case, however, for arguing that [p⁼] belongs equally with /p/ *or* /b/, as shown by the distribution of features, and therefore that *speak* could be transcribed equally as /spik/ or as /sbik/. The choice of /p/ is usually preferred, because of the *spelling*: English has a long-established tradition of spelling these words with 'sp', 'st', 'sk'. The spelling, however is not a reliable guide; in Gaelic, words with these sounds are spelt 'sb', 'sd', 'sg', even though the pronunciation is the same as English /sp–, st–, sk–/. One is tempted to suggest that if the techniques of phonemic transcription had been pioneered by Welsh- or Gaelic-speaking, rather than English-speaking, linguists, a transcription with /sb–/, for *speak*, etc. would have been preferred. In fact, the choice of /p, t, k/ vs /b, d, g/ is arbitrary; both are possible, neither is ideal.

To overcome this difficulty, the Prague School phonologists use the term 'archiphoneme'. An archiphoneme consists of the shared features of two (or more) closely-related phonemes, but excludes the feature which distinguishes them (Trubetskoy 1969: 79). Thus the archiphoneme of /p, b/ consists of the features *bilabial* and *plosive* (but excludes *voicing*, which separates them); the archiphoneme of /s, z/ is $\begin{bmatrix} \text{alveolar} \\ \text{fricative} \end{bmatrix}$; the archiphoneme of /m, n, ŋ/ is: [nasal]; and so on.

For transcription purposes, the symbols /P, T, K/ can be used to represent the archiphonemes of /p, b/, /t, d/ and /k, g/. In generative phonology, the transcription problem does not arise, since segments (phonemes) are represented not by alphabetic symbols but as a matrix of distinctive features.

Defective distribution

Neutralization, as a concept, must be distinguished from *defective distribution*, to which it is superficially similar. Defective distribution means that a phoneme is found in some environments but not others, i.e. its distribution (in terms of environments) is incomplete. For example, /h/ can occur initially in a syllable, but not finally; it can precede (in some accents) a glide, namely /hj–, hw–/, but not (in English) a liquid /hl–, hr–/. /ŋ/ occurs finally, but not initially; it may also follow a short vowel, but not a long vowel. /f/ can occur initially (*fine*), medially (*wafer*) and finally (*knife*), but not before another obstruent word-initially (/fθ–, ft–/, etc.).

Defective distribution poses problems for the definition of neutralization. If, for example (taking the case of /ŋ/), we can have /peɪn/ 'pain' but not */peɪŋ/, could we not say that there is a neutralization of /n, ŋ/ in the environment of a preceding long vowel? It is true, after all, that /n, ŋ/ contrast in other environments (*sin, sing*) but not in this one. And, likewise, if /fl–/ is possible but not /hl–/, could we not say that the opposition /f, h/ (cf. *feet–heat*) is neutralized before a following /l/?

If *neutralization* were to be extended in this way, it would become so broad a term as to be virtually meaningless. In order to confine the term to the sort of examples we have already given as illustrations, the Prague School phonologists limited neutralization to 'closely-related' phonemes; before two phonemes can be neutralized, they must have common qualities which do not occur in other phonemes (cf. Fischer-Jørgensen 1975: 29ff.). Thus /p, b/ can neutralize because they are the only *labial plosives* in the language: they share these two features, but no other sounds share them. Similarly /i, ɪ/ can neutralize because their common features, [close] [front] and [unrounded], are peculiar to those sounds alone. /n, ŋ/, however, cannot neutralize because their common property ([nasal]) is shared also by /m/. So any neutralization of nasals must involve all three of them, /m, n, ŋ/. And there cannot be a neutralization of /f, h/ before /l/, since the features common to these, ([voiceless], [fricative]), are also shared by other phonemes, namely /ʃ, s, θ/.

As an answer to the problem this is not entirely satisfactory. First, there may be cases which 'slip through the net'. Second, and more important, why should we wish to restrict neutralization in this particular way? The answer to the latter question must be left until the next section. First, let us consider an example which may elude Trubetskoy's requirement on 'closely-related' phonemes.

In English, initial /s–/ can precede a plosive or a nasal but initial /ʃ–/ cannot. In German, it is the other way round. Since /s, ʃ/ contrast in most other environments in English (including 'before a plosive' – cf. *least–leashed*), could we not say that the contrast is neutralized, word-initially before another obstruent or nasal? If Trubetskoy is correct, then we could, since the 'closely-related' requirement is, in this instance, satisfied: /s, ʃ/ share the features [voiceless], [fricative], [strident], and they are the *only* sounds to have these features. Yet it seems somehow unsatisfactory to include this as a case of neutralization. Why?

The 'psychological reality' of neutralization

The key to the concept of neutralization lies in its effect on

1   the knowledge or 'competence' of the speakers and
2   their observable behaviour.

In most of the illustrations of neutralization given earlier, speakers indicate uncertainty about the status of the sound which occurs in the neutralizing environment. For example, in general American, where short and long vowels are neutralized before /r/, speakers are unable to identify the vowels of *near*, *square*, *mirror*, *fairy*, etc. unambiguously. Normally, identification of a sound presents no problems for the speaker; the final sounds of *graph* and *enough*, for instance, or the initial sounds of *schedule* and *charade*, are unambiguously assigned to /f/ and /ʃ/ respectively, despite the unusual spellings 'ph', 'gh', 'sch' and 'ch'. The vowels of *put*, *good* and *should* are easily identified as /ʊ/, even though their spellings differ considerably. It is therefore somewhat unusual when a speaker is unable to say whether the vowels of *near*, *mirror* match the vowel of *hit* or of *heat*.

Trubetskoy (1939: 78) noted this phenomenon. 'The psychological difference,' he observes, 'between constant and neutralizable distinctive oppositions is very great. Constant oppositions are perceived clearly even by those members of the community who have had no phonetic training. . . . In neutralizable oppositions, perception fluctuates: in positions of relevance [i.e. where the sounds *do* contrast] both members are clearly distinguished; in positions of neutralization on the other hand, it is often not possible to indicate which of the two had just been produced or perceived.' As an example, he cites French /e/ and /ɛ/; from a purely phonetic point of view, the difference between /i, e/ is no greater than between /e, ɛ/. But 'the closeness of the /e, ɛ/ relationship is apparent to any Frenchman' – because /e, ɛ/ is neutralizable, while /i, e/ is not.

Since 'psychological' aspects of this kind were unfashionable at the time, Trubetskoy himself did not attach great importance to these observations. In addition, speakers' 'knowledge' (such as the Frenchman's intuitions that /e, ɛ/ are 'closely related', or Americans' uncertainty about the identity of the vowel of *near*) is not always easily and clearly available. Take the case of *cold, bolt, golf* and the other words in Exercise 2 above; if speakers are uncertain whether to identify this vowel with the vowel of *got* or of *goat*, how would we know, since they are not normally required to perform such a task?

One method of finding out is to observe what they do when (and if) learning phonemic transcription. If the identity of the *cold* vowel is in doubt, it will sometimes be transcribed /ɒ/, sometimes /oʊ/; students might even *ask* which symbol they should use in such words. There are, however, problems in this approach. For instance, students may be told of a 'rule' for the formation of regular plurals in English, namely that plurals are realized by /s/ after voiceless sounds (except for the stridents, /s, ʃ, tʃ/), and by /z/ after voiced sounds (except for /z, ʒ, ʤ/). Once such a rule is given, their transcriptions will simply follow it: their 'naïve' reactions have been spoilt. If such 'rules' are not given, their transcriptions produce interesting results; the /s, z/ neutralization, which applies to possessives and present-tense verbs (for example, *give–gives, hit–hits*) as well as to plurals, is transcribed almost randomly with /s/ or /z/; and /t, d/ in the positions of neutralization behave likewise. There is some preference for /s/ in the plurals and for /d/ in the past tense, which can be attributed to the regular spellings –s, –es, and –d, –ed.

Another source of evidence about speakers' knowledge comes from spelling mistakes. If speakers do not distinguish *latter* from *ladder* and *kitty* from *kiddy* (cf. the data in Exercise 4, p. 107), then we can expect the spellings of these words to fluctuate (for example, 'kiddy' for 'kitty' and vice versa – cf. Lehmann 1953, mentioned in Wells 1982: 250). A New Zealand student spelt 'Val' as 'Vell'; how could such a spelling be possible, unless she heard the vowel of the unfamiliar word 'Val' as being identical with that of the familiar word *well*? In spelling unfamiliar words (especially names), we extend the familiar by analogy. Proper names are a potentially rich source of evidence; in New Zealand, the confusion of *Alison* with *Ellison* is clear evidence of the neutralization of /e, æ/ before /l/.

Orthographic evidence may not always be available, for various reasons. The neutralization of voicing after /s–/, for instance, cannot be observed through the spelling, because of our tradition of using 'p', 't', 'k' (or 'ch') to the exclusion of 'b', 'd', 'g'. Surprisingly, students *transcribing* words such as *speak*, *steam*, etc., do occasionally choose /sb–/ and /sd–/, in defiance of the spelling tradition. From careful listening, they have detected the similarity between [p⁼] and [b]. This has been confirmed experimentally: Davidson-Nielsen (1969) removed the initial /s–/ from tape-recordings of such words, and asked listeners to identify what remained. Results showed that they heard /b, d, g/ more frequently than /p, t, k/.

The neutralization of /ɒ, oʊ/ in *cold, golf*, etc., cannot be observed from spelling mistakes for a different reason, namely that only one spelling is available. Letter 'o' is regularly used both for /ɒ/ (in *rot*) and /oʊ/ (in *rote*). Nor could we expect the spelling to identify the neutralizations of *writing/riding*, *betting/bedding*, because in this case the related words *write, ride, bet, bed* still retain the t/d contrast.

Role of 'psychological reality'

Neutralization has, as we have seen, important consequences for speakers' knowledge and behaviour. In an earlier section, the problem of *limiting* neutralization, so as to exclude cases like the 'neutralization' of /s, ʃ/ before /p, t, k/ word-initially, was discussed but not resolved. We might now propose that neutralization should be defined, and limited, by its 'psychological' consequences: a neutralization can be said to occur *only* if there is uncertainty about the identity of the sound in the position of neutralization. This would exclude not only cases like the 'neutralization' of /f, h/ before /l/ (i.e. cases which are really instances of defective distribution) but also the more difficult cases like the 'neutralization' of /s, ʃ/, since speakers are in no doubt that the sound which occurs in a word like *speak* is /s/, not

/ʃ/ (unless they are drunk!). The advantage of defining neutralization in this way is that it becomes a 'real' language phenomenon (as opposed to an artificial construct of the phonologist). In addition, neutralization helps to explain speakers' uncertainties, and these in turn can be used as evidence suggesting the existence of a neutralization (if we are not already aware of one).

Exercise 5

1   Students often find difficulty in choosing a symbol to transcribe the *stressed vowel* of the following words. Does this provide evidence of a neutralization? If so, what is it?

during	fury
curious	maturity
mural	purify

2   Is there a similar neutralization of /i, iə/ in the same environment? Find five words to illustrate the phonemic contrast of this pair and five words in which the contrast is neutralized.

Exercise 6

In the following words, the unstressed vowel shown in italics could be an allophone of either /i/ or /ɪ/. What kind of evidence could indicate whether or not a neutralization is involved?

ar*e*a	luck*i*est
cur*i*ous	chrom*i*um
jov*i*al	med*i*an
prett*i*er	allev*i*ate

Exercise 7

In Chapter 2 (p. 63), the distribution of nasals before a following plosive was shown to be restricted: /p, b/ are always preceded by /m/ (*lamp, amber*); /t, d/ by /n/ (*ant, sand*); /k, g/ by /ŋ/ (*sink, finger*). Suggest evidence both *for* and *against* regarding this distribution as a case of neutralization.

Conclusion

Neutralization is said to occur when a contrast or 'opposition' between two phonemes is 'suspended' (i.e. fails to apply) in some particular phonetic environment. The sound which occurs in the neutralizing context is usually intermediate between the two phonemes, for example the [t⁼] of /st–/ is like /t/ in one respect but like /d/ in another. The common features shared by a pair of phonemes is known as the archiphoneme, and it occurs in the neutralizing context. Other things being equal (which they rarely are), speakers will have difficulty in knowing which phoneme a 'neutralized' sound belongs to.

Defective distribution means that a sound does not occur in all possible environments; for instance, /h/ can precede a glide, but not a liquid. Defective distribution is similar to neutralization, but speakers do not confuse the 'missing' phoneme with any other phoneme. For example, since the initial sound of *steam* is unambiguously /s/ and not /ʃ/, this is a case of defective distribution (stated as: /ʃ/ does not occur in word-initial clusters, except /ʃr–/); it is *not* a case of the neutralization of /s, ʃ/. It would however be most inappropriate to apply the term 'defective distribution' to the neutralization involved in /sp–, st–, sk–/, because an arbitrary choice would be forced upon us: *which* set of phonemes are defective? /p, t, k/? or /b, d, g/?

Neutralizations have sometimes been obscured by 'rules' which treat the data in an entirely different way. For instance, there is an oft-quoted 'rule' for English regular plurals, to the effect that voiceless sounds are followed by /s/ (*locks*) and voiced sounds by /z/ (*logs*). Such rules are misleading, because the sounds which occur, after obstruents at least, are neither /s/ nor /z/, but the archiphoneme of /s, z/; /s, z/ cannot contrast in this neutralizing environment.[1] Students reveal this fact in transcription by using the symbols s and z inconsistently in such environments.

Marking and universals

Marked and unmarked

The concept of *marking* and its values 'marked' and 'unmarked' is a way of showing that, when two linguistic elements are related in some way, the relationship may not be between 'equals', but that one element is somehow more 'basic' than the other. The 'basic' element is said to be the *unmarked* member of the pair and the other the *'marked'* member. Marking is used not only in phonology, but also in other areas of linguistics, and it may be useful to see how the term is used elsewhere before we turn to phonological marking.

To take an example from semantics: the relationship between pairs of 'opposite' terms such as *high–low, long–short, old–young* is not an equal one, because in a neutral context, one term is preferred to the other. Speakers are more likely to inquire about the *height* or *length* of an object rather than the *lowness* or the *shortness* of it. In doing so, the questions are more likely to be formulated as: 'how *high* is it?' and 'how *long* is it?' rather than 'how *low* is it?' or 'how *short* is it?' (though the latter are, of course, possible). For these reasons, *high*, *long* (and *old* – cf. 'how old is he?' as a way of inquiring about age) are regarded as the *unmarked* ('basic') terms of their pairs, and *low*, *short*, *young*, as the *marked* terms.

For a grammatical example of marking, consider singular and plural. Which is 'basic'? The singular form (for example, *ship*) or the plural (*ships*)? The singular form appears in a wider range of contexts than the plural; thus in compounds, we find *shipyard, shipwright, ship-shape*, etc. but not **shipsyard*, etc. even though a *shipyard* is a 'yard for ships', plural. Likewise, we have *toothache* and *toothpick*, even though these refer to an ache of the *teeth*, and a pick for the *teeth* (plural). This suggests that *ship*, *tooth* are the unmarked 'basic' forms and that *ships*, *teeth* are marked. In most cases too, the plural is 'marked' in a literal sense, since the /–s/ is the 'mark' which conveys plural meaning. The singular is thus unmarked in the further sense that it is also the simplest form, the form to which things are 'added'.

Exercise 8

Of the following pairs of terms, which would be the unmarked term, and why?

dog – bitch	wide – narrow
failed – fail	she – he
shallow – deep	regular – irregular

'Natural' and 'phonological' marking

The concept of marking was applied to phonology originally by the

Prague School, where it was linked to neutralization. When an opposition between a pair of sounds is neutralized, the sound which actually occurs in the neutralizing position can, if it is identifiable with *one* of the phonemes,[2] be regarded as the unmarked member of the pair. For example, when the opposition *voiced–voiceless* is neutralized syllable-finally in German, it is the *voiceless* sound which occurs, hence *voiceless* is the unmarked term and *voiced* the marked. Voiced sounds are considered to be marked in the additional sense of requiring the presence of an extra feature, voicing.

Trubetskoy was careful to distinguish between the two components of markedness:

1 presence of an extra feature, which he called natural marking; and
2 occurrence in the position of neutralization, which he called phonological marking.

Naturally marked oppositions would include *nasality* (i.e. [+ nasal] is marked); *aspiration*; *rounding* (for vowels); and *palatalization*; similarly, *velarized, retroflex* and *ejective* consonants, etc. are 'naturally marked' in relation to their 'plain' equivalents, since they are all characterized by the presence of an extra feature.

The notion of marking has been taken over by generative phonologists, and extended considerably in usage, following from their interest in language universals. Some sounds, and sound systems, are found to be much more common throughout the languages of the world than others; within individual languages too, some sounds occur much more frequently than others. Generally speaking, the commoner, more frequent sounds are also phonetically less complex, i.e. less 'marked'. For example, velarized consonants, or retroflex consonants, are much less common among languages generally than their simple counterparts. Furthermore, a language will have *fewer* of the complex sounds (by comparison with the simple equivalents) in its inventory of phonemes, and they will occur *less frequently* in use.

We can add to this the evidence from language acquisition and from language change.

1 In language acquisition, children will acquire the simple, unmarked sounds *earlier* and *more easily* than they acquire the marked sounds, and they will tend to replace *marked* sounds with unmarked during early stages of acquisition.

2   In language change, marked sounds will tend to be replaced by their unmarked equivalents. For example, Old English had an aspirated /l, r/, written hl–, hr–, which has since been replaced by simple /l, r/ as in *lord* (< *hlaford*) and *ring* (OE *hring*); similarly the rounded, labialized [r], *wr–*, as in *write, wrench*, has been replaced by simple /r/. In Modern Chinese, a retroflex pair of consonants, [tʂ, tʂʻ], is currently disappearing in favour of the simple equivalent consonants, [ts, tsʻ].

According to the generative view, then, marking has been greatly widened in scope. To summarize, *unmarked* sounds:

1   'lack' a certain characteristic, for example voicing, velarization;
2   occur in the position of neutralization;
3   within a language, are greater in number (than their marked equivalents);
4   have a higher frequency of occurrence;
5   are acquired earlier by children;
6   replace their marked equivalents during early stages of acquisition;
7   replace their marked equivalents historically.

The importance of marking in generative phonology is that it explains, or at least describes, universal characteristics of human language, as well as events and properties in particular languages. Marking is part of the innate, universal structure of language.

Vowel systems

Marking among vowels can be illustrated by the fact that some vowel systems are much more frequent among the world's languages than others. It is very common, for example, for languages to have front vowels which are unrounded, and back vowels which are rounded; and for the most open vowel to be back and unrounded, rather than front, or rounded. Thus a system like:

i   u

e   o

a

is far more typical than a system such as:

y   u

ø   ʌ

æ

This suggests that the unmarked values for rounding are:

[−round] for front vowels and open vowels
[+round] for back vowels

This marking pattern is confirmed by two further observations:

1   That languages which have front, rounded vowels, like French and German, will *also* have front unrounded vowels and back rounded vowels. We do not find languages whose only front vowels are rounded ones.[3]

2   The *number* of front rounded vowels never exceeds the number of front unrounded ones, and is usually less. French, for example, has four unrounded vowels /i, e, ɛ, a/, but only three rounded, /y, ø, œ/ (and in many dialects the distinction between /ø, œ/ is being, or has already been, lost, thereby reducing the rounded vowels to two).

In language development, children are found to acquire the front unrounded vowels before the rounded ones, and to replace the latter by the former until the rounded vowels have been mastered. Language change shows a similar process; for example, those Creole languages, such as Haitian Creole, which developed from French, and which in many ways represent a simplification of French's more complex features, replaced the front rounded vowels with their unrounded equivalents, /y/ becoming /i/, and /ø/ becoming /e/, as in /di/ = French 'du', /lin/ = French 'lune'.

In sum, the evidence shows that front rounded vowels are in all respects more marked than front unrounded vowels, and the same is true of the back vowels, except that in this case [−round] has the marked value. The markedness of the feature *rounding* is thus determined by the context. The unmarked values are [−round] for front vowels, [+round] for back vowels.

Other vowel dimensions which can be distinguished by marking are as follows:

marked	*unmarked*
nasal vowels	oral vowels
voiceless vowels	voiced vowels

The general picture of vowel systems which emerges from the investigations of language universals by, for example, Greenberg (1966) and of language acquisition by Jakobson (1941) is that the least marked vowel is an open, back, unrounded vowel, symbolized [ə] or [ʌ] or [a]. This vowel is present in all known languages, and is acquired very early by children (cf. [mama] and [dada]). Note that in English, [ə] is the commonest vowel, and the one to which all others reduce when unstressed.

Next in order of marking is a simple triangular vowel scheme:

i   u

a

containing one front unrounded, and one back rounded, vowel. This pattern is found in a wide range of languages, and Jakobson claims that the child acquires /i, u/ next after /a/. In English, this scheme represents the gliding component of the diphthongs; all diphthongs glide either 'upwards' towards [i] or [u], or 'inwards' towards [ə].

The next stage is the addition of the two mid vowels [e, o] to the scheme, to give:

i   u

e   o

a

The mid vowels [e, o] often arise historically from the merging of sequences of the more 'primitive' vowels; thus the sequence [ai] becomes [e], and [au] becomes [o]. This change is well documented for a number of languages, for example ancient Greek [ai] as in [haima] ('blood') becomes Modern Greek [e] ([ema]), Latin [ai] becomes French [e] (*Caesar→César*), Latin [au] becomes Romance [o] (Lat. *causa* → Fr. *chose*, Ital. *cosa*, Lat. *pauper* → Fr. *pauvre*, etc.).

Consonants

Some consonants (either singly or in a series) can be quite clearly assigned a 'marked' value on the basis of their rarity, complexity, and lateness of acquisition. These are:

> palatalized (and velarized, etc.) consonants
> retroflex consonants
> ejectives
> implosives
> clicks
> breathy or 'murmured' consonants (cf. Ladefoged 1971: 12ff.)

In other cases, however, assignment of markedness values to a feature is more problematic.

Voicing

Sonorants, that is nasals, liquids and glides, are 'naturally' or 'spontaneously' voiced. Although languages may have voiceless sonorants, they are uncommon, and they always presuppose a voiced equivalent. For sonorants, therefore, the unmarked value of voicing is [+ voice]. For obstruents, on the other hand, the voicing values are less obvious. It is generally claimed that [− voice] is the unmarked value, the evidence being that in the position of neutralization, it is the voiceless member of a pair which is preferred. This would be true if, for example, English /sp–, st–, sk–/ had /p, t, k/ rather than /b, d, g/. But, as we have seen, the sound in question is in fact intermediate between the two. There are, however, many languages in which a voiceless sound represents a neutralization in word-final position, for example in German, Russian, Thai, Korean and Vietnamese (cf. Kim 1972; Sanders 1977). Leaving aside this evidence from word-final neutralization for the moment, we find other evidence which is much less conclusive. In the position of neutralization, for example, it is usual to find either an indeterminate sound (as in English plurals after an obstruent) or *both* members of the pair, as in Russian, where obstruents are voiced or voiceless, depending on the voicing of the following obstruent.

The issue might be resolved by languages which have a set of obstruents without a voicing contrast. For example, if such languages always had /p, t, k/ rather than /b, d, g/, this would show that [−voice] is the unmarked value. Unfortunately, the evidence is again inconclusive: generally, the sounds which occur are voiceless but also *unaspirated*, i.e. as much like /b/, etc. as like /p/, etc. Alternatively, both voiced and voiceless allophones of the single phoneme may be found, in different environments. One such language, Maori, has mainly voiceless unaspirated sounds;[4] another, Korean, has voiced and voiceless allophones of a single phoneme (cf. Kim 1972). There is much evidence, from a variety of languages, that where no voicing contrast obtains, *voiced* allophones occur in medial (intervocalic) positions, and *voiceless* allophones in final positions. The preference for a voiceless sound in this position might explain why word-final neutralizations (as in German, Russian, etc.) favour the voiceless member of the pair.

In language acquisition, the evidence is again mixed. It appears that children first acquire a *voiced* stop in word-initial position, and a *voiceless* one in word-final position, so that in the initial stages, voiced and voiceless are in complementary distribution. Thus *dog* is pronounced [dɒk], *bridge* is [bɪt], *teeth* is [dit], etc. (cf. Smith 1973:3).

In sum, the evidence from various sources suggests that voicing values may be contextually determined. The unmarked values are [−voice] in final position, [+voice] medially, and possibly [+voice] initially – though this is by no means certain.

Place of articulation

Dental or alveolar sounds have the best claim to represent the unmarked place of articulation, on the grounds

1 that all languages have sounds at one or other of these points,
2 that languages have *more* alveolar phonemes than, say, labial or velar phonemes, and
3 that alveolar sounds are acquired very early.

The evidence is not altogether clear; English, for example, has more alveolar phonemes than any other, and the alveolar sounds are highly frequent in use; also, young children tend to replace velars and palato-alveolars with alveolars (*cake* is [deɪt], *shirt* is [dɜt], *chair* is [dɛː]). On the other hand, labials are acquired just as early as alveolars, and there is no evidence that young children replace *labials* (as they do velars) with alveolars; labials are also just as widespread among the languages of the world, and almost as frequent, as alveolars. Thus it would seem that, in the marking stakes, labials and alveolars have a roughly equal claim to being 'unmarked'. Chomsky and Halle find themselves unable to decide this issue as far as the plosives are concerned; they propose three equally unmarked sounds, /p, t, k/ (*SPE*: 413).

Among the fricatives, the unmarked or basic member is generally claimed to be /s/, which is found very widely distributed; some languages have /s/ as their *only* fricative, and it is claimed that if a language has more than one fricative, /s/ will be among them. In English, /s/ has the highest frequency and it is the only fricative which can precede a plosive and a nasal word-initially (/sp–, st–, sm–/, etc.). In company with /z/, it also has a wide range of grammatical functions: it marks not only the plural of nouns, but also the possessive of nouns (*John's*, *Pat's*, etc.), the third person singular of present-tense verbs (*take-s*, *laugh-s*, etc.), and the contracted form of *is* and *has* (as in 'Pat's away today'; 'Jack's got measles', etc.). In English, /s, z/ are undoubtedly the pre-eminent fricatives.

On the other hand, the claim that languages with fricatives must include /s/ among them is not true (Maori, for example, has two fricatives, /h/ and bilabial /ɸ/), and there is a remarkable historical tendency for /s/ to change into /h/. Thus, Latin *sex* (six) and *septem* (seven) correspond to Ancient Greek *hex* and *hepta*; it is generally assumed that Latin preserved the earlier (Indo-European) /s/, which became /h/ in Greek. Similarly, in many modern dialects of Spanish, word-final /s/ is being replaced by /h/ (Hooper 1976: 32ff.). In Polynesian languages too, an older (Proto-Polynesian) /s/ has sometimes been replaced by /h/, as in Maori.

Evidence from language acquisition suggests that /f/ is acquired as early as, if not earlier than, /s/ (for a summary, cf. Crystal 1981: 34ff.). Both /f/ and /s/ may be replaced, during early stages of language development, by /h/. /h/ could thus claim to be the unmarked fricative on a number of counts, including the fact that it is the simplest from an articulatory point of view, since no tongue contact is required (cf. Lass 1976: 156ff.). Apart from /h/, the choice between a labial fricative (/f/) and an alveolar one (/s/) seems equally balanced, just as it is for the plosives /p, t/.

Among the nasals, Chomsky and Halle claim /n/ as the unmarked member, mainly on the basis of its wide distribution and the fact that it is alveolar. Again, however, the claim cannot be substantiated from language acquisition, where /m/ and /n/ seem to have equal claims to priority. For all three categories, therefore (plosive, fricative and nasal), labial and alveolar enjoy equal marking status.

Syllables

Markedness values can be applied not only to classes of segments but also to sound-sequences and, in particular, to syllable types. The archetypal unmarked syllable is claimed to be the sequence CV, and on the basis of universals and similar evidence, the claim is well justified. Other possible candidates would be VC and CVC, which are also very common syllable structures; but not all languages permit final consonants, whereas they all permit initial ones. We also find that young children are much more likely to delete a final consonant than an initial one. Thus [ti] and [kʌ] are quite normal early attempts at *teeth* and *cup*, whereas [it] and [ʌp] would be unusual. In language change it is final consonants which weaken, change or disappear, whereas initial consonants tend to be well preserved. So the initial position is 'stronger' than the final position, which supports the hypothesis that CV is the unmarked syllable type. We should perhaps add that V alone deserves equal claim as an unmarked syllable, since all languages have syllables consisting of just V, and such a syllable can be claimed as possibly the earliest of all child utterances – the vocalization. Languages readily combine V with CV, as CVV, VCV.

Further implications about syllable structure derived from the study of universals were discussed in Chapter 3. After CV, V, VC and CVC, the most likely pattern of consonant cluster is:

obstruent   +   approximant   +   vowel

If a language has more 'marked' clusters, such as 'fricative + stop + vowel' (for example, /sp–, st–/), it must also have clusters like /kl–/ and /fr–/. Likewise, the sequence: obstruent + nasal + vowel (/pn–, θn–/, etc.) is relatively 'marked'. A language with such clusters will also have the 'easier' (less marked) clusters of consonant + approximant.

Laws of implication

Closely connected with marking are the 'laws of implication', several of which have been alluded to indirectly. Laws of implication simply mean that before a language can have X, it must also have Y; i.e. the presence of X *implies* that Y is also present. But the reverse is not true; there will be languages which have Y, but which do not have X. For example:

> the presence of front rounded vowels implies the presence of front unrounded, and back rounded, vowels.

If a language has /y/, it will also have /i/ and /u/. There are no languages whose only front vowels are rounded ones. But there are languages with front unrounded vowels which do *not* have front rounded vowels, i.e. the reverse of the original statement is not true. Thus the implication goes one way only.

Manner of articulation

Two further cases of markedness, with associated laws of implication, should be mentioned. They concern the relationship between plosives, fricatives and affricates. Jakobson (1941) claims that, of the three classes, children always acquire plosives before fricatives, and fricatives before affricates. It is common for children to replace fricatives with the corresponding ('nearest') plosive, *fish* being pronounced [b̥ɪt] or [b̥ɪ], *sock* as [d̥ɒk], *this* as [d̥ɪt], etc. Language universals confirm this relationship: languages with fricatives always have plosives as well, but the reverse is not true, as there are languages with plosives but with no fricatives. Plosives are thus 'prior' to, or less marked than, fricatives, both in acquisition and as a universal. In terms of the 'laws of implication', fricatives *imply* plosives. Similarly, affricates are not acquired by the child until at least some plosives and fricatives have been mastered; and languages that have affricates are also found to have plosives and fricatives too. Of the three classes, then, affricates are the most marked; they *imply* plosives and fricatives.

Conclusion

By introducing evidence from language acquisition and universals into the concept of markedness, the notion has clearly been extended in significant ways from the original Prague School conceptions of *natural* marking and *phonological* marking. The principle of phonological marking, based on what happens in neutralizations, is in any case of rather limited value, because neutralizations in favour of one member of a pair are rather uncommon – usually both members are involved (as with /s, z/ in English final clusters, for example, /–ps/ but /–bz/, etc.); or alternatively, an *intermediate* value is involved, as with plosives after /s–/ in English.

One of the disadvantages in extending the notion of markedness is that it runs the risk of becoming completely circular, and hence meaningless. It is easy to fall into the trap of stating that a category (let us say nasal vowels) is marked because its occurrence is rare, and of then arguing that the category is rare because it is marked. Marking, in itself, does not *explain* anything; it merely summarizes a series of observations – observations which might otherwise go unnoticed and unrelated. Marking does not explain *why* (say) nasal vowels are rarer in languages generally, and *why* they are acquired later than oral vowels. Such explanations must be sought elsewhere – perhaps from articulatory or auditory phonetics. Nasal vowels, for example, could be 'rarer' and more 'difficult' because of their acoustic properties: listeners are unable to distinguish *between* nasal vowels as easily as they distinguish between oral vowels. The latter thus offer better opportunity for maximal contrast between one vowel and another (cf. Lindblom 1972; Liljencrants and Lindblom 1972).

Markedness, therefore, does not give any real explanation of the evidence it provides, but serves the useful purpose of drawing our attention to facts about acquisition and universals which may enrich the study of a particular language and of language in general. Seeking genuine explanations for those facts is a further stage which may extend into physical phonetics and acoustic phonetics on the one hand, or outside language altogether and into, say, psychology, on the other. In many cases, evidence of a marking or implicational relationship exists, but there is as yet no proper explanation as to why.

Exercise 9

If Jakobson's claim that *velar* consonants imply *alveolar* consonants is correct, which of the following statements are true, and which false?

1   Children acquire velars earlier than alveolars.
2   A language will have more alveolar than velar consonants.
3   Children during early stages of acquisition replace velars with alveolars.
4   [k] has a higher frequency than [t].
5   A language with [s] must also have [x].

Exercise 10

Which of the sounds in each pair below is unmarked relative to the other, and why?

1	[y, u]	5	[t, t']
2	[p, f]	6	[ʃ, s]
3	[ʃ, ʧ]	7	[t, s]
4	[ã, a]	8	[g, d]

Exercise 11

Which of the contrasting segments in each of the following pairs is unmarked for voicing, and why?

1	[bef, bev]	5	[efɪk, evɪk]
2	[bɪzɪn, bɪsɪn]	6	[bant, band]
3	[sɒk, zɒk]	7	[tas, das]
4	[lɪʧ, lɪʤ]	8	[satam, sadam]

5 Phonology and morphology

In Chapter 1 we saw how the pronunciation of a speech sound or phoneme can vary according to its position in the word, and how the variation is usually quite regular and can be stated in the form of 'rules' which predict the variants, or allophones, which will occur in each position. In this chapter we shall look at variation of a different kind, involving not so much interchange between allophones, but between related phonemes. Look at the following data:

Exercise 1   English regular plurals

From the data given, state the distribution of /S/, (i.e. the archiphoneme of /s, z/), /z/ and /əz/ in plurals:

/S/

/ʃɪpS/	ships	/kraʊdS/	crowds
/boʊtS/	boats	/nɒbS/	knobs
/breθS/	breaths	/haɪvS/	hives

/əz/		/z/	
/bʌsəz/	buses	/tɪnz/	tins
/wɒtʃəz/	watches	/plʌmz/	plums
/wɪʃəz/	wishes	/sɒŋz/	songs
/snizəz/	sneezes	/dɒlz/	dolls
/brɪdʒəz/	bridges	/pʌdl̩z/	puddles

We find here not variants of a single phoneme, but an interchange between more than one phoneme or sequence of phonemes, as variants of the *morpheme* 'plural' ('morpheme' is further explained in the next section). From the limited data above, an approximate rule could be stated as follows: if the noun ends in an obstruent (/p, t, b, v/, etc.) then the plural is /S/; if the noun ends in a (voiced) sonorant, the plural is /z/; but if the noun ends in one of the sounds /s, z, ʧ, ʤ, ʃ/, then the plural is /əz/. Further data could be added to confirm or refute this proposed rule; for instance, the plural of *pill*, which ends in a sonorant, is /pɪlz/; likewise, the plural of *shoe* and *toe*, with sonorants (in this case vowels) finally, is /ʃuz/ and /toωz/. /əz/ is confined to the five sounds mentioned, plus /ʒ/, the voiced counterpart of /ʃ/, as in *mirage*, though there are few nouns ending in /ʒ/ in English. For the sake of conciseness, the rule can be reformulated so as to state the exceptions first; once they are out of the way, the generalizations about obstruents and sonorants is valid for the rest of the data:

$$| \text{ plural } | \rightarrow \begin{cases} \text{/əz/ / [+ strident]} \_\_ \\ \text{/S/ / [− son.]} \_\_ \\ \text{/z/ / [+ son.]} \_\_ \end{cases}$$

Interpretation: the morpheme (shown between upright parallels) 'plural' is pronounced:

1   as /əz/ when it is preceded by a *strident* sound – strident being a term which includes the six sounds /s, z, ʧ, ʤ, ʃ, ʒ/, and only those six;
2   as /S/ (a sound intermediate between /s, z/) after an obstruent ([− son.]); and
3   as /z/ after a sonorant ([+ son.]).

The curly brackets around the three conditions mean that, in 'reading' the rule, one starts at the top – the first condition – and works downwards. If the first condition applies, then apply it, and skip the others; if the first condition does not apply, then go to the second, and so on. This curly bracket convention is useful, because it enables the exceptions to be stated concisely, without special clauses (for example, /S/ after obstruents, *except* /s, z, ʧ/, etc.) – which would be cumbersome.

Morphemes

Morphemes are minimal units of meaning. Very often, a *word* is itself a minimal unit of meaning, for example, *ship*, *toy*, *potato*, but a word may contain more than one minimal unit, i.e. more than one morpheme. *Ships* contains two morphemes, *ship* and 'plural'; *unhappy* also contains two morphemes, *un* (meaning 'not') and *happy*;

unlucky contains three, *un*, *luck*, and *y*, the latter being a morpheme whose 'meaning' is to convert a noun into an adjective (compare *wind–windy*, *dust–dusty*, *sun–sunny*, etc.). 'Simple' words like *ship*, *toy*, etc. are said to contain, or consist of, only one morpheme.

Exercise 2

Identify the morphemes in the following words:

stealing	wasted
improper	useful
regulation	faster
football	recycle
badminton	violinist

Sometimes, a sequence of sounds may *look like* a morpheme, without actually being one. In *badminton*, for example, we can see the sequence *bad*, and even *mint* and *on*, but *bad* in *badminton* has no meaning and is therefore not a morpheme, and neither is *mint*, nor *on*. Morphemes have to be meaningful. *Badminton* cannot be further subdivided into meaningful parts, and is therefore a single morpheme. But *badly*, of course, would be two morphemes, since the sequence /bæd/ here has the meaning 'bad'.

In the examples given so far, we have been able to divide up the words into their component morphemes. Sometimes this is not possible, or at least not easy. *Geese* and *feet*, for example, are obviously the plurals of *goose* and *foot* in just the same way as *ducks* and *boots* are the plurals of *duck* and *boot*. But whereas we can divide *ducks* into '*duck*' and '*s*', *geese* and *feet* cannot be divided. In this case, we recognize that there are still two units of *meaning*, i.e. two morphemes, *goose* (or *foot*) and 'plural', but the two morphemes are 'fused' into a single form. In terms of meaning, *geese* is exactly parallel to *ducks*, but the meaning 'plural' is realized in a different way: instead of *adding* a phoneme, for example /S/, there has been a *change* of phoneme, in this case the vowel /u/ of *goose* being replaced by the /i/ of *geese*.

Exercise 3

Identify the morphemes of the following words, and describe the changes which take place when the morphemes are combined.

men	broken
women	kept
loaves	cacti
wrote	criteria
sank	pianist

'Fused' morphemes which involve an internal vowel change, such as *foot–feet* and *write–wrote*, are not part of the *regular* patterns of English morphology – they are usually referred to as irregular forms of the plurals or the past tense (*broke*, *sank*) or the past participle (*broken*, *written*).

Lexical and grammatical meaning

Morphemes 'have meaning'. 'Having meaning' is normally interpretable in a straightforward way, as when it is said, for example, that the two morphemes of *boots* have the meanings 'boot' and 'plural'. In some cases, however, the notion of 'meaning' has to be extended a little. For example, we would all agree that *windy*, *dusty*, *sunny*, etc. each consist of two morphemes, 'wind', 'dust', 'sun' and '-y'. Similarly, *regulation* in Exercise 2, above, has two component morphemes, 'regulate' and '-ion'. The meanings of *wind*, *dust*, *sun* and *regulate* are obvious. But what of the meanings of '-y' and '-ion'? To answer this, we must consider what these morphemes *do* – what function do they perform? On the basis of many examples, it appears that the function of '-y' is to convert a *noun* (*wind*, etc.) into an *adjective* (*windy*, etc.). Similarly, '-ion' converts a *verb* (*regulate*, etc.) into an (abstract) *noun* (*regulation*, etc.). These morphemes have a *grammatical* meaning; their main purpose is to convert one part of speech into another. Other morphemes, like *wind* and *regulate*, have a 'lexical' meaning: they have meaning 'in themselves'. In saying that morphemes 'have meaning', we include both lexical *and grammatical* meaning as part of what it means to 'have meaning'.

Exercise 4

In the following words, which morphemes have 'lexical' meaning, and which 'grammatical'? What conversions do the 'grammatical' morphemes bring about?

suddenly	piteous
brightness	substandard

> intensity   developmental
> jealousy   careful
> knitting   examiner

Allomorphs

The plural morpheme of English has, as we saw earlier, three regular variants, /əz, S/, and /z/, whose occurrence is predictable on the basis of the preceding sound. The variants of a morpheme are known as *allomorphs*, in the same way as variants of a phoneme are called allophones. The allomorphs are the 'physical realizations' of the morpheme, and are usually therefore presented as phonemes or as a sequence of phonemes. The morpheme, being a unit of meaning, is rather more abstract, and should therefore be represented in such a way as to show that we are *not* referring to the sound-sequence, but to the meaning, for example, 'plural' or 'past'. In addition, the parallel line notation can be used to mean 'morpheme', for example | plural | | past |, and lexical morphemes like *ship*, *toy* can be shown in normal orthography:

> | ship | | toy |

We shall represent *feet* as a combination of the morphemes | foot | and | plural |.

Exercise 5

The regular past tense morpheme in English, | past |, has three regular allomorphs, /əd/, /T/ (the archiphoneme of /t, d/) and /d/, as in *waited* /weɪtəd/, *laughed* /lɑfT/, and *rowed* /roʊd/. Work out the rule determining which allomorph will occur, and present a set of data similar to that of Exercise 1 to show the distribution of each allomorph. The rule is similar to the 'plural' rule.

Exercise 6

The morpheme | in– |, meaning 'not', has the allomorphs /ɪm–, ɪn–, ɪŋ–/. From the following data, work out the distribution of these allomorphs:

/ɪm–/	/ɪn–/	/ɪŋ–/
impossible	intolerable	incomplete

imprecise	indecent	inconsiderate
imbalance	insolvent	ingratitude
	inability	incoherent
	inequality	

We have so far illustrated allomorphs mainly in connection with *grammatical* morphemes like |plural| and |past|. Lexical morphemes can also have variant forms or allomorphs, though less commonly. For example, *wife* has two allomorphs, /waɪv-/ which occurs in the plural *wives*, and /waɪf/ which occurs elsewhere, namely in the singular *wife*, the possessive *wife's*, and in compound forms (*wife-swopping*). Similarly, *knife* and *loaf* have allomorphs /naɪv-/ and /loʊv-/ for the plural, but /naɪf/ and /loʊf/ elsewhere.[1] This allomorphic alternation between voiced and voiceless sounds is found in other words too: *path* and *wreath* have the allomorphs /pɑð-/ and /rið-/ in the plural and /pɑθ, riθ/ elsewhere; *house* has /haʊz-/ in the plural, but /haʊs/ elsewhere. In subsequent sections we shall see further examples of allomorphic variation involving lexical items.

Morphophonemics

The study of the relationship between phonemes and morphemes, exemplified in the preceding sections, is called – or rather, *was* called, until the advent of generative phonology – *morphophonemics*. Morphophonemics was always treated separately from phonemics: phonemics (phonology) studies relationships between sounds (particularly between contrasting sounds within a language), and the variant realizations (allophones) of each sound or group of sounds. Most pre-generative phonologists took the view that phonemes should be related to morphemes only *after* the phonemes of the language have been established and described. Morphophonemics studies the ways in which phonemes can alternate as realizations (allomorphs) of the same morpheme. Thus there are three 'levels' involved altogether, the morpheme, the phoneme, and the (allo)-phone (i.e. phonetic) corresponding to our three notations, | |, / / and [ ]. For example:

morpheme	|wheel|	|plural|
phoneme	/wil/	/z/
(allo)phone	[wiːɫ]	[z̞]
(=phonetic)		

The top level shows the meanings; the second level shows the contrastive sounds by which those meanings are realized in concrete terms; and the bottom (phonetic) level is a more precise guide to the actual pronunciation, showing the (allo)phones.

This view of the relationship between levels, and particularly that of phoneme to phone, was held by the majority of pre-generative phonologists, including those of the major 'schools' – the Prague School (Trubetskoy and Jakobson), the American 'structuralists' (Twaddell, Bloomfield and the 'post-Bloomfieldians', Bloch, Trager, Hockett, Harris, Wells, Pike, etc.), and the British phoneticians (Daniel Jones, Ward, Abercrombie, etc.). Although there were disagreements as to how the phoneme should be defined and whether it should be given a relatively 'concrete' definition (for example, Jones – 'a group of related sounds') or a more abstract interpretation ('the phoneme . . . is meaningless as applied to any particular linguistic element: it is a negative, relational, differential abstraction', Twaddell 1935: 74), there was general agreement that two 'levels' were involved, the phonemic, based on contrasts, and the phonetic, which represented the finer details of actual pronunciation. In other words, pre-generative phonology was based on the principles outlined in Chapter 1.

Generative phonology brought many changes of principle but one of the most significant was the argument that there are not *three* levels involved (see the diagram above, p. 132), but only *two*. The intermediate phonemic level was abolished; the top level was renamed 'systematic phonemic', and the bottom level came to be referred to as 'systematic phonetic'. In the following sections we shall see why these changes were proposed.

Problems of analysis

While pre-generative phonology worked well for the majority of sounds in a very wide range of languages, there remained a number of problems with sounds which could either be analysed in more than one way (competing solutions) or for which there was no adequate solution at all. For example, in Danish there is a contrast, word-initially, between [tʰ] and [d] as in *tag* ('roof') vs *dag* ('day'), and another contrast word-finally between [d] and [ð] as in *hat* ([had]) 'hat' vs *had* [hað] 'hate'. However, [ð] does not occur initially nor [tʰ] finally, so there is no contrast between these two sounds. This means that, in reality, only two sounds are contrasted in each position.

Danish speakers indeed feel that only two phonemes are involved:
first, /t/, with realizations [tʰ] initially and [d] finally; and second, /d/,
realized as [d] initially and [ð] finally. We are then faced with the
problem of having assigned the same sound, [d], to more than one
phoneme. But if that were allowed, how could a proper analysis ever
be achieved? Strictly speaking, then, we require three phonemes, /t, d,
ð/. But this in turn is uneconomical; the distributions of /t, ð/ are
defective; and the solution runs counter to speakers' intuitions. A
diagram can show the pattern of relationships as follows:

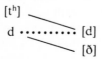

Phoneme theory forces us to 'read off' the phonemes horizontally,
when a diagonal matching would be more satisfactory for several
reasons.

In a carefully-argued paper, Chomsky (1964) draws attention to
several other problems raised by traditional phonemics. Some
examples had been noted earlier by Bloch (1941), as problems of
overlapping, similar in many ways to the Danish example. Some of
Bloch's examples will illustrate the difficulties.

The flap [ɾ]

In many English dialects, the intervocalic sound in *butter*, *betting*,
kitty, etc. is pronounced as a flap, symbolized [ɾ] (Chomsky uses the
symbol [D]). The flap is in free variation with [t] and would be treated
as a variant (allophone) of the phoneme /t/. But the same sound *also*
occurs as a possible pronunciation of /r/ after /θ, ð/, as in *three*,
gathering (for example, /θri/, pronounced [θɾi]). We are then faced
with an awkward choice; either we assign the flap to two different
phonemes, which accords with native-speaker intuitions but is
theoretically unsatisfactory; or we treat the flap as belonging to the
same phoneme, transcribing *three* as /θti/ if it belongs to /t/, or
alternatively transcribing *butter* as /bʌrə/ if it belongs to /r/ –
a solution which would run counter to all intuitions. Bloch calls
this a case of *overlapping* – one sound overlaps two phonemes. The
intuitively-correct solution is, however, permissible, he says, provided one takes *context* into account; [ɾ] belongs to /t/ intervocali-

cally, but to /r/ after /θ, ð/. The Danish example could be treated similarly; assign [d] to /d/ *word-initially*, and to /t/ *word-finally*.

In these two cases, the overlapping is only *partial*, and can be resolved by reference to the phonetic context. But there are also cases of what Bloch calls *complete* overlapping, where the same sound, under the same conditions, may be assigned now to one phoneme, now to another.

English vowel length

In English as in many languages, vowels are *longer* when followed by a voiced sound and *shorter* when preceding a voiceless sound. The [ɪ] of *bit* is shorter than the [ɪ] of *bid*, and the [eɪ] of *safe* shorter than the [eɪ] of *save*. The difference is quite considerable, especially for the diphthongs, where the long variant may be twice as long as the short variant (Wiik 1965, quoted in Gimson 1970: 95, calculates averages of 357 msecs and 178 msecs respectively). Since the distinction applies to all vowels, we could formulate a statement of the allophones along the following lines, using the raised dot to show length:

$$/V/ \rightarrow [V] / \_\_ [-\text{voice}]$$
$$[V^{\cdot}] \text{ elsewhere}^2$$

The problem is this: in American English, /ɒ/ is pronounced as an unrounded back vowel [ɑ]; distinguishing by length, *pot* (voiceless) is pronounced [pɑt], while *pod* (voiced) is [pɑ·d]. However, in the same accents, it so happens that there are minimal pairs distinguished by these two vowels. Thus, *bomb* is [bɑm], but *balm* is [bɑ·m]; *bother* is [bɑðr̩] but *father* is [fɑ·ðr̩]; likewise, *sorry* and *starry*, etc. There must, therefore, be two phonemes here, /ɑ/ and /ɑ·/. But this produces some odd effects, because *Pa'd*, in a phrase like *Pa'd go if he could*, is /pɑ·d/, while *pod* is /pɑd/. Yet, phonetically, according to Bloch, *Pa'd* and *pod* are identical.

So we have to assign the same utterance, [pɑ·d], once to /ɑ·/ and once to /ɑ/. This, says Bloch, is inadmissible: 'the apparent intersection of the phonemes of *pot* and *balm* reveals the fact . . . that the analysis we have made is faulty, even though we have proceeded . . . according to sound principles and usually valid methods' (1941 – reprinted in Makkai 1972: 66ff.). The only acceptable solution is to identify *pod* with *balm*, transcribing *pot* as /pɑt/ and *pod* as /pɑ·d/, even though this 'destroys the neat parallelism' shown by the allophonic vowel-lengthening rule, and produces a system which is 'lopsided'. We should note at once that this solution is not satisfactory either, because native speakers would surely identify the vowel of *pot* and *pod* as 'the same vowel', no matter what result phonemic theory arrives at. And if the theory produces results which are counter-intuitive, it is the theory which is wrong, not the intuitions.

Chomsky (1964: 91) uses Bloch's example to point out a weakness of 'traditional' phonemics, namely the need to state the same rule twice. He bases the argument around a well-known Russian example from Halle (1959), in which a rule of voicing assimilation has to be stated twice; first to convert morphemes into phonemes (for sounds like /t–d/ which are *phonemically* distinct in Russian), and second to convert phonemes into allophones (for sounds like [ʧ–ʤ] which are allophones of one phoneme). If, however, we dispense with the 'phoneme' and convert morphemes directly to (allo)phones, the rule need only be stated once – a great advantage, since clearly the same process is involved in both cases. Bloch's example is similar: the rule of vowel-lengthening has to be stated twice. The first time, as a morphophonemic rule, it applies only to /ɑ/;[3] the second time, as a phonetic (allophonic) rule, it applies to all other vowels *except* /ɑ/. Thus:

morpheme	|pod|	|spade|
Lengthening of /ɑ/		
phoneme	/pɑ·d/	/speɪd/
Lengthening of vowels (except /ɑ/)		
phone	[pɑ·d]	[speɪ·d]

In later sections we shall meet further examples which create difficulties for 'traditional' phonemics but which can, apparently, be handled more effectively under the generative method.[4] In the next section let us see how the generative approach might work for English. First, study the following data.

Exercise 7

Examples were given earlier of allomorphs of lexical morphemes such as /naɪf, naɪv–/ as allomorphs of | knife |. The alternation here is of /f/ and /v/. Each set of data below exemplifies an alternation of two phonemes, which takes place when an affix is added to the end of the word.

Example: create – creation
/krieɪt/ – /krieɪʃən/
/t/ changes to /ʃ/

1   fanatic – fanaticism
    toxic   – toxicity
    classic – classicist
    critic – criticism
    medic   – medicine

2   democrat – democracy
    subvert   – subversive
    pirate   – piracy
    complacent – complacency
    permit   – permissive

3   malice – malicious
    race   – racial
    depress – depression
    sense   – sensual
    suffice – sufficient

4   revise – revision
    enclose – enclosure
    confuse – confusion
    erase   – erasure
    incise – incision

The alternations exemplified in this data are quite regular, and can be expressed in the form of a rule; for example, in set 1, /k/ becomes /s/ when the affix begins with the vowel /ɪ/; hence:

$$k \rightarrow s \: / \underline{\quad} + ɪ$$

where the 'plus' symbolizes the affix boundary. Similarly, in set 2, /t/ becomes /s/ under the same conditions, and we can combine the rule with that of 1 (cf. Chomsky 1964: 71):

$$\text{Rule 1} \quad \left\{ \begin{array}{c} k \\ t \end{array} \right\} \rightarrow s \: / \underline{\quad} + ɪ$$

Set 3 illustrates a different rule; /s/ changes to /ʃ/, for example, *malice*, /mælɪs/, becomes *malicious*, /məlɪʃəs/, etc. It seems that this change takes place when the affix begins with /ɪ/ or /j/, followed immediately by a vowel. The affixes *-ious*, *-ial*, etc. can be seen to begin with /ɪ, j/ in examples like *ceremon-ial*, *harmon-ious*, *rebell-ion*. But when the preceding consonant is /s/, the sequences /sɪ/ or /sj/ coalesce into /ʃ/.[5] This happens only when another vowel follows immediately (compare *expression* with *expressive*). The rule can be formulated as:

Rule 2 $\left\{\begin{array}{c} s \\ z \end{array}\right\} + \left\{\begin{array}{c} \text{\i} \\ j \end{array}\right\} \rightarrow \left\{\begin{array}{c} \int \\ 3 \end{array}\right\} / \underline{\quad} V$

Now look at the following data:

Exercise 8

From the data given, work out which two phonemes are in alternation:

5	relate	– relation	6	magic	– magician
	confident	– confidential		logic	– logician
	convert	– conversion		silica	– siliceous
	Egypt	– Egyptian		music	– musician
	infect	– infectious			

Set 5 illustrates a relationship between /t/ and /ʃ/ (for example, /rɪleɪt–rɪleɪʃən/); set 6 a relationship between /k/ and /ʃ/ (/mædʒɪk–mədʒɪʃən/). The environment requires an affix which begins with ɪ or j, followed immediately by a vowel, as in sets 3 and 4 above (if ɪ/j are not followed by a vowel, /t/ and /k/ change to /s/ – compare *permit–permissive–permission*, or, *electric–electricity–electrician*).

The rule for sets 5 and 6 combined is therefore as follows:

Rule 3 $\left\{\begin{array}{c} k \\ t \end{array}\right\} + \left\{\begin{array}{c} \text{\i} \\ j \end{array}\right\} \rightarrow \int / \underline{\quad} V$

Now it is clear that there are similarities between Rule 3, and Rules 1 and 2. In fact, Rule 3 seems to be the result of combining Rules 1 and 2, if they apply in that order. Chomsky points out, however, that if these rules are simply stated independently in order to show the relationship between alternating phonemes, as would be done in traditional morphophonemics, then the fact that Rule 3 is simply the product of Rules 1 and 2 (and is therefore unnecessary as an independent rule) cannot be captured. A better solution, then, is to let Rules 1 and 2 apply, in order, to the morphemic representation; the output, after the rules have applied, will correspond to the pronunciation. A typical 'derivation' might be as follows:

	logic–ian	*president–ial*
	/lɒdʒɪk + ɪən/	/prezɪdent + ɪəl/
Rule 1	lɒdʒɪs + ɪən	prezɪdens + ɪəl
Rule 2	lɒdʒɪʃən	prezɪdenʃəl
Output	lɒdʒɪʃən	prezɪdenʃəl

In some of the other examples, only Rule 1, or Rule 2, would apply, thus:

	fanatic–ism	*malic–ious*
	/fənætɪk + ɪzm/	/mælɪs + ɪəs/
Rule 1	fənætɪs + ɪzm	N/A
Rule 2	N/A	məlɪʃəs
Output	fənætɪsɪzm	məlɪʃəs

Exercise 9

Using Rules 1 and 2, provide derivations similar to those above for the following:

  expression; expressive; enclosure; conversion; plasticity

Exercise 10

1 What alternation is involved, in the following pairs of words?

persuade	– persuasion
corrode	– corrosion
decide	– decision
evade	– evasion
provide	– provision

2 Suggest a small modification to either Rule 1 or Rule 2 which will enable this additional alternation to be accounted for.

Further rules will be needed to account for other types of 'morphophonemic' variation. These will then be incorporated into the sequence of rules at the appropriate points. For instance, we shall need a rule to convert /z/ to /s/ in certain circumstances, for example *abuse* (vb) – *abuse* (noun), *advise* (vb) – *advice* (noun); the circumstances will include a following *-ive* affix, for speakers who pronounce *corrosive*, *decisive*, etc. with /s/ rather than /z/. In the latter cases, the /d/ of *corrode*, *decide* must be converted to /z/ by an extension to Rule 1 (cf. Exercise 10, 2 above); then at the next stage /z/ will be converted to /s/ by the new rule:

Rule 4　z → s / __ + ɪv

Three more rules capture generalizations which have already been discussed:

1　*Vowel lengthening*　Vowels are pronounced with a long allophone finally and before a voiced sound: compare *rice* [raɪs], *rise* [raɪ·z], *rye* [raɪ·]. The rule is formulated as follows (cf. p. 135, above).

Rule 5　V → [V]/ __ [− voice]
　　　　　[V·] elsewhere

2　*Past tense*　The past-tense rule selects /T, d, əd/ as the appropriate allomorph in each case.

$$\text{Rule 6}\quad |\text{past}| \rightarrow \begin{cases} \text{əd/t, d \_\_} \\ \text{T/[−son.] \_\_} \\ \text{d/[+son.] \_\_} \end{cases}$$

3　*Flapping*　/t/ is pronounced as a flap in words like *butter*, *betting*, *kitty*. This rule is not found in all English dialects, but is common to many of them. The relevant environment is a *stressed* vowel in the preceding syllable, and an *unstressed* vowel in the following syllable. Thus, of the two /t/'s in *potato*, only the second occurs in the right environment for the rule to operate, giving the pronunciation [pəˈtʰeɪɾoʊ], but not allowing [pəˈreɪtoʊ], nor [pəˈreɪɾoʊ]. The rule must also be extended to /d/ as well as /t/ in many American dialects:

Rule 7　t, d →　[ɾ] / ˈV __ V̆

where ˈV means 'stressed vowel', and V̆, 'unstressed vowel'. This rule, and its consequences, will be discussed again later (p. 144).

The rules, with suitable labels, can be summarized as follows:

1 Velar softening:

$$\left.\begin{cases} \begin{cases} k \\ t \end{cases} \to s \\ d \to z \end{cases}\right\} / \underline{\hspace{1em}} +_1$$

2 Palatalization:

$$\begin{cases} s \\ z \end{cases} + \begin{cases} \mathrm{I} \\ \mathrm{j} \end{cases} \to \begin{cases} \int \\ 3 \end{cases} / \underline{\hspace{1em}} V$$

4[6] Z-devoicing:

$$z \to s \ / \underline{\hspace{1em}} +_{\mathrm{IV}}$$

5 Vowel lengthening:

$$V \to \begin{cases} [V] \ / \underline{\hspace{1em}} [-\text{voice}] \\ [V\text{·}] \text{ elsewhere} \end{cases}$$

6 Past tense:

$$+d \to \begin{bmatrix} \text{əd} & / \begin{cases} t \\ d \end{cases} \underline{\hspace{1em}} \\ T & / \ [-\text{son.}] \underline{\hspace{1em}} \\ d & / \ [+\text{son.}] \underline{\hspace{1em}} \end{bmatrix}$$

7 Flapping:

$$\begin{cases} t \\ d \end{cases} \to [\mathrm{r}] \ / \ {}'V \underline{\hspace{1em}} V$$

The sounds, in the rules above, have deliberately not been assigned a notation of / / or [ ]. In generative phonology, / / represents the abstract, underlying, level known as 'systematic phonemic'; [ ] represents the systematic phonetic level, approximately corresponding to the actual pronunciation.

We shall now illustrate the rules, and the ordering sequence, with some sample 'derivations' which proceed, step by step, from the underlying representation to an approximate pronunciation.

	corrosion	*corroded*	*delighted*
	/kə'roωd + ıən/	/kə'roωd + d/	/dı'laıt + d/
Rule no.			
1	kə'roωz + ıən		
2	kə'roωʒən		
4			
5	kə'roω·ʒən	kə'roω·d + d	di'laıt + d
6		kə'roω·dəd	dı'laıtəd
7		kə'roω·rəd	dı'laırəd
Output			
(phonetic):	[kə'roω·ʒən]	[kə'roω·rəd]	[dı'laırəd]

corrosive
/kə'roɔd + ɪv/

1	kə'roɔz + ɪv
2	
4	kə'roɔs + ɪv
5	kə'roɔs + ɪv
6	
7	

Output: [kə'roɔsɪv]

The derivations show that the ordering of these rules is quite important. The flapping rule (7) has to follow the past-tense rule (6), because the latter provides the unstressed vowel which is needed as (part of) the environment for Rule 7 (as in *delighted*). The vowel length rule (5) has to follow the devoicing rule (4), because otherwise in words like *corrosive* the long allophone would be inserted, then have to be changed again when z becomes s. Rule 4 has to follow Rule 1, since Rule 1 provides the /z/ which is necessary for Rule 4 to apply. In the sequence as given, the flapping rule (7) has been put after the vowel length rule (5). The result is that a word with a 'voiced' origin, like *corroded*, ends up with a long vowel allophone before the flap, while a word with a 'voiceless' origin (*delighted*) is pronounced with a *short* vowel before the flap (see the derivations). If the rules had been put in the opposite order, both types would receive a long vowel, because the flap is *voiced*; so we would have the output [dɪ'laɪ·rəd] as well as [kə'roɔ·rəd]. Which output is correct? Do speakers differentiate vowel length here, or not? A minimal pair might help to provide an answer. Do speakers distinguish, for example, *rated* and *raided*, or *petal* and *pedal*? If they do, then Rule 5 must be ordered before Rule 7. If they do not, Rule 7 will precede Rule 5. The order of the rules will be determined by what the speakers do. We shall discuss this again in connection with Chomsky's well-known example of *writer* and *rider*.

One further point about the ordering of the rules is that the past-tense rule 6 has to follow Rule 1. If the order were reversed, there would be nothing to stop the first /d/ of *corroded* from changing to /z/, by Rule 1, thus giving the incorrect output of [kə'roɔ·zəd] for *corroded*. We want Rule 1 to apply for *corrosive* (and *corrosion*), but not for *corroded*. Since the rule had to be formulated so as to apply before +ı, *corroded* can only be excluded by representing it, at the earliest stage, *without* the /ı/ vowel.[7] Hence the representation of past tense as simply +d.

It will be noted that the 'morphemic' representation given at the top of the derivation is sometimes quite abstract, i.e. quite different from the eventual pronunciation. Thus *corrosion* appears as /kə'roʊd+ıən/, though in the final output, neither /d/ nor /ı/ occur. Conversely, elements of the final output are sometimes not to be found in the initial (or 'underlying', as it is often called) representation; [ʒ] in *corrosion*, for example. And third, a morpheme may be given the *same* representation at the underlying level, even when it finally appears in a variety of different forms. Thus *corrode* has the same underlying representation for all three versions, *corroded*, *corrosive* and *corrosion*. Similarly, the representation of *electric* would be the same, /ı'lektrık/, for each of the words derived from it – *electrical* (which has [k]), *electricity* (which has [s]), and *electrician* (with [ʃ]). The notion of a *constant* underlying form, and an *abstract* underlying form which may differ sharply from the eventual pronunciation, later became strongly characteristic of 'orthodox' generative phonology, as developed in *Sound Pattern of English* (Chomsky and Halle 1968). The notion of 'abstractness' will be the subject of a later section.

The phonemic level

Chomsky uses the ordered set of rules, and the typical derivations given above, to argue that an intermediate phonemic level (he calls it 'taxonomic phonemic', roughly equivalent to 'traditional-phone-mic') is both unnecessary and impossible. Unnecessary, because the ordered rules take the derivation from the underlying 'morphemic' representation through to the 'surface' phonetic output, without the need to refer to any specific 'level' on the way; and impossible (or at least problematic), because there is no obvious point in the derivation which corresponds exactly to a taxonomic phonemic level. Some of the rules are clearly 'morphophonemic' in nature: they convert 'phonemes' into other 'phonemes', for example, Rules 1, 2, 4 and 6. Other rules are clearly phonetic in nature; they convert 'phonemes' to '(allo)phones', for example, Rule 5. Now, if the phonetic rules all followed the morphophonemic rules in the ordering, one could take the point at which the phonetic rules start, and the morphophonemic rules finish, as being the 'phonemic' level. But as we can see, this does not happen; the rules are intermixed. Rule 6, a morphophonemic rule, *follows* Rule 5, a phonetic rule; and there are some rules in the scheme which are not clearly classifiable as either 'morphophonemic' or 'phonetic'. Rule 7 is an example; it provides 'allophones' of t and d and is thus phonetic, but it also neutralizes the contrast between the *phonemes* /t/ and /d/ and is thus 'morphophonemic'. Chomsky concludes that an intermediate phonemic level creates more problems than it solves. He suggests relabelling the underlying representation as 'systematic phonemic', and the surface output, corresponding to a modified version of the actual pronunciation, 'systematic phonetic'. In effect, what he is doing is to make the phonemic level more abstract, extending it 'upwards' to take in morphological as well as phonological information.

Writer and *rider*

The difficulties of traditional phonemic theory are nowhere more apparent than in the analysis of this minimal pair. Chomsky claims that in certain dialects, these are distinguished even when /t, d/ are pronounced as a flap, [ɾ]; *writer* is [raiɾ], but *rider* is [rai·ɾ]. Whether speakers *do* make this distinction is not at all certain – many of those who use [ɾ] for both /t/ *and* /d/ do not preserve the distinction, and the situation is much more complicated than Chomsky admits (for a reappraisal, see Rudes 1976) – but let us for the moment assume that Chomsky has got his phonetic facts right. If this is a minimal pair, the only proper solution under the traditional model is to make separate phonemes for /ai/ and /ai·/, for they alone are responsible for the distinction. And this solution will have to be extended to all vowels, since similar differences appear elsewhere (for example, *petal–pedal, rating–raiding*). Vowel length thus becomes phonemic for all English vowels, when they precede [ɾ]. But this is an odd situation because, in all other environments, vowel length is only allophonic: *write* and *ride* do differ in length, but they none the less share 'the same' vowel. Suppose, however, that we accept a phonemic distinction before flaps; we still have the problem of relating the two phonemes /ai, ai·/ to the single phoneme /ai/ in *write* and *ride*. And somehow, the contrast /t, d/ is also involved, as the conditioning environment for vowel lengthening.

For Chomsky, the data can be explained according to the rules and derivations outlined earlier, using Rules 5 (vowel length) and 7 (flapping). The derivations proceed as follows:

	writer	*rider*
Underlying	/raɪt + ɾ̩/	/raɪd + ɾ̩/
Rule 5	raɪt + ɾ̩	raɪ·d + ɾ̩
Rule 7	raɪɾ + ɾ̩	raɪ·ɾ + ɾ̩
Output	[raɪɾɾ̩]	[raɪ·ɾɾ̩]

In traditional phonemics, *as practised*, it is doubtful whether anyone would have adopted the proposed *theoretical* solution, namely to make two phonemes /aɪ, aɪ·/. Like Chomsky, they would represent *writer* and *rider* as /raɪtɾ̩/ and /raɪdɾ̩/, with the flapping rule (Rule 7) to convert /t, d/ to phonetic [ɾ]. They could not, in this case, have made *writer* distinct from *rider*. So the question of whether *writer is* distinct from *rider* (and likewise for other pairs) is an important one.

There are other major issues here too. One is that phonemic distinctions may often be carried not just by the phonemes them-selves, but by neighbouring sounds in the sequence. The distinction between *write* and *ride* is conveyed to the listener not only by voiceless [t] vs voiced [d], but by short [aɪ] vs long [aɪ·]. At the moment, phonologists regard the voicing distinction as crucial ('distinctive') and the vowel-length difference as supplementary ('allophonic', 'redundant'). But this could change with time – it could be that speakers come to perceive the vowel length as crucial, and the voicing distinction as supplementary, in which case the voicing distinction might disappear altogether. The difference between *write* and *ride* would then have to be shown as one of vowel length, and a historical sound change would have taken place: one phoneme, /aɪ/, would have split into two, /aɪ, aɪ·/. Such changes are known to have occurred in the past: the vowels of *path* (/ɑ/) and *pat* (/æ/), for example, were originally the same vowel /a/; this vowel had allophones, [æ, ɑ], which eventually led to a split into two distinct phonemes, /æ, ɑ/.

If Chomsky's 'phonetic facts' are correct, then a historical change of some kind has been initiated. Speakers, anxious to preserve a distinction between *writer* and *rider* (and the many other pairs similarly affected), but unable to do so via /t, d/ because both sounds have been replaced by [ɾ], have *transferred* the distinction to the vowel length; it is now only the difference between [aɪ] and [aɪ·] which maintains the distinction. So in a sense, it would be quite right to say that there is a (traditional) phonemic contrast here between /aɪ/ and /aɪ·/. It is quite possible that this distinction of vowel length might spread to other phonetic environments, eventually taking the historical change through to completion. But this would require favourable conditions, for there are many other possible avenues of development. One is that speakers fail to preserve the distinction between *writer* and *rider*, in spite of *write* vs *ride*, and that Chomsky's phonetic facts are wrong, or perhaps limited to a minority of speakers. In this case the /t, d/ contrast is said to be *neutralized* in this particular environment (namely, the environment of the flapping rule). Historically, the *loss* of distinctions like this is quite common. A third possibility is that speakers *do* preserve the distinction, but not through vowel length (Rudes 1976). In several North American accents, for example, and especially in Canada, there is a difference of vowel *quality* before voiced and voiceless sounds: *write* is pronounced [rʌɪt] or [rəɪt], whereas *ride* is [rɑɪd] or [raɪd]. Before voiceless sounds, the diphthong starts from the mid instead of the open position. Here again, we have two phonetically distinct allophones, which could easily split into separate phonemes at a later stage. For these speakers, *writer* and *rider* are distinguished as [rʌɪɾ̩] and [raɪɾ̩]. However, not all vowels have distinct allophones like this before voiced and voiceless sounds; it seems to be only the wide diphthongs, /aɪ/ and /aʊ/, which are affected.[8]

Chomsky uses the *writer–rider* example to point out the theoretical shortcomings of traditional phonemics. There are certainly problems, but as we have seen, these could be overcome without the need to resort to the generative apparatus of ordered rules. More important perhaps, are the other matters brought to light by this discussion: first the fact that distinctions can be *transferred* to neighbouring phonemes (or shared with them); and second, the possibility that we are witnessing sound changes in progress. The final example, discussed in the next section, further illustrates these two points.

The example of *can't* and *hand*

The nasalization of vowels before a following nasal consonant is another case which Chomsky adduces as posing problems for a traditional-phonemic analysis. Although there are no phonemic nasal vowels in English as there are in French, it is normal in most dialects for some nasality to 'spread' on to the vowel when a nasal follows, the velum being lowered early in anticipation of the nasal; for example, *can* is pronounced [kʰǽn]. In some dialects, however, if the nasal is followed by a voiceless plosive, the vowel carries all the nasality and the nasal consonant is dropped; so although *hand*, with a voiced plosive, is pronounced [hǽnd], *can't*, with voiceless /t/, is pronounced [kǽt].[9] This would embarrass a traditional phonemic analysis, since there are now minimal pairs distinguished only by vowel nasality, namely *can't*, [kǽt] vs *cat* [kæt]. This would require two phonemes /ǽ, æ/, a solution which is counter-intuitive for two reasons: first, because native speakers still transcribe *can't* as /kænt/; and second, because the nasal phoneme, /ǽ/, would occur *only* in this limited environment. Chomsky's solution is to propose two rules which apply in order: the first is a rule of vowel nasalization, the second a rule of nasal consonant deletion:

$$\text{Rule 8} \quad V \rightarrow [+\text{nasal}] \, / \, \underline{\quad} \begin{bmatrix} C \\ +\text{nasal} \end{bmatrix}$$

$$\text{Rule 9} \quad \begin{bmatrix} C \\ +\text{nasal} \end{bmatrix} \rightarrow \emptyset \, / \begin{bmatrix} -\text{tense} \\ V \end{bmatrix} \underline{\quad} \begin{bmatrix} -\text{voice} \\ -\text{contin.} \end{bmatrix}$$

Interpretation: a vowel becomes [+nasal] when preceding a nasal consonant (Rule 8). In Rule 9, a nasal consonant becomes zero(ø), i.e. is deleted, when followed by a voiceless ([−voice]) plosive ([−continuant]) and preceded by a lax ([−tense]) vowel (note that the deletion only takes place after lax, i.e. short vowels). Derivations would be as follows:

	can't	*hand*	*can*
Underlying	/kænt/	/hænd/	/kæn/
Rule 8	kǽnt	hǽnd	kǽn
Rule 9	kǽt	N/A	N/A
Output	[kǽt]	[hǽnd]	[kǽn]

Once again, it is the side issues raised by this example which may be of greater significance than the theoretical question. As in the case of *write* and *ride*, it appears that the characteristics and distinctiveness of one phoneme, the nasal, have been transferred to, and are shared by, a neighbouring phoneme, in this case the preceding vowel. So long as the nasal itself remains, the nasalization of the vowel is merely supplementary, 'allophonic'. But it is quite possible that vowel nasalization could become the *critical* feature for the listener's perception of the presence of a nasal. Such a change is known to occur quite regularly in the history of languages: the nasal vowels of French and Portuguese developed, historically, from sequences of oral vowel + nasal consonant.

When historical changes like this take place, they do not happen all at once; they spread from environment to environment, until all the environments have been affected; the change is then complete. Typically, a change of this kind starts in a voiceless environment, with lax vowels, and with words of high frequency. It spreads to the voiced environments (as in *hand*), and then to word-finals (as in *can*), but never to environments where the nasal is followed immediately by another vowel, as in *spanner* or *running*. At the same time it may also spread to tense (long) vowels and to words of lesser frequency. Whether these changes will ever take place in English depends, of course, on many factors: the conditions have to be favourable. At present then, we are witnessing only the initial stage of a *potential* historical change. In this regard, a traditional-phonemic minimal pair, /æ̃, æ/, can be accepted as a correct solution, but limited for the moment to the 'voiceless plosive' environment. The generative analysis is wrong to the extent that it treats *can't* and *hand* as exactly parallel phonemically (/kænt, hænd/); they are *not* parallel, because *can't* is already in opposition to *cat* and the nasality of the vowel has become 'significant'; for *hand*, the nasality of the vowel is still 'incidental'.

One final point about the ordering of these two rules, as 8 and 9. For orthodox generative phonology, rule ordering is considered very important. It has since been attacked as unnecessary, for example, by the adherents of 'natural' generative phonology (cf. Hooper 1976), who argue that rules *need* not be ordered, and *should* not be ordered, since there is no evidence that native speakers' mental processes 'work' in such a way: ordering lacks 'psychological reality'. Whatever the merits of this issue, it is as well to point out that, in the case of Rules 8 and 9, the same outcome can be achieved without ordering by a small modification to Rule 9, namely:

$$\text{Rule 9a} \qquad \begin{bmatrix} C \\ +\text{nasal} \end{bmatrix} \rightarrow \emptyset \ / \ \begin{bmatrix} V \\ -\text{tense} \\ +\text{nasal} \end{bmatrix} \ - \ \begin{bmatrix} -\text{voice} \\ -\text{contin.} \end{bmatrix}$$

Rule 9a states that a nasal consonant deletes only if the preceding vowel includes the feature [+ nasal]. It is claimed that such a rule is more 'natural', because it shows *why* the nasal consonant can delete: deletion is possible *only* if the crucial 'nasality' feature has been 'transferred' on to the vowel. The original Rule 9 does not show this, and is therefore less 'natural'. One might suggest that a rule of the form:

9b   A nasal consonant can delete (before a voiceless plosive), if, and only if, it has fully transferred its distinctive nasal property to the preceding vowel.

would be even more specific, and hence the most 'natural' of all. But it would be difficult to convert such a statement into a concise notation.

Vowel alternations

In an earlier section (p. 143) it was noted that the underlying representation of a word may differ quite markedly from its actual pronunciation. *Magician*, for example, would be represented as /mædʒɪk + ɪən/, although neither /k/ nor /ɪ/ are actually pronounced, and the [ʃ], which *is* pronounced, fails to appear in the underlying form. Representations of this kind appeared in Chomsky's 1964 paper. In subsequent publications (*SPE* 1968), the possibilities inherent in this theoretical view were extensively developed. For instance, to explain the vowel relationship /ɪ ~ aɪ/ in pairs like prov*i*de–prov*i*sion, div*i*ne–div*i*nity, they posit an underlying representation /prəvīd, dɪvīn/, etc. (where /ī/ represents a tense vowel) which is converted by appropriate rules to the lax vowel [ɪ] in certain environments (*provision, divinity*, etc.) and to the diphthong [aɪ] in other environments (*provide, divine*, etc.). Likewise, *sane* has the underlying form /sæn/ (compare *sanity*), and *receive* is represented as /rɪsēv/ (compare *reception*). The underlying /ī, æ, ē/ are converted to surface [aɪ, eɪ, i] respectively by complex rules of *diphthongization* and *vowel shift*. These changes, it should be noted, reflect actual changes in the history of English (for example, *provide* was at one time pronounced with [iː]), but the posited rules themselves are *not* historical.

Abstractness

These examples are only the barest outline of the extensive proposals of *SPE*. For example, the summary of rules (Chapter 5) lists no fewer than twenty-four different phonological rules which are required to derive the phonetic output from the underlying representations. The question is: in a wider context, how valid are rules of this kind? And can phonemic representations like /prəvīd/ for *provide*, which depart radically from what native speakers would normally expect of a phonemic representation, be justified? To illustrate the lengths to which 'abstractness' is taken, *SPE* has the representations /rixt–i–ɔs/ for 'righteous', /ab = kēd/ for 'accede', and /re = duke = ǣt + iən/ for *reduction*.

Let us look briefly at some of the issues.

The 'free-ride' principle

First, there is the problem that *all* the lexical items of English have to be given a similarly abstract representation, even where no alternations are involved. While it might be acceptable to represent *keep* as /kēp/ because of the alternation with /e/ in *kept*, it is hardly reasonable to represent, say, *leaf* as /lēf/ and *pain* as /pæn/ if the vowels /e, æ/ never appear in alternation. The alternative, however, involves distinguishing between the phonemic representations of (the vowels of) *leaf* and *keep*, or *pain* and *sane*. To avoid this, *leaf* and *pain* are allowed to 'pass through' the rules so as to emerge as [liːf] and [peɪn], according to what has become known as the 'free-ride' principle for non-alternating morphemes.

Where does history stop?

Second, if it is permissible to recreate the history of the language in underlying forms, as reflected by contemporary alternations, then what is to stop the process from being extended to even greater depths? For instance, we know that, historically, there is a link between pairs like *two–dual*, *three–tertiary*, *foot–pedal*, and *tooth–dentist*. Would we really aim to link these pairs phonologically in a set of rules for Modern English? Such an undertaking would lead to unimaginably remote 'underlying forms', yet would only be an extension of the principles already proposed.

Psychological reality

Third, what is the reality of such representations for the ordinary speaker of the language? This question can be answered from two viewpoints: first, from the viewpoint of the child learning the sounds of his language (language acquisition); and second, from the knowledge of mature native speakers ('psychological reality').

The alternations exemplified in sets a, b, c of Exercise 11 apply very largely to the learned, Latinate component of the vocabulary of English. Words like *provision*, *cleanliness*, *sanity* and *abundant* are not part of the average child's early vocabulary during the years up to the age of, say $3\frac{1}{2}$, by which time the bulk of language-learning is complete. We are thus in the position of having to say that the child does not really learn the phonology of his language until he is, 1 familiar with such words, and 2 perceives their relationship with the forms *provide*, *clean*, *sane*, *abound*, etc. Alternatively, it must be argued that the proposed underlying representations are not part of the 'core' phonology of the language, the part that is learnt by young children. For a broad discussion of these issues relating to language acquisition, cf. Derwing 1973.

For the mature native-speaker, the question is, how real are the proposed relationships? Is it reasonable to suggest that the rules correspond to some mental reality? We need to know how strong is the link between, say, /ɪ, aɪ/, or between /d, z/ (cf. *decide–decis + ion*), or between /z, ʒ/ (*enclose, enclosure*). Sometimes the validity of a rule can be tested by observing whether speakers can extend the use of the rule to new or unfamiliar words. For instance, the 'plural' rule which alternates /əz, S, z/ can be tested by asking speakers to give the plurals of new or nonsense words, for example:

this is a /ræl/; these are ___

If the speaker offers plurals such as /rælz/, /krɪnz/, and /mɪʃəz/, for the nonsense words /ræl, krɪn, mɪʃ/, we can be reasonably certain that our 'plural' rule has been internalized and is a valid rule.

A rule may also be confirmed if it is found to occur 'spontaneously' in other contexts. For instance, the palatalization rule (Rule 2 above, p. 141) accounts for the change of /s + ɪ/ (or /s + j/) to /ʃ/ and of /z + j/ to /ʒ/, for words like *express-ion* and *enclos-ure*. But this rule is found much more widely, as an assimilation rule in fairly rapid speech, whenever the sequences /s + j/ or /z + j/ arise. Thus *(I) miss you, race your (car)*, in which final /s/ is followed in the next word by an initial /j/, are pronounced [mɪʃu] (or [mɪʃju]) and [reɪʃə] (or [reɪʃjə]), and similarly *lose your (keys)* becomes [luʒə] (or [luʒjə]). This particular rule is thus given strong support by speakers' actual behaviour patterns (see also below).

Testing the validity of the bond between /ɪ, aɪ/, /e, i/, etc. is not so easy. These alternations do not occur except in related pairs of words, so it would be necessary to test speakers' performances in nonsense or unfamiliar items. Given the nonsense word *recrane*, could speakers derive *recranity*, parallel to *sane, sanity*? Devising a suitable test poses problems in itself, since one cannot ask speakers to form 'abstract nouns' from 'adjectives' directly. There is also the problem that the new derivation will be influenced by the spelling; if the test is given in written form, the production of *recranity* could be ascribed to the influence of the letter 'a'. On the other hand if the test is given orally, there is still a possibility that the speaker mentally 'translates' /rɪ'kreɪn/ into its written form *recrane* and then produces the derivation on the basis of letter 'a'. Ideally, then, the test would have to be given to illiterate speakers. But how many illiterate speakers are sufficiently educated to know the Latinate vocabulary which the rules reflect? Alternatively, the test could be given to *pre*-literate speakers (children), but as we have already mentioned, young children are not familiar with the necessary vocabulary.

Experiments which minimize these difficulties can be devised, however. My students in a number of such experiments have tested the reactions of ordinary speakers in various ways. In one experiment (SM 1975), six subjects were each asked to complete a set of sentences, in which a derivation has to be supplied for a nonsense word, for example:

> Jane's (moraine)__ could get her into trouble
> The (aneceive)__ for the people was disappointing

If the vowel shift rule has psychological reality, subjects would be expected to complete the sentences with *moranity, aneception* or *anecevity*. Subjects were presented with written versions of the sentences but were asked to respond orally. The results showed that in fifteen out of the thirty-six responses, the derivative ending chosen was *-ness* (for example, *moraineness*); *-ity* was chosen in a further fifteen cases. The vowel shift /eɪ/ to /æ/ occurred in only seven responses out of eighteen possible, and the shift /i/ to /e/ likewise, in seven of eighteen instances. Oddly, not a single subject offered *aneception* for the second sentence, despite the 'obvious' parallels with *receive–reception, deceive–deception*, etc. Linguists have, it seems, tended to overestimate the knowledge and capabilities of ordinary speakers in matters of this kind: the validity of vowel shift was not strongly supported in any of these experiments.

Spelling mistakes

If vowel shift, and similar rules proposed in *SPE*, were valid, the present orthography for English would be about the best that could be devised for the language, as indeed Chomsky and Halle claim on a number of occasions. In practice, however, English-speaking children have great difficulties in mastering the spelling system, by comparison with, say, Russian or Spanish children – languages in which the orthography is much closer to a traditional-phonemic representation. Furthermore, if Chomsky and Halle are correct, speakers should not make spelling errors of the type 'professer' for *professor*, because of the existence of the derivative *professorial*, in which the vowel /ɔ/ clearly indicates that the spelling must be 'or'. As any schoolteacher will confirm, however, mistakes of this kind are not only common, but difficult to eradicate.[10] For further discussion, cf. Sampson (1970: 621ff.).

Rule validity 1

The evidence suggests then, that highly abstract phonemic representations such as /prəvīd/ for 'provide' and /sæn/ for 'sane' should be avoided, and that representations much closer to the 'surface' are required if 'psychological reality', i.e. the native speaker's knowledge and behaviour, is taken into account. The same questions can (and should) also be asked about the proposed phonological rules, such as Rules 1–9 outlined earlier (pp. 141, 147). Do they truly represent speakers' knowledge? Are they reflected by actual behaviour?

Notice first, that there is a great difference between a rule like 'past tense' (Rule 6) and one like the vowel shift rule (p. 149 above) which converts underlying /ī/ to surface [aɪ]. The past tense rule can be shown to be 'real' in a number of ways. While acquiring language, for example, children give evidence that the rule has been 'learnt' by extending it to verbs like *drink* and *teach*, producing *drinked* and *teached* – forms which they have not heard from adults, but which they create for themselves by productive use of the rule. Mature speakers, likewise, if presented with new verbs such as 'to *twain*' or 'to *proot*', would have no hesitation in deriving the past-tense forms *twained* and *prooted*. The vowel shift rule, by contrast, has never been shown to have 'productivity' of this kind, even though many pairs of items are related by it, such as 'provide–provision', 'clean–cleanliness', etc.

P rules and MP rules

In natural generative phonology (NGP) – one of the successors to 'orthodox' generative phonology (OGP) – three categories of rules are recognized, the P rules (=phonetic rules), the MP (morphophonemic) rules, and 'via' rules (Hooper 1976: 12ff.). P rules describe 'automatic', exceptionless phonetic processes, processes that take place below the threshold of speakers' awareness. Vowel lengthening is one such; speakers 'automatically' pronounce *rice* short and *rise*, *rye* long. As a consequence, any new words coming into the language would be expected to 'obey' the rule (for example, the vowels of *Grand Prix* take the 'long' allophone); the rule would also be applied to words of other languages; for example, English speakers pronouncing French *gite* ('resting-place') vs *Gide* (the writer) automatically give a shorter vowel to *gite* and a longer vowel to *Gide*.

Aspiration (of voiceless stops) is another such automatic process in English. A loan-word such as French *coup* will therefore be pronounced with an aspirated [kʰ] (despite the relative lack of aspiration of French /k/); and in learning French, English speakers aspirate the voiceless stops of words like *pension* and *corps*. Similarly, the distribution of 'clear' and 'dark' [l] is an 'automatic' P-rule; French borrowings such as *Mistral* or *Marcel* will be automatically given the expected [ł], and the 'unlearning' of such habits in order to achieve a more French-like pronunciation is not easy.

As will by now be apparent, there is a close parallel between the P rules of NGP, and the 'allophonic' or 'phonetic' realization rules discussed in Chapter 1. P rules include, in fact, all the phonetic adjustments resulting from co-articulation, such as the nasalization of vowels in the environment of nasal consonants, etc.

The MP rules of NGP are rules which have to be described in terms of morphological or lexical, rather than phonetic, environments. They are usually not 'exceptionless', and are not applied 'automatically'. They include rules such as the voicing of fricatives in certain plural words, for example *knives*, *hooves*, *houses*, a rule which is restricted both lexically (it only affects certain words) and grammatically (it applies only to *plural*, not to possessives – cf. *knife's*).

A third category of rules, known as 'via' rules, account for morphemic alternations which have no direct phonological motivation, such as velar softening (cf. Hooper 1976: 132) and vowel shift. Together, MP and via rules correspond to the 'morphophonemics' of pre-generative phonology. Since they are not automatic or exceptionless, justification on the basis of speakers' behaviour becomes more difficult.

It will be appreciated that the NGP rule categories represent a virtual return to the pre-generative model. The two-level system of OGP, with its single set of ordered rules, proved too problematic, because it incorporated such different types of rules, all within the same framework. The three-level pre-generative framework was, on the other hand, too rigid in separating the morphophonemics ('above' the phoneme) from the phonetic processes ('below' it). NGP accepts that *most* MP rules are 'above', and *most* P rules 'below' the phoneme, but that there may be some overlapping. The three models can be compared in diagram form:

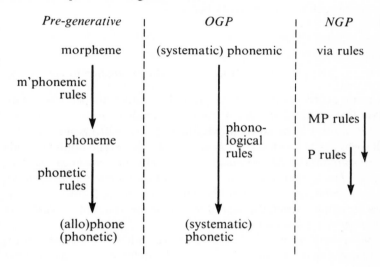

Pre-generative	*OGP*	*NGP*
morpheme	(systematic) phonemic	via rules
m'phonemic rules		MP rules
phoneme	phono-logical rules	P rules
phonetic rules		
(allo)phone (phonetic)	(systematic) phonetic	

Rule validity 2

Of the rules given earlier, in the generative framework (p. 141 above), velar softening and palatalization are not automatic P-rules and must therefore be justified in some other way. Palatalization (the rule which relates /s, z/ to /ʃ, ʒ/ as in *repress–repression*) can make at least some claim to 'reality' because it also operates in fast speech, where it can account for the conversion of the sequences /s–j/ and /z–j/ to /ʃ/ and /ʒ/, as in *miss you* and *as yet*. Velar softening – the rule which relates /k, t/ to /s/ and /d/ to /z/, as in electri*c*–electri*c*ity, pira*t*e–pira*c*y and corro*d*e–corro*s*ive[11] – gets no such support, and is therefore much more difficult to justify as forming part of the native speaker's competence.

Base forms and extended forms

A major question raised by any attempt to justify rules such as velar softening, is the issue of whether words like *division* are to be regarded as derived by rule from a base form (*divide*) or whether they exist as lexical items in their own right, relatively independent of the base. If it can be shown that they are independent, then there is even less justification for the 'rules' whose purpose is to relate them. In OGP, the 'derivation' view is taken for granted, based mainly on syntactic evidence such as the similarity between:

<blockquote>they decided to strike   electricity is produced</blockquote>

and

<blockquote>their decision to strike   the production of electricity</blockquote>

But there is also evidence in favour of the relative independence of the base (for example, *produce*) from its extended form (for example, *production*). For instance, as Matthews (1973: 49ff.) points out, not all verbs can form an extension in this way; there is no noun **salution* corresponding to the verb *salute*. Conversely, there are no verbs **tuit*, *nutrit*, *funct*, corresponding to the nouns *tuition* (cf. *education*), *nutrition* and *function*. Often where there *is* a related form, it is not the one we would expect; the base of *revolution* is *revolt*, not *revolute*; that of *solution* is *solve*, not *solute*.

More striking still is the fact that even where an extended form exists, speakers do not always use it, preferring instead a more 'productive' version. For instance, instead of:

<blockquote>I was surprised about their decision to withdraw</blockquote>

a speaker may say:

<blockquote>I was surprised about them deciding to withdraw</blockquote>

In this case, the speaker has preferred the usual, regular method for producing a noun from a verb, namely by adding -*ing*, instead of the existing de-verbal noun 'decision'. Similarly, a speaker may create the word *undecidedness* (with productive *un*- and -*ness*) instead of using the already-existing form *indecision*.

The most convincing evidence, however, of the relative independence of the extended forms is the fact that, in many cases, their
meanings diverge from the base. Matthews (1973) gives the example
of *generation*, which, although related in one of its senses to *generate*
(as in 'the generation of electricity' – cf. 'electricity is generated'),
nevertheless has other senses with little or no connection to the base,
as in *three generations ago*, or *the younger generation*. Other examples
of extended forms unrelated in meaning to their 'base' are *comprehensive* (for example, ~ *school*) which has little connection with *compre-
hend*, *solicitor vis-à-vis solicit*, and *dissolute vis-à-vis dissolve*. If native
speakers always produced the extended forms from the base by
means of psychologically-real 'rules', how could such divergences of
meaning come about? If *solicitor* was originally (at an earlier stage of
the language) derived from *solicit*, as we assume it must have been,
the intervening changes of meaning which have led to the separation
of meanings could only be possible if extended forms are, in peoples'
minds, relatively independent of their base.

The traditional distinction between *inflection* and *derivation* may
be useful in this context. *Inflections* include those forms which are felt
to be variants of *the same word*, whereas *derivations* are forms which
are in some sense 'new' or 'different' words from the base. Thus
defends and *defended* are *inflections* of the verb *defend*, since they are
simply variant forms of the verb, i.e. they are 'part of' the one word
defend. *Defence* and *defensive*, on the other hand are *derivations* of
defend, since they form 'new' words from the base. Inflections
normally apply to all instances of whatever category they apply to:
for instance, *all* verbs would be expected to inflect for third-singular-
present (cf. defend*s*) and past tense. Derivations, on the other hand,
often change the word-class (for example, verb (*defend*) becomes
noun (*defence*) or adjective (*defensive*)), and affect only *some*
instances of their category (for example, there is no derivative
*attackive, parallel to *defensive*). Orthodox generative phonology has
failed to distinguish between inflections, which because of their
global nature may genuinely incorporate phonological rules, and
derivations like *provide–provision*, which can be linked only by MP or
via rules: instead, OGP has assumed that *all* extended forms can be
derived from a single underlying base. As Hogg observes, 'if we
accept the traditional view that derived forms are much less closely
linked than inflectional forms, the presence of phonetically-unrelated
alternations [he gives the Latin example *honor–honestus*] is no longer

troublesome, since there is no need to suppose that they must share the same underlying morpheme' (1979: 57).

Models of language activity

This issue is connected with questions as to the nature of language activity as a mental process. There seems to be a choice of two possible models: first, we store a relatively small number of lexical items (morphemes), and make maximum use of rules to extend and combine them; but the rules, in this model, must be fairly complex. Second, we store a relatively large number of lexical items, with a correspondingly smaller and simpler set of rules.

As an example of what might be regarded as 'simple' rules, take the rules for the formation of regular plurals and past tenses in English. In writing a dictionary, or a grammar, of the language, it would be pointless to list each plural and past tense form for every noun and verb, when the vast majority of plurals and past tenses are formed perfectly regularly. It is much simpler, and more economical, to put plural and past-tense 'rules' into the grammar, and to list (i.e. make specific mention of) only the exceptions. In the dictionary, therefore, *require* will not have its past tense specified (it will be assumed to be regular) but *write* and *catch* will have their past forms mentioned specifically (since *wrote* and *caught* are irregular). Since it is simple and economical for grammars/dictionaries to operate on such a basis, it is generally assumed that our mental processes work in the same way: past tenses and plurals are not 'stored' individually for each noun and verb, but are 'generated' for each item on each occasion by application of the appropriate rules.

This last assumption, however, although generally held, is not as obvious as it seems. For instance, there must be some mechanism for storing the information that *require* is regular, as well as the fact that *catch* is not. It could be then argued that it is just as economical to store the regular past tenses individually, as to store the information that regular verbs *are* regular.

Generally, however, there is no disagreement about the advantages of treating processes such as plural and past tense as being generated by rule. The arguments focus on the more complex, less psychologically 'real' processes, such as vowel shift and velar softening. In these cases, if linguists prefer a smaller number of lexical items, and a set of complex rules to generate the extended forms (as in *provide–provision*), then that is their choice (and this is clearly the choice favoured by OGP),[12] but there is not much evidence that our mental processes work that way. Rather, the evidence suggests that we store a larger number of lexical items, and that whatever phonological rules exist are relatively simple and straightforward. Given the fact that our mental store must have a capacity of several thousand items anyway, this argument seems reasonable.

Substantive evidence

The relative merits of the two models are discussed by, among others, Skousen (1973). Skousen's account of phonological processes in Finnish is interesting because he initially favoured an orthodox generative approach to the data, but then rejected it in favour of rules which could be shown to be 'real' for the speakers of that language. Some rules, such as stress assignment and vowel harmony, could be shown to be 'real' because speakers maintained them even when contrary tendencies emerged. For instance, in one dialect, the stress assignment rule could have changed completely when speakers came to insert an extra vowel in a consonant cluster, for example, *kylmä* → *kylymä*. But the stress rule remained constant, and the new vowel was simply incorporated within it. Compound words, too, adopt the stress pattern of a simple word, once they lose their original sense, which again indicates the strength and independence of the stress rule. Similarly, the validity of the vowel harmony rule is confirmed by the fact that loan-words always adapt to it. Finnish borrows many words from Swedish; the changes that are made illustrate well the natural phonological rules of Finnish. So, for example, Swedish *bärja* ('to get along') becomes Finnish *pärjä*, and *läkare* ('doctor') becomes *lääkäri*, both of these showing the vowel harmony rule in operation. The 'reality' of this rule is also confirmed by the fact that, in fast speech, it extends across word-boundaries (it normally applies only *within* the word).

These rules are thus supported by what Skousen calls *substantive* evidence: evidence based on speakers' behaviour, as shown by dialect forms, by the adaptation of loan-words, by stylistic changes in fast speech, and by more purely 'internal' changes such as compounding. Skousen found, however, that many of the previously-proposed generative rules of Finnish phonology, such as 'consonant gradation' and palatalization, lacked the support of substantive evidence. These rules were established on the basis of morphemic alternations, and could even be stated in terms of a phonetic environment. But there are two reasons which suggest these rules are not natural phonological rules:

1   There are numerous exceptions to the rules, but speakers make no attempt to bring the exceptions into line; rather, it seems that they simply memorize the exceptions. The phonetic environments of the rules have a historical explanation, but it seems that present-day speakers are not aware of these environments (i.e. they have not internalized them in the form of a rule).

2   Recent loan-words fail to conform to the rules. For instance, there is an assumed rule of palatalization:

$$t \rightarrow s / \_\_i$$

(/t/ becomes /s/ when followed by /i/)

but the loan-word *äiti* 'mother' remains as *äiti* and has not become *äisi*; the loan-word *synd* 'sin' has become *synti*, and not *synsi* as it should, if the palatalization rule were 'real'. The importance of loan-words in the validation of phonological rules is also emphasized by Shibatani (1973).

Skousen concludes that rules such as consonant gradation and palatalization in Finnish belong, if they belong anywhere, in a separate component of the grammar: they are *not* part of the phonology of the language.

Skousen also mentions Hale's (1971) data from Maori, which is a well-known example of the same problem. Here, the analysis which, to the linguist, appears simple, economical and obvious, is found, on further investigation, *not* to be the analysis which native speakers themselves make, as indicated by their behaviour. Instead of formulating a phonological rule, the speakers seem to prefer to memorize the items individually. The conclusion is that our mental processes apparently favour less economical storage and simple rules, rather than an economical lexicon and relatively complex rules.

Conclusion

The arguments which have occupied many phonologists during the 1970s have centred on the level of abstractness which can be admitted into a phonemic representation, and on the restrictions which need to be imposed to avoid unrealistically-abstract analyses. The traditional phonemic analysis was rejected for being too 'concrete', too close to the surface, too concerned with actual pronunciation. Orthodox generative phonology is now criticized in turn for being too far removed from the surface, for having lost touch with the intuitions and real knowledge of the ordinary speaker of the language. This problem can be put in another way: the linguist always 'knows' much more about his language than the ordinary speaker – he has knowledge of the history of the language, of phonological patterns in other languages, of varieties within his own language, etc. Should the rules that are proposed, then, reflect the knowledge of the linguist? or of the ordinary speaker, who has no access to this specialist knowledge? The generally accepted view now is that any phonological rule proposed by linguists should be subject to validation on the basis of the behaviour or the knowledge of ordinary speakers. In general, this means that phonemic representations will be relatively close to the 'surface'; and that phonological rules should be simple and transparent, rather than complex and obscure. Abstract representations, and the complex rules required to bring them to the surface, must be regarded as suspect, however ingenious they might appear.

6 Connected speech

Hitherto, we have looked at sounds and sound patterns either individually, or within the context of small units such as the word or the syllable. But language in everyday use is not conducted in terms of isolated, separate units; it is performed in connected sequences of larger units, in sentences and longer utterances. In this chapter we shall be concerned with what happens to sounds when words are connected into larger units. There are, as we shall see, some remarkable differences between the pronunciation of a word in isolation and of the same word in connected speech, but the changes which take place are mostly quite regular and predictable.

The major processes involved are: first, the *deletion* or loss of sounds; second, *assimilation*, which involves a sound changing in order to become more like a neighbouring sound; third, *vowel reduction*, which is the process of replacing a 'full' vowel with [ɪ] or [ə]; and fourth, *insertion*, i.e. the *addition* of a sound to the existing sequence.

If we listen carefully to the actual sounds a speaker produces in a block of connected speech, and transcribe what we hear phonetically, we may be quite surprised at the results. Here are some examples, taken from everyday conversation, and transcribed on the basis of what was actually *said*, rather than what might have been written:

> [ɫˈɑs mə ˈmʌm]
> I'll ask my mum

> [vjə ˈfaʊndʒ ə ˈkiz]
> have you found your keys

> [zɪ ˈbin]
> has he been

Although these utterances look non-standard, they were spoken by members of an educated family (my own!) speaking standard English in everyday situations. Gillian Brown (1977: 53ff.) reports that the kind of changes illustrated here are typical not only of standard English, but also of quite formal situations in which the speaker is being reasonably 'careful'. She presents a wealth of examples from television newsreaders, political discussions, and speeches, etc. So we must assume that phonetic simplifications of this kind are part of normal, standard connected speech.

Non-standard English

Phonetic simplification is not of course confined to standard English, but it is important to make the distinction between *simplified forms* of standard English, and *non-standard* forms. Sometimes the same process may be involved in both, for example, deletion of /h/. Loss of /h/ is widespread in the non-standard speech of most of England apart from East Anglia, but it also affects fast or casual pronunciations of *standard* English. Standard English (SE) deletes the /h/ of *him*, *her*, *he*, *his*, etc., as in:

>(SE)   [twɪst ɪz ɑm]   'twist his arm'
> [wɪl i əksept]   'will he accept'

Non-standard English (NSE), however, deletes /h/ in lexical items like *how*, *head*, *hurt* as well as in grammatical items like *he*, *his*; for example:

>(NSE)   [aʊ dɪd i ɜt ɪz ed]   'how did he hurt his head'

The SE equivalent would be:

> [haʊ dɪd i hɜt ɪz hed]   (note the deletions in *he*, *his*)

In NSE, the deletion of /h/ is thus *extended* to items where it would not be permitted in SE. Other processes may also be extended similarly, for example, NSE [ɪnt ɪt] for *isn't it* extends the deletion process by allowing deletion of /z/. Another example from Midlands NSE shows deletion of /l/ before another consonant:

> [oʊʤə taɪt]   (or more simply, [oʊʤə])   'hold yer tight'

(the cry of the Nottingham bus conductor as the vehicle lurches forward) shows deletion of [l] before the [d] of *hold*, as does:

[koʊd ɪnt ɪt]   (cold, isn't it)

with [l] deleted before the [d] of *cold*. In standard English, [l] has been deleted, historically, in words like *talk*, *walk* and *should*, but is now deleted in only a small range of items, such as *alright* ([ɔraɪt]), *already*, *also*.

Since the same processes are found in both casual standard, and non-standard, pronunciations, it is important that the two should not be confused with each other.

'Fast' and 'casual' speech

The term 'connected speech' to describe these events is only one of many terms which have appeared in the literature. Some writers, perhaps a majority, consider that *speed* or tempo is the main source of the differences; they therefore distinguish fast or allegro speech (the musical terms *allegro* (fast), *presto* (very fast), *andante* (rather slow) and *largo* or *adagio* (very slow) are sometimes employed) from slow, or normal speech. Others base the distinctions on *care* of articulation (or lack of it), differentiating between *careful* and *casual* styles of speech. Quite frequently, speed and care are linked, so we read of 'fast, casual speech', etc. On Brown's evidence, however, and also that of Hewlett (1980) and Shockey (1973), it seems that the simplifications we are concerned with are found just as much in so-called 'careful', 'formal' speech, as in casual speech. So the real distinction seems to be between *full* forms like /hæv/, /mʌst/, /ɪz/, etc. which are attributed (perhaps wrongly) to 'careful' speech, and the *simplified* or *reduced* forms (/v, məs, z/, etc.), which are attributed to 'casual', 'fast', etc. speech.

Exercise 1

What would be the full form of the sentences below, given in phonetic transcription as typically pronounced? Give the orthographic version first, then the 'full' form in a phonemic transcription. As you will appreciate, it is impossible to leave spaces corresponding to all the word boundaries. Example:

Phonetic   [dʒə wɒnə help]

Orthographic   do you want to help
Phonemic   /du ju wɒnt tu help/

1 [ˈwɒʧə ˈduɪn]
2 [snɒʔ ˈraɪt]
3 [ˈwɒrə jə ˈplænz]
4 [a ˈwoʊmp bɪ ˈlɒŋ]
5 [aɪŋənə ˈtel ðm̩]
6 [ə sədəv ˈgleɪz km̩ˈoʊvrɪz aɪz]

Exercise 2

What might be a typical 'reduced' pronunciation of each of the following sentences? There may be several possibilities for each. Give them in phonetic transcription.

1 it's a nice day today
2 let's go for a walk
3 don't be so stupid
4 because we can't get back again
5 it's as much as I can do to breathe
6 is that her problem

Why simplify?

One point about simplified utterances like the ones illustrated is that, in the normal course of conversation, the reductions themselves go quite unnoticed by the listener. The listener is mainly interested in the meanings the speaker aims to convey and not in the precise phonetic detail with which he conveys them.[1] So long as the meaning is recoverable, the listener is satisfied. We have to regard the omissions and reductions then as a kind of economy on the part of the speaker – who aims not to give more information than is necessary. The speaker assumes, usually correctly, that the listener will not notice the 'omissions'. Paradoxically, this makes the omissions difficult to observe; being so used to ignoring them, we have to make a conscious effort to realize that they occur at all.

Ambiguity

A question often asked about phonetic reduction is whether it leads to excessive ambiguity. On the face of it, one would expect a great deal of ambiguity to arise, particularly in cases where a whole word is reduced to a single phoneme (for example, /z/ for *has*), or deleted altogether (for example, *(it)'s dinnertime*). The load carried by a single phoneme can become enormous; /z/, for example, can represent the reduced forms of *has*, *is* and even *does*, as well as 'plural' and 'possessive' for nouns, and 'third-person-singular-present' (3sg.) for other verbs. The single phoneme /ə/ can represent the reduced forms of *are*, *or*, *her* and sometimes *of* (as in *cup o' tea*, *friend o' mine*, *six o' clock*), as well as the indefinite article *a*, the comparative of adjectives (*rich-er*), and the agentive *-er* (*sing-er*). But in spite of the meaning-load carried by the same sounds, ambiguity rarely arises because the syntactic functions are quite different, and the rest of the context will make the intention clear. Thus in:

[z̧ ned goʊɪŋ] (is Ned going?)

[z] can only be the reduced form of *is*; in:

[z̧ned gɒn]

it must be derived from *has*; in

[nedz̧ brekfəst]

it must be 'possessive'; and so on. It seems that the language has rather cleverly arranged matters so that the same sound can represent many different meanings without at the same time creating unacceptable levels of ambiguity.

Full forms

On hearing a sequence like:

[vjə 'fɪnɪʃt]

the listener presumably 'reconstructs', from this minimal phonetic string and the rest of the situation or context, the interpretation:

have you finished?

In its full form, without any reductions, the sequence would be:

/hæv ju 'fɪnɪʃt/

But how can we be confident that this *is* the corresponding full form? The fact is, that we cannot be completely certain, but it is often possible to relate the simplified form to a full form which occurs in other environments, for example (for /hæv/)

/jes wi hæv/	'yes we have'
/aɪ θɪŋk aɪ hæv/	'I think I have'
/wi hæv fɪnɪʃt/	'we have finished'

The full form of the word occurs either under emphasis, as in 'we *have* finished', or when it is final in the sentence, as in 'yes we have'. Note that, in the latter position, reduction is not acceptable; we do not find:

*/jes wi həv/   */jes wi əv/   */jes wiv/

as possible pronunciations for 'yes we have'; and similarly

*/aɪ θɪŋk aɪv/

is disallowed as a realization of 'I think I have'.

We thus 'reconstruct' the full form of a reduced item on the basis of its occurrence in other environments, thus linking [v] to *have*, [jə] to *you*, etc. Sometimes, however, it is not possible to be certain about a full form. For example, *I'll* and *we'll* could be reductions of either (I/we) *will* or (I/we) *shall*. When the full forms occur, either of these is acceptable, for example

I hope I will/shall
Will/shall we need it
I *will*/*shall* be sorry (emphatic)

You'll and *they'll* are more clearly relateable to *will* (rather than *shall*), cf.

I suppose you will
We know they will, won't they

There is at least one remarkable case where speakers quite regularly reconstruct the 'wrong' full form; both *of* and *have* reduce to [əv], and there are certain environments in which the full form hardly ever surfaces; for example, after modal verbs, *must have*, *should have*, *could have*, etc., *have* is almost invariably pronounced in its reduced form:

[mʌst əv]   [ʃʊd əv] etc.

Even in sentence-final position (where full forms are usually required), we find:

[aɪ mʌst əv]   [wɪ ʃʊd əv] etc.

And whereas emphasis can be given to *must*, etc. (we *must* have), it cannot be given to *have* (*we must *have*, etc.). The result is that many children, and quite a few adults, reconstruct *of* from the reduced form [əv], and we get utterances like:

[aɪ ʃʊd ɒv]   [ðeɪ mʌst ɒv]

and the corresponding orthographic forms in writing ('I should of', 'they must of').

Basis of description

In a description of the processes of deletion, assimilation, etc., we aim to show the relationship between the full form of a word and its corresponding reduced form(s). In principle we could start either from the simplified forms or from the full forms, but in practice it is easier to start from the latter, because in the course of reduction, information gets lost, and may not be uniquely recoverable, as for example in the case of [z] which could derive either from *has* or from *is*. So although it is the reduced form which the listener actually hears, the description is based on the reconstructed full forms.

Some examples will show how this might proceed.

1   The phonetic sequence:

[zɪ 'bin]

derives from the unreduced sequence:

/hæz hi bin/

Between the full form and the reduced form we can propose a stage-by-stage reduction of the material:

a   hæz hi bin
b   həz hɪ bin
c   əz ɪ bin
d   z ɪ bin

At stage *b*, vowel reduction takes place; the full vowels /æ, i/ are reduced to [ə, ɪ] respectively in *has, he*. Stage *c* represents the *deletion* of /h/; and stage *d* marks another *deletion*, of the already-reduced [ə] vowel.

2   The unreduced sequence:

/aɪ kɑnt get jɔ fɒt aʊt/

is actually pronounced as:

[a kɑŋk geʔʧə fɒɾ aʊʔ]

By the process of vowel reduction /aɪ/ becomes [a] and the /ɔ/ of *your* becomes [ə]. Then there are assimilations; first the /t/ of /kɑnt/ changes to velar [k] under the influence of the immediately following velar, /g/. Then the nasal /n/ assimilates to the velar [k] which now follows it, giving the sequence [ŋk] instead of /nt/. The sequence /t–j/ in *get your* also undergoes an assimilation – in this case the sounds mutually influence each other, so that the sequence: alveolar (t) + palatal (j) becomes the *palato-alveolar* [ʧ]. (This process corresponds to the palatalization rule, cf. Chapter 5.) However, the speaker compensates for the fact that two segments have been rolled into one by adding a [ʔ] (glottal stop) before [ʧ], thus preserving the *timing* of the original. Without the glottal stop, the resulting sequence would be [geʧə]; this pronunciation may in fact be possible, but in many cases there is a difference between the reduced pronunciation of *get your*, and the sequence [eʧə] as in *ketchup*.

These examples show how the reduced pronunciation can be derived from the full form via the operation of a set of processes; deletion, vowel reduction, and assimilation. In the rest of the chapter, we shall look at each of these processes in turn. *Insertion*, a less common process than the others, will also be mentioned.

Exercise 3

The words given below normally occur in their reduced or simplified form. Construct sentences in which the word will most probably be pronounced in its full form.

Example: *from*   Full form: /frɒm/
           Sentences   I know who that's from
                        Is the letter *from* them or *to* them

Words:

        for   the   some   am   could

Exercise 4

Of the following pronunciations, which can be regarded as standard English, and which as non-standard? The orthographic form is given alongside each.

[ɪn ɪt]	isn't it
[gənə]	going to
[aɪ eɪt ɪm]	I hate him
[kʊdṇ ɪt]	couldn't it
[kʌp ə ti]	cup of tea
[geɾɪŋ əlɒŋ]	getting along
[av gɒrɪt]	I've got it
[lɒs mɪ bʊk]	lost my book
[mʌs bɪ kreɪzɪ]	must be crazy
[pleɪn fʊpbɔl]	playing football
[ən aɪdɪər əv maɪn]	an idea of mine

Deletion

One of the commonest processes of reduction is the *deletion* of consonants and vowels. Among the consonants, perhaps the most obvious 'casualty' is /h/, which as we have already seen, is deleted almost entirely in many varieties of non-standard English, and in standard English is regularly lost under certain conditions. The conditions are, first, that it is mainly grammatical items that are affected, particularly the pronouns *he, him, her*, the possessive pronouns *his, her*, and the auxiliary verb *have* and its parts, including *has* and *had*. The second condition is that the items must be unstressed (as indeed they usually are). If stressed, we would regard the deletion of /h/ as non-standard, for example

	'not for him'	'yes I have'
Standard	['nɒt fə 'hɪm]	['jes aɪ 'hæv]
Non-standard	['nɒt fər 'ɪm]	['jes aɪ 'æv]

Apart from /h/, other consonants are lost when they occur as the last consonant in a syllable-final cluster, as in:

[fɜs taɪm]	first time
[lɑs naɪt]	last night
[neks wik]	next week
[mʌs bɪ]	must be

Again, there are conditions which limit the extent to which this process applies. First, it only happens when the cluster is followed by another consonant (in the next word). If a vowel follows, the consonant remains. Compare the following with the examples just given:

[fɜst əv ɔl]	first of all
[lɑst ɪn]	last in
[nekst oʊvə]	next over

Another condition is that it is mainly /t/ and /d/ which are affected. Examples of the deletion of /d/ are:

[stæn stɪl]	stand still
[ə θaʊzən taɪmz]	a thousand times
[reɪz ðə mætə]	raised the matter

Other consonants can be deleted occasionally, but the restrictions seem to be tighter. For example, /k/ can be deleted in *ask* when another consonant follows:

[ɑs ðə poʊsmən]   'ask the postman'

but other words ending in /–sk/ are much less likely to lose the /k/; for example

? [rɪs mə nek]   'risk my neck'

Deletion can also affect vowels, but mainly this is confined to the unstressed vowels [ə] and [ɪ]. The grammatical items are again the ones most affected. We have discussed examples like *has* → [həz] → [əz] → [z], and *have* →[v].

If the consonant following the [ə] is a liquid or a nasal, what usually happens is that the consonant becomes syllabic; look at the following series of changes:

/fɪʃ ænd ʧɪps/

[fɪʃ ənd ʧɪps]	(vowel reduction)
[fɪʃ ən ʧɪps]	(C deletion)
[fɪʃ n̩ ʧɪps]	(V deletion)

At the final stage, the sequence: [ə]+nasal becomes: syllabic nasal. Similar examples are:

[fr̩ ɪnstəns]	'for instance'
[sm̩ bʌɾə]	'some butter'
[beɾə ðn̩ ðæt]	'better than that'
[aɪkn̩rid]	'I can read'
[wɒɾl̩ wɪ du]	'What'll we do'

An unstressed vowel can be deleted from lexical items too, under certain conditions. One common type of environment is an unstressed initial syllable, as in:

[spoʊz]	suppose
[bliv]	believe
[plis]	police
[krekt]	correct

In these examples, the resulting consonant cluster is one which occurs quite normally elsewhere, for example /sp–, bl–, kr–/. But we also find deletions of [ə] which result in 'impossible' clusters, as for example in:

[pteɪtoʊ]	'potato'
[ktoʊniæstə]	'cotoniaster'
[vrɒnɪkə]	'Veronica'
[mlɪʃəs]	'malicious'

It was proposed earlier (Chapter 2, p. 72) that such items be given the [ə] in their 'underlying' (phonemic) representation. There will then be a distinction between items like *potato* and *correct*, whose clusters derive from [ə]-deletion, and items like *train* and *crook* whose clusters are part of the lexical composition itself. The difference is that the former have *alternative* pronunciations with [ə], while the latter do not. Thus *correct* can be pronounced either [krekt] or [kə'rekt], but *crook* can only be pronounced [kr–]. Native speakers are aware that the former type have two alternative pronunciations, and the latter only one; it is therefore reasonable to give *correct* the lexical representation /kərekt/; a rule of [ə]-deletion then optionally converts this to [krekt].

The unstressed vowel [ə] can undergo deletion not only in word-initial syllables, but also word-medially, as in *governor*, *different*, *temporary*, *interrupt*. Zwicky (1972) points out that deletion occurs most frequently when the consonant following the [ə]-vowel is a liquid or nasal, the reasons being that these are the most 'vowel-like' consonants, and that the loss of [ə] often results in a readily-acceptable cluster like [fr–] and [pr–]. If the consonant after [ə] is an obstruent, deletion does not occur; *prohibitive*, *fallacy*, and *noticeable* cannot be pronounced *[prə'hɪbtiv], *['fælsɪ], *['noʊtsəbl]].

Exercise 5

1   What 'impossible' clusters may result from vowel deletion in the following? Example: 'is the water off' [zðwɔtrɒf]

> it's never open
> there's no excuse
> thank you
> is that it
> bananas

2   Find five more 'impossible' clusters from similar data.

Exercise 6

The following items all have a [ə] vowel medially. In which of them can [ə] be deleted? Does the data support Zwicky's observation above?

general	utterance
possible	character
consonant	opening
considerable	ventriloquist
vertical	similar

Insertion

While the *deletion* of segments is a very common process in connected speech, we also occasionally find segments being inserted. In view of the fact that speakers generally try to economize on the information given and *reduce* the output to the limits of intelligibility, it seems surprising that segments should actually be inserted, and we shall require some explanation for it. The most probable explanation is that the insertion somehow makes the sequence 'easier' to pronounce or articulate, i.e. the speaker would have to make a greater effort to *suppress* the insertion than is required to include it. Look at the following data.

Exercise 7

1   What sound has been inserted in the following items?
2   Can the environment of the insertion be stated in the form of a rule?

[prɪnts]	prince
[traɪʌmpf]	triumph
[kɒrɪntθ]	Corinth
[leŋkθ]	length
[əmʌŋkst]	amongst
[wʌnts]	once
[wɔmpθ]	warmth
[nɪmpf]	nymph
[tentθ]	tenth

The words in the list above have alternative pronunçiations *without* the voiceless plosive, for example [prɪns] for *prince*.

The rule is that a voiceless plosive can be *inserted* when a nasal is followed by a voiceless fricative. In the examples given, the sequence occurs at the *end* of the syllable, but we can also find examples of these sequences across syllable boundaries: *mincing, chancellor, Corinthian*.

The reason for the insertion of a voiceless plosive in these environments is one of articulatory timing. To move the articulators from a nasal stop to a following oral continuant (namely a fricative) requires two changes: the raising of the velum to shut off the nasal cavities, and the release of the oral closure. If the timing of these changes is perfectly synchronized, then no insertion takes place; but if the velum rises *before* the oral closure is released, the airstream is momentarily completely checked, and the acoustic result is a voiceless plosive. In this case, then, insertion is caused by articulatory timing; it may be 'easier' for the speaker to achieve the movements separately than to synchronize them precisely.

'Linking' r and 'intrusive' r

Another example of insertion in connected speech is the so-called 'linking' [r]. Look at the following data:

hear	[hiə]	hearing	[hiərɪŋ]²
wear	[weə]	wearer	[weərə]
pure	[pjuə]	purest	[pjuərəst]
star	[stɑ]	starry	[stɑri]
stir	[stɜ]	stir up	[stɜr ʌp]
store	[stɔ]	store away	[stɔr əweɪ]
director	[dərektə]	director of	[dərektər əv]

Based on this data, there seems to be a rule that when a word which ends in a vowel is followed by another word (or morpheme) which *begins* with a vowel, an [r] is inserted between the vowels. The rule only applies under certain conditions, the first of these being the type of vowel. Linking [r] follows only the vowels /iə, eə, uə, ɑ, ɜ, ɔ, ə/, each of which is given one example in the data above. If the word-final vowel is a diphthong which glides to [i] or [u], no linking [r] appears. The [i]-gliding diphthongs tend to insert a [j], and the [u]-gliding diphthongs a [w], as in:

| [seɪjɪŋ] | saying |
| [tʃuwɪŋ] | chewing |

What do the vowels which receive linking [r], /iə, eə, uə/, etc., have in common? It could be suggested that they all involve a centring glide, towards [ə]. This is only plausible for /ɑ, ɔ/ if we can accept that phonetically these vowels have a small final off-glide, [ɑə] and [ɔə]. If so, then we have a symmetrical relationship between the end-points of the diphthongal glides and the sounds which are inserted:

i   u   j   w

ə   r

Thus [i]-glides insert [j], [u]-glides insert [w], and [ə]-glides insert [r].

The second condition on linking [r] is that it applies only for speakers of those accents which do not pronounce [r] in syllable-final position – the accents, like RP, which are called *non-rhotic*. Speakers of r-pronouncing (or *rhotic*) accents (cf. Chapter 8) can represent words like *hear*, *star*, etc. as /hir/ and /star/, and there is therefore no question of any insertion.

Before we consider a third possible condition on the occurrence of linking [r], look at the following data:

[mɑ]	ma	[mɑr ən pɑ]	ma and pa
[sɔ]	saw	[sɔr ən æksɪdənt]	saw an accident
[rʌʃə]	Russia	[rʌʃər ən poʊlənd]	Russia and Poland
[drɔ]	draw	[drɔr ə sɜkl]	draw a circle
[lɔrə]	Laura	[lɔrər æʃli]	Laura Ashley
[diploʊmə]	diploma	[diploʊmər ɪn drɑmə]	diploma in drama
[aɪdɪə]	idea	[aɪdɪər əv hɪz]	idea of his

In this data we again find words ending in some of the same vowels as before: /iə, ɑ, ɔ, ə/, but this time the words do not have a letter 'r' in the spelling. Nevertheless, the same process of insertion of [r] may take place, whenever the word is followed by another word beginning with a vowel. This [r] is sometimes distinguished from 'linking [r]' as 'intrusive [r]', on the grounds that speakers are 'putting in an [r]' where there 'shouldn't be one'. It is clear, however, that linking and intrusive [r] are both part of the same phonetic process of [r]-insertion.

Why do speakers insert these [r]s, both linking and intrusive, and [j, w] after [i, u]-glides? The answer is that it is apparently easier, from an articulatory point of view, to put these sounds in, than to leave them out. In effect, a sequence of two vowels, VV, is being interrupted by a consonant-like sound, to give a sequence VCV. We know from other evidence (cf. Chapter 4) that the 'optimal' or 'basic' syllable types are CV and V; thus the insertion changes a non-optimal pattern, VV, into a more 'basic' one, VCV. This is particularly 'natural' when the first V is a long or diphthongal vowel.

In summary, insertion takes place in connected speech in order to facilitate the process of articulation for the speaker, and not as a way of providing 'extra' information for the listener. We have suggested that speakers would have to work harder to *suppress* the insertions than they do in admitting them.

Vowel reduction

A number of words have alternative pronunciations involving a 'full' form which appears in positions of stress, and a 'reduced' form with [ə] in unstressed positions. Thus *to* is [tu] in *to and fro* but [tə] in *want to come*; *for* is [fɔ] in *Who are you looking for?* but [fə] in *looking for John*, etc. The process by which a full vowel becomes [ə] in unstressed positions is known as vowel reduction.

'Grammatical' vs 'lexical' items

The words which undergo vowel reduction are mainly monosyllabic 'grammatical' items.[3] Examples of 'grammatical' classes are:

> auxiliary verbs (forms of *be*, *have*, *do*)
> pronouns (*I*, *me*, *my*, etc.)
> articles (*a*, *the*)
> demonstratives (*this*, *that*, *there*)
> the negative *not*

Certain lexical items are also subject to vowel reduction:

1   Suffixes which have become closely attached to their stem, such as *-man* in *postman*, *milkman*, *chairman*, and *-ful* in *handful*, *doubtful*, *careful*.
2   Polysyllabic words in which the position of primary stress may vary. Compare:

> photograph – photography – photographic
> diplomat   – diplomacy   – diplomatic
> phonology   – phonological
> Canada   – Canadian

Stress-timed rhythm

Vowel reduction in English takes place because of the nature of the patterns of rhythm and stress. Rhythm in speech, like rhythm in music, is based on the idea of a strong beat or accent which recurs at regular intervals of time. In music, the unit of rhythm is the bar; each bar begins with a strong beat, and is allotted approximately the same amount of time: the regularity of the time intervals can be clearly heard by tapping each strong beat. The unit of speech corresponding, approximately, to the *bar* in music is the *foot*.

In speech, the type of rhythm depends on the language spoken. Some linguists divide languages broadly into two groups, those whose rhythm is based on the syllable (known as *syllable-timed* languages), such as French and some other Romance languages, for example Spanish, and those with a rhythm based on the *foot* (see below, p. 179), such as English and the other 'Germanic' languages, which are known as *stress-timed* languages (Pike 1946; Abercrombie 1965: 17). In a syllable-timed language the speaker gives an approximately equal amount of time to each *syllable*, whether the syllable is stressed or unstressed, and this produces a characteristically even, rather staccato, rhythm. In a stress-timed language, of which English is a good example, the rhythm is based on a larger unit (the foot), and can best be explained with some examples.[4]

In the examples that follow, we shall assume that the sentences are spoken in a rhythmic manner. In practice, however, there are many factors which can disrupt the potential rhythm of a sentence, and we find very often that sentences are not spoken rhythmically at all – the rhythm may only be potential, or latent. For example, the speaker may pause at one or more points in the utterance; he may be interrupted; he may make false starts, repeat a word, or, in rapid speech, slur a number of words together, etc. All these factors, which come under the general heading of hesitation phenomena, can disrupt the rhythm, so that in assuming that a sentence is spoken rhythmically, we are referring to an ideal realization from which 'performance' factors are absent.

With this proviso, let us take an example to illustrate a stress-timed rhythm. The sentence

How did you manage to keep so calm?

can be spoken with a strong beat on the syllables *how, man-, keep, calm*. We can mark the accents in the usual way, namely 'how did you 'manage to 'keep so 'calm

Each accent occurs at an approximately equal time interval, so that *how did you* takes roughly the same amount of time as *manage to* and *keep so*. We can thus regard the accent marks as equivalent to bar lines in music, the only difference being one of terminology – we talk of *feet* instead of *bars*. The sentence above, then, can be divided into feet in the following way:

|how did you | manage to | keep so | calm

A sentence can begin with one or more unstressed syllables before the first complete foot, just as a line of music can begin with an up-beat before the first complete bar. For example:

I | wonder | why he | did
there's a | lot of | work to be | done

We can observe that the amount of time given to each *syllable* must vary considerably, because some feet have three syllables, others two, others only one, yet the total time allotted to each foot is the same. The rhythm of English is thus quite different from that of a (syllable-timed) language which assigns an approximately equal time to each *syllable*. From a practical viewpoint we can predict that foreign learners with a syllable-timed background will have difficulties in adapting to an English type of rhythm, and conversely, those with English as a native language will tend to impose English rhythmic patterns on to other languages.

One way of allotting time to the syllable in English would be to share out the foot equally, giving one-third of the total time to each syllable of a three-syllable foot, half the total time to each syllable in a two-syllable foot, etc., for example (assuming a speech rate of one second per foot):

	how did you	manage to	keep so	calm
secs	.33 .33 .33	.33 .33 .33	.5 .5	1.0

Speakers do not actually do this, however; they allot more time to some syllables and less to others, making the distribution unequal. Broadly speaking, lexical (i.e. content, or high information) items are given more time, while grammatical items, which are usually low in information, are given the least time. In the sentence illustrated, the lexical items are *manage, keep, calm,* while *did, you, to, so* are grammatical items. We must bear in mind, however, that the distinction between lexical and grammatical is not an absolute one (*how,* for instance, is neither purely lexical nor purely grammatical), and can therefore be only a rough guide to the allocation of time.

The unequal distribution of time means that, in the sentence above, *keep* will get about two-thirds of a foot while *so* gets the remaining one-third; *manage* will occupy three-quarters of its foot, leaving only one-quarter to *to*; *how* will get about a half, *did* and *you* about a quarter each. The result is that the time allotted to each successive syllable varies greatly, and the rhythm of the sentence consists of an alternation of 'long' syllables with 'short' ones, there being possibly two or three short syllables between each long one. The rhythm is thus at once both regular and irregular; the regularity is provided by the strong 'beat' at the beginning of each foot, and the irregularity by the unequal distribution of time *within* the foot. Poetic metres can make skilful use of this interplay between the regular and the irregular, which is characteristic of natural speech (cf. Abercrombie 1965: 16).

Exercise 8

1   Divide each of the following sentences into feet according to the rhythm with which the sentence might normally be spoken. (Note that there may be more than one possibility.)
2   Which syllables are given the most time, and which the least? Is there a correlation with the distinction lexical vs grammatical?

> Could you find me some decent notepaper?
> He always turns up at the critical moment.
> The tape's got jammed in the cassette.
> You really shouldn't have said it like that.
> I wish you could've seen his expression.

Rhythm and vowel reduction

Rhythmic patterns have consequences elsewhere in the phonology, for they determine the incidence of [ə]. Not only does [ə] occur exclusively in unstressed syllables, but it is also *the* characteristic vowel of the short, unstressed syllables which occur between the full (stressed) ones. [ə] is the most frequent sound of English; in continuous text it represents about 11 per cent of all sounds; and if we add the occurrences of /ɪ/, which is closely related to [ə] in unstressed syllables (cf. Gimson 1980: 104ff.), we get a figure close to 20 per cent – nearly one sound in five is either [ə] or unstressed [ɪ]. This high frequency of [ə] is the result of the rhythmic pattern: if syllables are given only a short duration, the full vowel which they might otherwise have had is reduced.[5]

English rhythm thus prefers a pattern in which long (stressed) syllables alternate with short (unstressed) ones. The effect of this can be seen even in single words, where a shift of stress is often accompanied by a change of vowel quality: a full vowel becomes [ə], and [ə] becomes a full vowel. Compare *photograph* with *photography*; in both words, full vowels appear in the stressed positions, alternating with [ə] in unstressed positions – /ˈfoʊtə, græf/ (/græf/ has a secondary stress), /fəˈtɒgrəfi/. It would be impossible to have [ə] in a stressed syllable (*ˈfətə, grəf), and almost as impossible to have a full vowel in every unstressed syllable (*foʊˈtɒgrafi). The process of vowel reduction is peculiar to languages which, like English, are stress-timed; it does not normally occur in syllable-timed languages, which retain full vowel qualities in all positions. The reason is not because syllable-timed languages have no stressed syllables: many of them alternate stressed with unstressed syllables just as English does. But the difference is in the rhythm; in English, many of the unstressed syllables are allotted very little time, whereas in a syllable-timed language each syllable gets a more equal share of time, whether it is stressed or not (cf. Pointon 1980). One can predict, again, that a foreign learner with a syllable-timed first language will find difficulty in using [ə] appropriately, and will seek to maintain a full vowel in all positions.

Phonological vs grammatical conditioning

A wide variety of vowels can undergo vowel reduction. Examples among the short vowels are:

/e/ /ðem/ → [ðəm] 'them'
/æ/ /ðæn/ → [ðən] 'than'
/ɒ/ /wɒz/ → [wəz] 'was'

etc.

Long vowels (including diphthongs) also reduce; for example:

$$/u/ \quad /tu/ \quad \rightarrow [tə] \quad \text{'to'}$$
$$/ɔ/ \quad /fɔ/ \quad \rightarrow [fə] \quad \text{'for'}$$
$$/ɑ/ \quad /ɑ(r)/ \rightarrow [ə(r)] \quad \text{'are'}$$

Grammatical words with /ɪ/, however, do not reduce to [ə]. When unstressed, they retain [ɪ]. Examples are:

is	this	if
him	in	with
his	it	its

Of the grammatical categories whose items are subject to vowel reduction (pronouns, etc.), it appears that not all instances of each category behave alike. Some items reduce; others do not. For example, the pronouns *you* and *them* reduce to [jə, ðə m] in unstressed environments, but *I* and *they* never reduce completely (to [ə]) no matter how weakly stressed. Similarly, the prepositions *to* and *from* regularly reduce to [tə, frəm], but *on, off* do *not* reduce. The causes are partly phonological (the diphthongs /ai, ei/, etc. reduce, by losing their glide, to [a, e], etc. rather than by complete reduction to [ə]) and partly semantic – prepositions which are more purely *grammatical* (*to, for, from, of*) are more likely to reduce fully to [ə] than the more 'lexical' prepositions *on, off, down*, etc.

Exercise 9

1   Which of the following *prepositions* reduce to [ə] in unstressed positions?

on, off; to, from; up, down; for; at; by; of; in, out.

2   Which of the following *pronouns* can reduce to [ə]?

I, me; you; they, them; he, him; she, her; we, us; it.

3   Which of these *possessive pronouns* can reduce to [ə]?

my; your; his; her; their; our.

Acceptability

Vowel reduction varies considerably from speaker to speaker and from context to context. Educated speakers are not fully convinced that reduction to [ə] is respectable, even though observation of their behaviour shows that [ə] is normal (and unnoticed) in phrases like *want to stay*, *not for me*, etc. Attitudes are influenced to some degree by the fact that [ə] is clearly non-standard in certain lexical items, such as in the final syllable of words like *window*, *borrow*, *potato*. In between the acceptable and the non-standard there are words like *so*, *your*, *her*, which reduce to [ə] only in very fast or casual speech and in environments where the stress is minimal, for example *quite so certain*.

The ambivalent status of [ə] occasionally produces *hyper-corrections*; instances where a speaker substitutes a full vowel in a context where it has no justification, as when *about* is pronounced /eɪbaʊt/, or *reduce* is pronounced /ridjus/. Politicians seem to be particularly susceptible to this kind of hyper-correction, perhaps because many of them suffer a certain amount of linguistic insecurity, but the phenomenon can also be observed among newsreaders. *Police*, for example, which is pronounced [pə'lis] or even [plis] by educated RP speakers, regularly appears on the BBC World News as [poʊ'lis] or [pɒ'lis]. *Guerrilla* is another example, though there may be a question here of keeping this word distinct from *gorilla*. [ə] is good enough for an ape, perhaps, but a freedom fighter deserves the full vowel [ɜ], despite the rhythmic awkwardness of a full vowel immediately preceding the main stress.

Exercise 10

The following items can all undergo vowel reduction.

1 Which grammatical category (for example, modal verb, article, conjunction, etc.) does each item belong to?
2 Find two other members of the category which can also be reduced.

> Example *as*: *a* conjunction
> *b* other conjunctions which reduce: *and*, *but*, *so*.

a at   *b* would   *c* some   *d* am   *e* than

Exercise 11

The following is a list of modal or modal-like verbs. Underline any that do *not* undergo vowel reduction.

| can | will | shall | may | ought to | need | must |
| could | would | should | might | going to | dare | |

Assimilation

Assimilation takes place when one sound changes its character in order to become more like a neighbouring sound. The feature which can vary in this way is nearly always the *place* of articulation, and the sounds concerned are commonly those which involve a complete closure at some point in the mouth, that is, *plosives* and *nasals* (remember that nasals involve an oral closure).

Nasals

Nasal consonants are particularly susceptible to assimilation. We saw in Chapter 2 that, in morpheme-final clusters, the nasal is always *homorganic with* the following plosive, that is, they share the same place of articulation; if the plosive is labial the nasal will be labial ([m]), and so on. But the process is even more extensive than this. Look at the following data:

lamp	[–mp]	(bilabial)
symphony	[–ɱf]	(labio-dental)
tenth	[–n̪θ]	(dental)
hint	[–nt]	(alveolar)
inch	[–ṋʧ]	(palato-alveolar)
wink	[–ŋk]	(velar)

We can see from this data that the nasal's locus of articulation varies quite precisely according to the following obstruent. The nasal preceding /f/ is not just the nearest labial nasal, [m], but a labio-dental [ɱ] corresponding exactly to the labio-dental [f]. Similarly, the nasal preceding dental /θ/ is dental, and the one preceding /ʧ/ is palato-alveolar (for which we have used the symbol [ṋ]).

Nasal assimilation is sensitive not only to the locus of the following obstruent, but also to the (wider) environments in which it occurs.

The examples above illustrate its operation *within the morpheme*. It operates also across syllable boundaries, as in *symphony* ([–ɱf–]) and *concrete* ([–ŋk–]); and across morpheme boundaries, for example with the morphemes |in–|, |un–| 'not', as in:

[ʌmprədʌktiv]	'unproductive'
[ʌmbitn̩]	'unbeaten'
[ɪŋkəmplit]	'incomplete'
[ʌŋgreɪʃəs]	'ungracious'

In this case the assimilation is optional: pronunciations with [ɪn–, ʌn–] are also possible ([ʌnprədʌktɪv], etc.). There is also optional assimilation across word boundaries:

[ɪɱ fækt]	'in fact'
[ɪŋ keɪs]	'in case'
[·tʃeɪŋ gæŋ]	'chain gang'

Yet, despite the fact that nasal assimilation occurs across so many boundaries, it does *not* occur before plurals and past tenses, as in [rɪŋz] 'rings', [rɪŋd] 'ringed', etc., even though the nasal and the obstruent fall within the same syllable. This sensitivity to particular environments requires some explanation. Clearly, assimilation cannot be, in NGP terms, a P-rule, since it is neither 'automatic' nor exceptionless. It must therefore be an MP rule, with its environments specified in terms of words and morphemes. But a general statement to the effect that 'assimilation occurs, optionally, across morpheme boundaries' would be inaccurate, since it occurs across some (*un-beaten*, *in-fact*, etc.) but not others (*sing-s*, *sum-s*, *wrong-ed*). Perhaps the reason why it does *not* take place in the latter cases is because if it did, essential properties of the lexical items (*sing*, *sum*, *wrong*, etc.) would be damaged or lost; *sing-s* and *sum-s* would, for example, become *sin-s* and *sun-s*; whereas in the assimilation of |in–, un–|, no essential information is lost. Assimilation is thus (possibly) determined by broader factors such as the need to preserve essential properties of lexical items.

Plosives

The other major type of assimilation, apart from the nasals, involves the alveolar plosives /t, d/ before another plosive. Look at the following data:

[ðæp pis]	that piece	[hab pəteɪtoͻz]	hard potatoes
[ðæp bɔɪ]	that boy	[hab bɑgɪnz]	hard bargains
[ðæt dɪʃ]	that dish	[had taɪmz]	hard times
[ðæ*t* ʧ3ʧ]	that church	[ha*d* ʧ iz]	hard cheese
[ðæk kɪd]	that kid	[hɑg keɪs]	hard case
[ðæk gɜl]	that girl	[hɑg goͻɪŋ]	hard going

Assimilations like these are, of course, optional, though they do occur very frequently in informal conversation. What happens is that the alveolar plosive retains its 'voicing' feature (for example, *that*, in the data above, always ends in a voiceless plosive, and the final segment of *hard* is always voiced) but shifts its locus in sympathy with (i.e. assimilates to) the locus of the following plosive or affricate. This change can be expressed in the form of a rule:

$$
\begin{bmatrix} \text{alveolar} \\ \text{plosive} \end{bmatrix} \rightarrow \begin{bmatrix} \alpha \text{ locus} \\ \text{plosive} \end{bmatrix} / \_\_ \begin{bmatrix} \alpha \text{ locus} \\ \begin{Bmatrix} \text{plosive} \\ \text{affricate} \end{Bmatrix} \end{bmatrix}
$$

The notation [α locus] means a variable locus: the symbol α is used for variable values of a feature. Normally a rule must have at least two α's in it, so that whatever value is given to one α can also be given to the other.

One interesting fact is that /t, d/ are the only plosives which are subject to assimilation. /p, b/ and /k, g/ do not assimilate, but keep their own locus whatever the locus of the following plosive. Thus for

'black pan'	we do not find	[blæp pæn]
'black box'	we do not find	[blæp bͻks]
'black tin'	we do not find	[blæt tɪn]

A phrase like [raɪp bə'nɑnəz] can therefore mean either *ripe bananas* or, by an assimilation from /t/, *right bananas*. But [raɪt tə'mɑtoͻz] can only mean *right tomatoes* because the /p/ of *ripe* never assimilates, and [raɪk kͻn] can only mean *right corn* by assimilation of the /t/. The condition [alveolar] on the left-hand side of the assimilation rule is therefore correct.

Assimilation of /t, d/ can combine with nasal assimilation. In a phrase like *can't bear*, the /t/ of *can't* assimilates to [p], and the nasal /n/ then assimilates to this [p], giving as the pronunciation, [kɑmp beə]. These double assimilations·are particularly common when the contracted negative (*n't*) follows an auxiliary verb: *can't, don't, isn't, won't*, etc.

Exercise 12

Give an 'assimilated' pronunciation (use square brackets) for each of the following. Say whether the assimilation is *optional* or *obligatory*.

comfort	Great Britain	improbable
input	congress	don't bother
sunglasses	unbecoming	stand there
hot pies	in person	can't guess

Progressive assimilation

The assimilations considered so far have been *regressive* in type; this term is used when the influence goes 'backwards' from a 'later' phoneme to change an 'earlier' one, as when the /f/ of *fact* changes *in* to [ɪŋ]. Less commonly, assimilation may be *progressive*: an earlier sound influences a later one. An example of this is the palatalization process, mentioned previously (Chapter 5, p. 155). The sounds /s, z/ and /t, d/ assimilate to palato-alveolars when followed by the palatal /j/. Look at the following data:

1	*a*	[feɪʃ jə pɑtnəz]	face your partners
	b	[naɪʃ jɒt]	nice yacht
	c	[æʒjə seɪ]	as you say
	d	[ɪt wəʒ jestədeɪ]	it was yesterday
	e	[nɒt əʒ jet]	not as yet
2	*a*	[kɑntʃə si ɪt]	can't you see it
	b	[lɔk ətʃə hænz]	look at your hands
	c	[pleɪ ə tʃun]	play a tune
	d	[glædʒ ə keɪm]	glad you came
	e	[maɪ dʒuti]	my duty
	f	[hædʒ ə brekfəst]	had your breakfast

An interesting question which arises is the accuracy of the phonetic transcription given in the data above. It is sometimes stated that no [j] remains, once the assimilation has taken place, giving pronunciations such as:

[æʒ ə seɪ]   'as you say'
[feɪʃ ə pɑtnəz]   'face your partners'

The problem is that the *as you* of 'as you say' does not sound quite like the [–ɪʒə–] of *vision*, nor is *face your* quite like *gracious*, and (for a minimal pair) *press your* is not identical with *pressure*. In the first members of each pair, the [ʃ] and [ʒ] are longer.

We can account for this by proposing that a double assimilation takes place. First the /s, z/ assimilate to /ʃ, ʒ/, and then the /j/ in turn assimilates to the preceding sound, taking on the friction and locus of /ʃ, ʒ/. The palatal semi-vowel /j/ thus becomes a palato-alveolar fricative. Hence, at the first stage of the assimilation, /s + j/ becomes [ʃj], and at the second stage this becomes [ʃː], i.e. a long [ʃ] (and similarly, /z + j/ becomes [ʒː]). These 'long' sounds may not be equal in length to two segments [–ʃʃ–], [–ʒʒ–], but they preserve a trace of the lost /j/, showing that the pronunciation originates from two sounds rather than one.

Voicing assimilation

The assimilations discussed so far involve mainly changes affecting place (locus) of articulation. Another type of assimilation affects the voicing feature: in particular, voiced sounds become voiceless when followed by another voiceless sound. Look at the following data:

[faɪf pɑst]	five past
[hæf tə goʊ]	have to go
[lʌf tə goʊ]	love to go
[ʃis tɔkɪŋ]	she's talking
[əf kɔs]	of course
[dʌʃ ʃi]	does she

The sounds which assimilate their voicing are usually, as the examples show, fricatives; the environment is a voiceless obstruent in the following word. Grammatical items in particular are affected: the /v/ of *of*, *have* changes to [f], and the /z/ of *is*, *has*, *does* becomes [s]. A rule could be formulated as follows:

$$
\begin{bmatrix} + \text{voice} \\ \text{fricative} \end{bmatrix} \rightarrow [-\text{voice}] \ /\_\_ \ \# \begin{bmatrix} -\text{voice} \\ -\text{son.} \end{bmatrix}
$$

where the symbol # represents a word-boundary.

Assimilation vs co-articulation

As a process, assimilation is very similar in many ways to the *co-articulations* discussed in Chapter 1, in which, for example, the /s/ of *soup* has a rounded pronunciation, [ş], in anticipation of the rounded vowel, /u/. In both cases, segments change their properties through the influence of neighbouring segments, either preceding or following. And in both cases, changes of *locus* are very common, though other changes, in *manner* and *voicing*, are also possible. The difference is that co-articulations describe sub-phonemic, i.e. allophonic, effects, whereas assimilations involve an exchange at a 'higher' level, for example a change of phoneme. Co-articulations are 'automatic' and exceptionless, whereas assimilations may have exceptions, and are often optional rather than obligatory. For instance, [ðæp bɔɪ] for 'that boy' is an *assimilation*: there is a change of phoneme, and the process is optional, since the pronunciation [ðæt bɔɪ] is a possible alternative. Similarly, [ɪmbɔn], [ɪm pisəz] for 'inborn', 'in pieces' are assimilations, since they involve a phonemic change, and they are optional. In NGP terms, co-articulations belong among the P-rules, and assimilations among the MP rules.

Phonemic vs phonetic representation

The changes which take place in fast or casual speech, compared with the same words in isolation (or in what is called 'citation' form, i.e. the form in which the word would appear in a dictionary), bring a new dimension to the distinction between phonemic and phonetic representation. It was suggested earlier that words like *correct* and *crook* should be distinguished (even though both might be pronounced [kr–] in fast speech) because speakers know that *correct* has two pronunciations while *crook* has only one. One way to distinguish them is to assign different phonemic representations: /kərekt/ vs /krɒk/. An (optional) rule of *vowel deletion* then converts the former to [krekt], if it is applied, or to [kərekt], if it is not. The *similarity* between [krekt] and [krɒk] is shown at the *phonetic* level.

The same distinction could reasonably be extended to the other fast-speech processes. For example, *prince* would be distinguished from *prints* as /prɪns/ vs /prɪnts/, but at the phonetic level, after application of an *insertion* rule (cf. p. 174 above), identical pronunciations are possible. Similarly, *tune* and *chew* might be represented as /tjun/ vs /tʃu/, to allow for the fact that *tune* has two pronunciations, *chew* only one. The citation form, or lexical representation, of *that* will be /ðæt/, but assimilation rules may convert this to phonetic [ðæp, ðæk, ðæt̪], etc.

The only problem, in thus extending the phonemic–phonetic distinction, is in the treatment of vowel reduction. There are two types of problem here.

First, certain lexical items will be given rather unusual and perhaps unacceptable, phonemic representations. For example, on the basis of the full vowels which emerge in positions of stress, *photograph* will receive the representation /foʊtɒɡræf/ (cf. phot*o*graphy, phot*o*graphic). This might be acceptable, provided the vowel-reduction rule is formulated sufficiently carefully, in relation to stress-patterns, to ensure that the correct output is achieved in all cases. On the other hand, speakers may well prefer a phonemic representation which is closer to the 'surface', such as /fətɒɡrəfi/ for 'photography', rather than /foʊtɒɡræfi/.

Second, grammatical items such as *to, for, of, have*, which are usually pronounced in their reduced form and achieve their full form only rarely, will nevertheless be represented phonemically as /tu, fɔ, ɒv/, etc. Phrases such as *cup of tea, not for me*, will be given as /kʌp ɒv ti, nɒt fɔ mi/, etc. Again, this is somewhat counter-intuitive, and, if the phonemic representation is meant to reflect speakers' knowledge, it cannot explain, or account adequately for, their frequent confusion of *should have/should of* (cf. p. 168 above).

On the other hand, there are a number of advantages in treating vowel reduction in the same way as the other fast-speech processes. First, there are many occasions in which a speaker may be unsure of the actual vowel quality involved. For example, if asked to transcribe the sentence 'I met your uncle', speakers (for example, students learning transcription) hesitate between /jɔr/ and /jər/, feeling that the pronunciation does not exactly accord with either of them. In such cases, recognition of the *variation* between the full vowel, /ɔ/, and the reduced vowel, [ə], is of great value. The two symbols could, in fact, represent end-points of a continuous scale of variation, rather than an 'either-or' choice.

A second benefit of representing grammatical items in their full form is illustrated by the case of words like *to*. In traditional transcriptions this word is represented in three forms, as /tu/, /tʊ/, and /tə/. The presence of the intermediate value, /tʊ/, has always been questionable, for if we include it, there are many contexts where it is difficult to decide between the alternative representations /tu/ vs /tʊ/.

To in *he came to* is clearly /tu/, but in *where are you going to* it could be /tu/ or /tʊ/. Yet it is nonsense to make this a *phonemic* issue, for there is clearly no contrast in *meaning* between /tu/ and /tʊ/, and these phonetic events should therefore not be represented as if they were phonemic. Similarly, the choice between [tʊ] and [tə] is not a phonemic one, but a phonetic one, depending on degree of stress and also, perhaps, on style – for instance, a 'careful' pronunciation of *I'd like to look* might have [tʊ], a 'casual' one [tə].

In making a phonemic transcription, such decisions about *phonetic* events are best avoided; this can be achieved by adopting only one phonemic form (the full form) and the realization rules can then be used to indicate the actual pronunciation. These rules will need to be sensitive to stress levels in the sentence and to non-linguistic factors such as style. On this basis, phonetic [tʊ] is not treated as phonemic /tʊ/; it is simply one stage along the scale from /u/, the 'full' form, to [ə], the reduced form.[6]

In summary, it is useful to distinguish 'citation' forms from the 'actual pronunciations' (in connected speech) as 'phonemic' vs 'phonetic' representations. Items such as *correct* vs *crook* can have their differences, as well as their similarities, expressed by such means. Vowel reduction, however, causes some problems, particularly for highly-frequent grammatical items. Use of the full form runs the risk of being too abstract, but has, on the other hand, the advantage of letting us recognize vowel reduction as a scale. This in turn helps to overcome the problems of, first, identification of vowels of intermediate quality, second, continuous variation of vowel quality under different degrees of stress, and third, treating what is really only phonetic as if it were phonemic (the case of [tʊ]).

A note on 'stress-timed' vs 'syllable-timed'

A stress-timed language such as English or German is supposed, ideally, to have a rhythm based on feet of approximately equal time-length (*isochronous* feet). The notion of isochrony in rhythm was questioned many years ago by Classe (1939), who suggested that it is only maintained under certain limited conditions. Crystal adds that 'if one means by isochrony a direct perception of *regular* peaks of prominence . . . then English is not isochronous. . . . Such regularity [is] the exception, not the rule' (1969: 162). Nevertheless, Classe refers to an 'underlying tendency' towards isochrony, and Crystal (1969) to a 'subjective' isochrony, and many other writers including

Abercrombie (1965), Halliday (1967), and Lehiste (1979) take similar views.

Syllable timing as the alternative to stress-timing has also been subjected to criticism in recent years. Wenk and Wioland (1982) ask 'is French really syllable-timed?', and conclude that it is not: 'French syllables are produced and perceived in rhythmic groups, just as those of English . . .'. French rhythmic groups are established by a lengthening of the final syllable in each group, whereas English groups are deliniated by a stronger syllable at the *beginning*. French is thus 'trailer-timed', English is 'leader-timed'. Pointon (1980) asks similar questions about another classical example of a syllable-timed language, namely Spanish; he concludes that syllables in Spanish are *not* of equal length, but that their length is determined by a complex of factors, such as the number and type of segments they contain, and whether they are stressed or not. Spanish, however, '*sounds* syllable-timed to native English speakers', and this may be because its syllables are *more* equal in length than English syllables, and because Spanish syllables, unlike English, do not undergo vowel reduction. Languages other than those commonly mentioned are not always easy to classify into 'stress-timed' vs 'syllable-timed' which casts further doubt on the distinction. Thus Biedrzycki (1980) assumes that Polish is stress-timed, but despite this it 'still sounds rhythmically somewhat different from English'; and Balasubramanian (1980) concludes that the rhythm of Tamil 'can be called neither stress-timed nor syllable-timed' (p. 457).

The division of languages into 'stress-timed' and 'syllable-timed' is thus over-simplistic. Rhythmic differences across languages are perhaps not as great as was once thought. But despite the difficulties with this particular distinction, many writers seem to agree that the rhythmic alternation of stressed with unstressed syllables in sequence, and the avoidance of two consecutive stressed vowels, is a property common to many, if not all, languages. This 'rhythm rule' for English was noted by earlier writers such as Sweet (cf. Henderson 1971: 136) and Jespersen (1909: 156) and has been extensively discussed since. For a brief summary, including references to the existence of the 'rhythm rule' in other languages, cf. Bolozky (1982: 275).

7 Intonation

Intonation is the name given to the fluctuations of pitch in spoken utterances. It normally refers to the pitch patterns of a larger grammatical unit such as a phrase, clause, or sentence, though of course a sentence may consist of only a single word, in which case intonation can apply to it. Intonation and stress are related phenomena (see above, p. 178) and, indeed, some writers use the term 'sentence stress' for what we shall call intonation.

In this chapter our general aims will be: first, to present a concise, simple, yet adequate method for transcribing intonation, i.e. a suitable notation; second, to relate the pitch patterns to typical sentence functions such as statement, question, etc.; and third, to explore the role of intonation in grammatical structure, looking particularly at examples in which intonation resolves grammatical ambiguity.

Basic features

Intonation has three basic properties:

1 It is a language universal. There are no languages which are spoken as a monotone, i.e. without change of pitch. In 'tone' languages, pitch change can be used to make a difference between one lexical word and another, in the same way that /p/ and /b/ differentiate *pit* and *bit*: in Chinese, which is a good example of a tone language, *lán* (high rising tone) means 'blue', but *lǎn* (fall-rise tone) means 'lazy'. Non-tonal languages, like English and most other European languages, do not make such lexical distinctions. In the tone languages, however, when the individual lexical items are combined into phrases and sentences, there still emerges an overall pitch 'contour' which is not simply the sum of the individual (lexical) tones, but carries the same functions as intonation in other (non-tonal) languages. So tone languages have intonation, but *in addition* the tones can be used to make lexical distinctions.

2   Intonation is *functional*, i.e. it is used in a language for particular purposes and is never merely 'decorative' nor a way of avoiding speech becoming 'monotonous'.

3   Within any particular language, intonation is *systematic*; different speakers use the same patterns for the same purposes, though there may be (and usually are) dialect differences, just as segmental phonemes are systematic in the language as a whole, but each phoneme may be subject to different realizations according to the region, age, sex, etc. of the speaker.

The functions of intonation in English

We can group the functions of intonation under four general headings. Intonation serves:

1   To structure the *information content* of a sentence so as to show which information is new or cannot be 'taken for granted', as against information which the listener is assumed to possess or to be able to acquire from the context (i.e. 'given' information). This is explained further below (pp. 199ff.)

2   To determine the *speech-function* of a sentence, i.e. to indicate whether the sentence is intended as a statement, question, command, etc. (see below, p. 204).

3   To convey connotational meanings of 'attitude' such as surprise, annoyance, enthusiasm, etc. This can include whatever meanings are intended, over and above the meanings conveyed by the lexical items and the grammatical structure. For example the sentence:

   thanks for helping me last night

can be given more than one meaning. The difference between a 'sincere' intention and a 'sarcastic' one would be conveyed by the intonation. Note that in the *written* form, we are given only the lexis and the grammar. The written medium has very limited resources for marking intonation, and the meanings conveyed by it have to be shown, if at all, in other ways.

4   To characterize a particular *style* or *variety* of the language (the *stylistic* function). Talking to a baby usually requires a typical set of intonation patterns; so does telling a joke, or taking a service in church, or guiding a party of tourists. These patterns are typical of the style and tend to be used throughout the discourse, rather than in just one or two sentences.

The study of special or marked styles of intonation presupposes that we already have, as a frame of reference, a description of normal, unmarked intonation patterns. The norm is usually taken to be the informal conversational variety, though in reality this should perhaps be regarded as only one style among many.

We shall be concerned only with the first two of the four functions above, since these are the most fundamental, the most systematic, and perhaps the least subjective of the functions.

The notation of intonation

There are a variety of methods for recording intonational patterns in writing and we can look at the advantages and disadvantages of some of the commoner ones.

1 The 'linear' method. One of the simplest, introduced by Fries (1940), involves drawing a line around the sentence to show relative pitch heights, thus:

he's gone to the│of│fice

2 The 'crazy letter' method.[1] This is a variant of the 'linear' method; the syllables are written at different heights across the page. The method is particularly favoured by Bolinger (1972: 19ff.; 1975: 47ff.), for example;

ab   ny
I solutely de it

Bolinger's book of readings (1972) has the cover title:

   a
  ton t
    i
 in o
    n

Both of these methods can be called *expressive*, in that they reflect the pitch movements directly.

3 The 'levels' method. A number of discrete levels of pitch are recognized, and the utterance is marked accordingly. This method was favoured by the pre-generative American linguists such as Pike (1945), who distinguished four levels of pitch, and Trager and Smith (1951), who also recognized four levels, *low* (one step below the

'normal' level of the voice), *normal, high* (one step above 'normal') and *extra-high* (two steps above). Pike numbered his levels 1–4, starting from extra-high, while Trager and Smith also numbered their levels from 1–4, but starting from low. Since others who have adopted a 'levels' analysis have favoured the low-to-high numbering, we shall use this in our example:

$$^2\text{he's gone to the }^3\text{o- }^1\text{ffice}$$

This notation corresponds to the pattern shown linearly in 1, above. 4   The 'contour' method. This is favoured by most of the British phoneticians such as Jones (1956: 275ff.), Kingdon (1958), O'Connor and Arnold (1961) and, more recently, by Halliday (1970) and Crystal (1975: 11ff.). The basic difference between 'contours' and 'levels' is that 'contours' treat the pitch pattern of an utterance as a whole, instead of dividing it into sections each of which has its own 'level'. Fries's example (set out above) would be described as having a falling contour (more simply, a *fall*), or, in some systems, a *high fall*, possibly with the additional information of a 'mid' pre-nucleus. Since we shall be using a contour method ourselves, a more detailed account will be given later (below, pp. 203ff.). Lieberman (1965), in an important theoretical paper, showed that the 'contour' method has a number of distinct advantages, and that those who use 'levels' must also resort to 'contours'; the sentence used above in 3, for example, could be described as having a '231' contour.

One of the disadvantages of contours is that there has been no general agreement about the number of contours or 'tones' a system requires in order to provide an adequate description. The simplest (Daniel Jones) recognizes only two tones, a fall and a rise – easy to distinguish, but not sufficient to account for all the data. On the other hand a more complex system, such as O'Connor and Arnold's, has no fewer than ten different contours, which creates major problems when attempting to distinguish the meaning of each from all of the others. Our system, which attempts to combine adequacy with simplicity, uses three tones, a fall, a rise, and a fall-rise (see the discussion below, p. 204). Delattre (1965), one of the few American-based linguists to use contours, also proposed a three-tone system ('finality', 'major continuation', and 'minor continuation') which deserves wider recognition. Crystal (1975: 34) distinguishes seven tones, but it is interesting to note that, from the analysis of a very large body of material, the *fall* was found to be statistically the most frequent (51.2 per cent), followed by the *rise* (20.8 per cent) and the *fall-rise* (8.5 per cent). The compound *fall + rise*, which we shall also use, adds a further 7.7 per cent, so that in all, the three basic tones account for more than 88 per cent of Crystal's data (Crystal 1969b: 203; cf. also in Bolinger 1972: 120).

Intonation and meaning

A system of intonation aims in the first place to select, and represent, whatever elements or components contribute to a distinction in meaning, and in the second place to relate these to actual patterns of pronunciation. As with a phonemic analysis the linguist seeks to reduce the great variety of pronunciations actually observed, to a system which captures the meaningful and essential contrasts that can be conveyed. In a segmental analysis, the actual pronunciation of a word like *tribal* might be represented as [tʰɹʌiːbəɫ]. But if we want to exclude all the redundant or predictable information, such as the initial aspiration of [t] and the final darkness of [l], we represent the word as /traɪbl/. In this phonemic representation, only the elements which distinguish this word from other words, such as *treble*, or from possible words, such as /draɪbl/, are represented. Ideally we would like to be able to analyse intonation in the same way, but the problems are of a different kind. The difficulty, with intonation, is in deciding what constitutes a 'difference of meaning' and what does not. For example, the sentence 'he's gone to the office' could be spoken with either of the following contours:

In some respects, the meanings conveyed by these two different patterns of pitch would be the same. Both would be *statements* (perhaps in answer to a question), and both put the main emphasis on *office* rather than on some other word such as *gone*. But whereas one pattern is 'neutral' in attitude, the other might be interpreted as 'surprised' or 'impatient'. Thus there is both 'sameness' and 'difference' in meaning. In devising a system for intonation, we are faced with the problem that any difference of pitch pattern, however small, may be interpretable as a difference in meaning. This is one reason why linguists, who tend to be broadly in agreement over a segmental analysis, have never agreed on a system for intonation, and why the systems proposed differ so markedly.

It seems essential, by way of a solution to the problem, to distinguish between different *kinds* of meaning. In the example just quoted, we saw a difference in one type of meaning ('attitude') but identity in the speech function (statement) and in the focus of emphasis, i.e. identity in what we call the 'grammatical' functions of intonation. If we can separate the grammatical meanings from meanings which convey attitude or stylistic features, we have a better chance of working out a basic system of description. Since grammatical meanings are more likely to be agreed on, i.e. are less subjective, than attitudes, we should aim to describe these first. Crystal (1969a) and Halliday (1970) have both emphasized, in different ways, the importance of distinguishing different kinds of meaning, and of establishing a system on the basis of possible contrasts. Halliday in particular sees intonation as playing a major role in the grammar, though Cruttenden (1970) and Brazil (1975) both emphasize the difficulties of distinguishing 'grammatical' from 'attitudinal' meaning, and these problems should not be underestimated.

The major disadvantage of the 'linear' and 'crazy letter' methods of notation, described above (p. 195), will now be apparent. These notations are entirely 'phonetic': they are only a record of the pronunciation, and therefore offer no analysis of the patterns, nor show which parts are meaningful. The 'levels' method, unless converted to contours, can be criticized for the same reason. Whatever the disadvantages of a 'contour' method, at least it attempts to sort out the essential from the inessential, and to relate pitch patterns on the one hand to distinctions of meaning on the other.

Exercise 1

How many different intonation patterns can you think of for each of the two sentences below? Try putting the main emphasis on different words, as well as varying the pitch patterns:

> I wouldn't do that if I were you
> I've already got a headache

The nucleus

It has often been pointed out that, given a sentence with X number of words, almost any of the words can be highlighted by having a sentence-stress assigned to it. The choice of the word to be singled out in this way is determined by the context as a whole. For example, in the sentence

these peaches are bad

we can highlight *bad* (these peaches are *bad*), *are* (these peaches *are* bad), *peaches*, or *these*. The word highlighted in this way by the intonation pattern is called the *nucleus*, or *nuclear word*, and the larger unit of which it forms a part is called the *tone group*.[2] The tone group is the basic unit of intonation; we shall not attempt a precise definition at the moment, but provisionally:

1   the tone group usually contains one, and only one, nucleus – though we do recognize a compound pattern which requires two nuclei, one major, the other minor, within a single tone group (see below).
2   the tone group often corresponds to the *clause* in grammar, i.e. one clause normally consists of one tone group.

The tone group can be marked by putting slant lines at the beginning and end, and the nucleus can be shown by underlining (or using italics), for example:

/these peaches are *bad*/

Retrievable information

By putting the stress on one particular (nuclear) word, the speaker shows, first, that he is treating that word as the carrier of new, non-retrievable, information, and second, that the information of the other, non-emphasized, words in the tone group is not 'new' but can be 'retrieved' from the context. 'Context'[3] here is to be taken in a very broad sense: it may include something that has already been said, in which case the antecedents may be very specific, but it may include only something (or someone) present in the situation, and it may even refer, very vaguely, to some aspect of shared knowledge which the addressee is thought to be aware of. The information that the listener needs, in order to interpret the sentence, may therefore be retrievable either from something already mentioned, or from the general 'context of situation':

retrievable information—
$\begin{bmatrix} \text{from verbal context} \\ \text{from situational context} \end{bmatrix}$

Non-retrievable information

Non-retrievable information, given by the nuclear word, can be either *contrastive* or *non-contrastive* (simply 'new'). A contrastive nucleus may emphasize a change of polarity (positive–negative), for example

> A   /I *didn't* take your biscuit/
> B   /you *did*/

or it may contrast one lexical item with another:

> A   /these peaches look *bad*/
> B   /these peaches *are* bad/

A non-contrastive nucleus, on the other hand, simply presents some new information:

> /these peaches are *bad*/

Notice that the decision as to whether some information is retrievable or not has to be made by the speaker on the basis of what he thinks the addressee can take for granted from the situation, etc. The speaker must, in framing an utterance, make many assumptions, and he does this rapidly and to a large degree unconsciously. He then arranges his tone groups and assigns nuclear stresses accordingly. But in any particular situation, the speaker's assumptions run the risk of being wrong; what he takes to be retrievable information may not in fact be retrievable by the addressee. In this case there is a breakdown of communication, and the listener will probably seek clarification:

(A and B are passing the tennis courts)

> A   /there *isn't* anyone playing/
> B   /who said there *was*?/
> A   /*nobody*/

Dialogues like this, though not uncommon, are unsatisfactory

because vital information is missing. By putting the nucleus on *isn't*,
speaker A took 'anyone playing' as retrievable or 'expected' information. B responds with a request for an explanation, which A then fails
to fulfil. If A had put the original nucleus on *playing*, the conversation
could have proceeded normally. Another example:

> A /does *Emma* take dancing lessons?/
> B /who *else* does?/
> A /Jenny started three *weeks* ago/
> B /Emma goes *next* week/

This time, A highlights 'Emma' and treats 'taking dancing lessons' as
given. B has no memory of a previous mention of dancing lessons and
refuses to accept this information as 'given': her response is not a
reply to A's question but in effect a request for clarification of A's
intonation pattern. Once A has cleared that up, B replies to A's
original question.

Exercise 2

Use the following sentences for practice in identifying the nucleus of a
tone group. The exercise should preferably be done orally, in a group.
One speaker pronounces the sentence (having first determined which
(lexical) item he/she *intends* as the nucleus). The other(s) then identify
the nucleus.

1 You get all the sandwiches.
2 How many pounds did you buy?
3 The weather was quite exceptional.
4 There won't be another election.
5 When did the visitors go?

Position of the nucleus: marked vs unmarked

Out of the possible positions of the nucleus in a tone group, there is
one position which is normal, or unmarked, while the other positions
give a special or marked effect. In the examples:

> /these peaches are bad/
> /he's gone to the office/
> /how much did they pay/

the nuclei, in an unmarked pronunciation, would occur on *bad*, *office* and *pay* respectively. Nuclei elsewhere in these sentences would be 'marked'. The general rule is that, in the unmarked case, the nucleus falls on the *last lexical item* of the tone group. The marked nuclei (for example, *peaches*, *are*) are usually *contrastive*, whereas the unmarked nucleus is simply 'new' information.

One feature of marked nuclei is that they can easily be heard and identified as constituting the nucleus, while an unmarked nucleus is less easy to recognize. It is much easier to hear the nucleus of

/these peaches *are* bad/

than of

/these peaches are *bad*/

and the reason is that, in the unmarked case, the nucleus is predictable: the listener expects it to fall on the last lexical item, but since this expectation is only part of his intuitive 'knowledge of the language', he has to make an effort to bring it into conscious awareness. In learning to identify intonation patterns, for example, students find it much easier to recognize a nucleus when it occurs in an unexpected position.

'Last lexical item' is not the same as 'last word', since there may be one or more *grammatical* items following the final *lexical* item.[4] In the sentences

We didn't see him
He doesn't need it

the nucleus falls on *see* and *need* in the unmarked case, because *see* and *need* are the last *lexical* items, *him* and *it* being grammatical items. It is quite possible for a grammatical item to carry the nucleus, but when this happens the nucleus becomes marked, and the item is usually contrastive, as would be the case with nuclei on *we*, *didn't*, *he* in the sentences above. A nucleus on *him* or *it* here would likewise be marked, and these items would be contrastive.[5]

It is possible for the nucleus to be a marked one even when it falls on the last lexical item. This happens when the word is *contrastive*, as with the nucleus on *yesterday* in

(did you see John today?) /no I saw him *yesterday*/

where *yesterday* contrasts with *today*. Hence, in the truly unmarked case, the nucleus must not only be on the last lexical item, but also give new, rather than contrastive, information. Nuclei which fall elsewhere, or which fall on the last lexical item but are contrastive, are marked.

Elements of the tone group

We have seen that the nucleus is the most important constituent of the tone group. The rest of the tone group can be divided for convenience into the *pre-nucleus* and the *post-nucleus*. For example:

/how did you make such a   mess   of it/
     Pre-nucleus   Nucleus Post-nucleus

The pitch patterns of the post-nucleus are, as we shall see, entirely determined by the tonal movement on the nucleus itself, and there is therefore no need to consider the post-nucleus separately.

The pre-nucleus

The *pre-nucleus* can take a variety of pitch patterns. Variation within the pre-nucleus does not normally affect the *grammatical* meaning of the utterance, though it often conveys meanings associated with attitude. There are two common types of pre-nucleus: a *high* type in which the pitch gradually descends (often in 'steps') to the nucleus:[6]

Pattern A

for example,   how did you   make such a   mess of it

and a *low* type in which the pitch stays low until the nuclear word:

Pattern B

for example,   how did you make such a   mess of it

As the examples show, the different types of pre-nucleus do not affect the grammatical meaning of the sentence, but they can convey something of the speaker's attitude.

The tones

We have seen how intonation can be used to structure the information content of a clause or sentence; the second function of intonation is to indicate whether the sentence is intended as a statement, question, command, etc., i.e. to determine the speech-function of the sentence. Clearly, it is not always intonation alone which gives this information; sentences have their functions marked grammatically too. For example, a sentence which begins with a WH- word (*who, where, what,* etc.) is marked as being a question. Intonation and grammar thus combine to determine speech-functions, and as far as intonation is concerned this is done by the direction of pitch movements on and around the nucleus; the pitch may rise, or fall, or rise and then fall, etc. The crucial point for the pitch change is the nuclear word, together with any words that follow it within the tone group.

We shall begin, then, by describing a system of *tones*, i.e. a system of pitch changes centred round the nucleus. We shall distinguish three tones, a *fall*, a *rise*, and a *fall-rise* (cf. above, p. 196), with in addition a compound tone consisting of a fall plus a rise (*fall + rise*). Once the tones have been described, we can then relate each tone to specific sentence-functions such as statement, question, etc.

The nuclear tones: form

The tones are based on the pitch movements centred around the nucleus and any words that follow it in the post-nucleus. In this section we shall describe the shapes of these tones, in terms of their typical pitch patterns (rising, falling, etc.). In the following section, the *uses* or functions of each tone will be described. In the notation we have adopted, the tone of an utterance will be marked at the beginning of the nuclear word, using the marks ` for a *fall*, ′ for a *rise* and ˇ for a fall-rise, for example:

> /today is ˋ*Wednesday*/
> /is today ′*Wednesday*/
> /I can't believe it's ˇ*Wednesday*/

The falling *tone*

The pitch pattern of a *falling* tone requires a fall in pitch on the nucleus, and all syllables *following* the nucleus are spoken at the same low pitch to which the nucleus falls, giving the pattern:

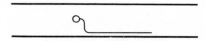

Since there is often a rise in pitch between the pre-nucleus and the start of the nucleus, it is easy to (wrongly) identify the contour as 'rising'. Thus the following is an example of a *fall*, not a rise, because tone is determined *on and after* the nucleus:

I'm | cold

The rising *tone*

When a *rising* tone is used, the rise in pitch may start on the nucleus and continue rising throughout the post-nucleus (Pattern C); alternatively the rise may be delayed until the end of the post-nucleus, so that the nucleus itself stays fairly level (Pattern D):

Pattern C

Pattern D

Very often, the pitch of the nucleus, in a rising contour, appears to have a 'kink' or 'wobble' in it; it actually falls before it rises:

For example:

is today   Wednesday

The rising tone, like the fall, is thus determined by what happens on *and after* the nucleus, i.e. by the direction *towards which* the nucleus turns rather than the pitch changes which occur before (or even sometimes within), the nucleus.

The fall-rise

The *fall-rise* has pitch-patterns rather similar to those of the *rise*, but there are two ways in which they may differ:

1 in the fall-rise, the changes in pitch take place *at a lower overall pitch* than in the rise;
2 in the fall-rise, the changes in pitch are smaller giving a smoother, less angular impression. Compare:

> is today ˊ*Wednesday* (rise)
> I can't believe it's ˇ*Wednesday* (fall-rise)

The rising tone is, as the example suggests, basically associated with *questions*. The fall-rise, on the other hand, is found mainly in utterances which are not intended as questions. The grammatical functions of the tones will be explained in the next section, and in a later section (see below, pp. 215–16) we shall re-examine the distinction between the rise and the fall-rise.

Exercise 3

Use the following phrases and sentences to practise identification of the nucleus and tone. As in Exercise 2, the sentences can be spoken by one person and described by the others.

1   those chocolates
2   really
3   intonation isn't easy
4   it's your turn to deal
5   what would you like
6   he was nearly arrested

The fall + rise

The compound tone *fall + rise* has a pattern which is simply a combination of a falling tone, coinciding with the major nucleus of the tone group, and a rising tone, coinciding with the minor nucleus. Major and minor nuclei, and the use of the compound tone, are explained in the next section.

The nuclear tones: grammatical functions

Having established the pitch patterns characteristic of each tone, we can now consider how they are used. Each tone is distinguished not only by its contour, but by the grammatical functions which are typically associated with it. It must be emphasized, however, that the descriptions which follow are merely general guidelines, which should be interpreted flexibly. For example, we (following Halliday 1967 and many others) suggest that a WH-question like

/where are you *going*/

is 'typically' given a falling tone, but there is no reason why it should not be spoken with one of the rising tones, which would add a connotation of 'politeness' or 'tentativeness'. As Cruttenden observes, 'no statistical evidence has [ever] been provided to prove that the norms usually established [i.e. our 'typical' uses] are of most frequent occurrence' (1970: 186). He prefers a more general statement about the meanings of the tones, meanings which are independent of the particular sentence type the tone is attached to. *Falling* tones, he suggests, 'seem to carry always an element of definiteness, rising tones an element of tentativeness. Definiteness may on occasions be interpreted as either sincere or abrupt; tentativeness . . . as polite or incomplete (1970: 187). These broader meanings should always be borne in mind in relation to the grammatical descriptions which follow.[7] Where necessary, unfamiliar grammatical terms will be briefly explained in footnotes.

The falling *tone*

A *falling* tone is characteristically found in the following contexts:

1   In statements, or answers to questions:

> /he's obviously feeling `better`/
> /it's a new `edition`/
> /I didn't `want` to/

2   In WH-questions:[8]

> /what do you `want/
> /where are the `keys/
> /how did `that happen/

3   In tag-questions[9] when the meaning is 'confirmation-seeking' (otherwise, tag-questions take a rising tone – see below). A tag-question with a falling tone does not have the effect of a true 'question' but merely invites the listener to agree with the speaker or simply signal that he/she is still listening:

> /he never stood a `chance/ `did he/
> /that was a nasty ˇsurprise/ `wasn't it/

The nucleus, in a tag-question, always occurs on the auxiliary verb, not the pronoun.

4   In exclamations (in writing, normally followed by an exclamation mark):

> /what a `disaster/
> /ˊamazing/
> /ˊdamn/

The rising *tone*

Typical contexts for the *rising* tone are as follows:

1   In *polar* questions (those which can be answered by *yes* or *no*)

> /is the ˊtoast ready/
> /have you got a ˊtelephone/
> /does it ˊwork/

2   In words or phrases intended as questions (but not otherwise grammatically marked as such):

> /you played for three ˊhours/
> /a ˊcharter flight/
> /book it ˊnow/

The intonation shows that these sentences are intended as questions in spite of the grammar, which indicates otherwise. In the first and last examples, the grammatical construction marks a statement and a command respectively; in the second example, the construction is unmarked as there is no verb. So in all three cases, the utterances are converted into questions by the intonation. In writing, each would be followed by a question mark to make this intention clear.

3 In WH-questions as 'echo' questions. 'Echo' questions occur when the speaker asks for a repetition of information already given. In these cases the nucleus always occurs on the WH- word itself. In 'ordinary' WH-questions, the nucleus never occurs on the WH-word.

    (/There are thirty-two `variations` on it/) /ˈhow many/

> /ˈwhat did you say/
> /ˈwhy did it break/

4 In tag-questions of the 'information-seeking' type. A tag-question with a rising tone has the effect of turning the preceding main sentence into a question (compare the 'confirmation-seeking' use, described above)

> /this is `Schubert`/ ˈisn't it/
> /we could sleep `outside`/ ˈcouldn't we/
> /they won't be ˘disappointed/ ˈwill they/

The meaning of these examples is approximately equivalent to:

> isn't this Schubert? couldn't we sleep outside?, etc.

    The use of the tag-question suggests that the speaker is fairly confident of his statement but would like the opinion of the listener; the straight question seeks the views of the listener directly.

The fall-rise *tone*

The *fall-rise* tone is normally found in utterances which require some further contribution before they can be taken as complete. In other words, the fall-rise signifies, in a very general way, incompleteness or non-finality. Delattre (1965) appropriately calls this tone a 'continuation'. Typical contexts are as follows:

1 In *subordinate* clauses, which require a main clause for completion:

> /when we ˘get there/ we'll have a good `meal`/
> /I'd `buy` you it/ if I could ˘afford it/
> /if he ˘comes/ we can tell him `then`/

2   In *main* clauses which are followed by at least one more main clause:

> /so I counted ˇ*ten*/ and then I ˋ*thumped* him/

3   In counting, or making a list. In this case, each element except the last may have its own separate fall-rise tone; the last element gets a falling tone, to signal the completion of the series:

> /ˇ*one*/ˇ*two*/ˇ*three*/ˇ*four*/ˋ*five*
> /you've had ˇ*fish*/ˇ*chips*/ˇ*peas*/ˇ*vinegar*/ what ˋ*more* do you want/

4   In sentence-modifiers,[10] when they occur at the beginning or at the end of the clause they belong with:

> /ˇ*obviously*/ we'll have to ˋ*accept* it/
> /ˇ*fortunately*/ they were all ˋ*away*/
> /you'd find a brown ˋ*mark* on it/ˇ*usually*/

5   In phrases and sentences where the speaker wishes to convey a sense of non-finality because the statement is a personal opinion (and the speaker is willing to be contradicted) or because an alternative is implied:

> /he's a pretty lousy ˇ*player*/
> /he's not ˇ*that* bad/
> /I don't ˇ*think* so/
> /I ˇ*expect* so/
> /we ˇ*were* going to buy it/ (but . . .)

The compound fall + rise *tone*

The *compound* tone, consisting of a *fall* followed by a *rise* within the same tone group, occurs when a tone group is felt to have two points of emphasis, a major one which coincides with the *fall*, and a minor one coinciding with the *rise*. Typical grammatical contexts are as follows:

1   In clauses with an adjunct of place or time, the *rise* (minor point of emphasis) occurs on the adjunct:

> /my ˋ*brother* lives over ʹ*there*/
> /we're going up ˋ*north* on ʹ*Sunday*/
> /there's some ˋ*cream* in the ʹ*fridge*/

2 In clauses in which more than one lexical item is highlighted:

> /I've ˋ*posted* your ´*letter*/
> /the ˋ*library*'ll ´*help* you/
> /ˊ*you* can get the ´*meat*/

3 The compound tone is particularly common in clauses containing a verb of 'feeling' such as *like, enjoy, appreciate, hate*:

> /he really ˋ*likes* those ´*ginger biscuits*/
> /they don't ˋ*approve* of ´*children*/
> /I'm ˋ*cross* with your ´*aunt*/
> /I'm ˋ*sorry* about the ´*mess*/

The tone group

So far in this chapter, we have used single sentences or short phrases to illustrate different patterns of intonation, and most of these have, therefore, consisted of only one tone group. In longer utterances, the information is broken down into shorter 'pieces' of about a clause or less in length. These 'pieces' are the tone groups; the purpose of the tone group is, in fact, to mark off a unit of information, breaking up longer utterances into easily digestible components. It is up to the speaker to decide *how many* tone groups to assign, and *where* to make the divisions. Here is a (made-up) example of an extended utterance, separated into tone groups and marked for nuclei and tones:

> /in ˇ*writing*/ a ˇ*fall-rise* tone/ is often shown
> by a ˋ*comma*/ and a ˇ*fall*/ may be marked by a full
> ˋ*stop*/ a ˇ*question-mark*/ corresponds to a ˋ*rising*
> tone/ except in ˇ *WH* questions/ which are normally
> spoken with a ˇ*fall*/

Here is another example, transcribed from a tape recording:

> /anyway thank you very much ˇ*indeed*/ for two. . .
> lovely ˋ*holiday* tapes that we've had from you/
> I think you sent them to ˋ*Janet* ˇ*first*/ and then
> ˇ*we* had them/ and . . . now we've sent them on to
> ˋ*Richard*/ what a lovely holiday you seem to have
> ˋ*had*/ you make me quite ˇ*jealous*/

Non-nuclear stress

One further addition to the system is needed before our account of the grammatical contrasts conveyed by intonation is complete. This is the *non-nuclear stress*, which occurs in the *pre-nuclear* part of the tone group. A lexical item in the pre-nucleus may be stressed, and the stress is meaningful, but it is not a *nuclear* stress because the nucleus of its tone group occurs elsewhere.[11] Some examples will help to show how a non-nuclear stress can contrast with, on the one hand, nuclear stress, and on the other hand, absence of stress:

/you drink the *beer*/

1   If *you* is unstressed, it is pronounced with [ə] and the meaning is approximately: 'one drinks the beer' (it could occur as a reply to: 'what do you do if there's no wine?').
2   If *you* receives a *non-nuclear* stress, it is pronounced with a full vowel (/ju/), there is a nucleus elsewhere in the tone group (for example, *beer*), and it refers in meaning to one or more specific persons. There may be a contrast involved:

/'I'll drink the ˇ*wine*/ 'you drink the ˋ*beer*/

(non-nuclear stress is marked by the normal stress mark).
3   If *you* receives a *nuclear* stress, it has a full vowel *and* a pitch change, the meaning refers to one or more persons, and because the nucleus is occurring on an item other than the last lexical item (see, p. 202), the meaning would normally be contrastive:

/ˋ*you* drink the beer/ ˇ*I*'ve/ had ˋ*enough*/

For another example contrasting all three possibilities, compare the pronunciation of *are* in the following:

1   unstressed: /you are ˋ*naughty*/ (equivalent to 'you're naughty')
2   non-nuclear stress: /you 'are ˇ*naughty*/ (context: speaker has just been given an expensive present)
3   nuclear stress: /you ˋ*are* naughty/ (in reply to: I'm ˋ*not* naughty)

The grammatical contexts in which non-nuclear stress is found, typically include the following:

1   Within a *noun-phrase*, when the noun is modified by an adjective

or a classifier. The nucleus is assigned to the noun, and the adjective (or classifier) takes a non-nuclear stress:

> /a 'rolling `stone`/
> /a 'hollow `tree`/
> /a 'German `textbook`/
> /the 'Berlin `Wall`/

Ambiguous examples which can be distinguished by intonation, such as 'Greek professor' (meaning *a*, professor who is Greek, or *b*, professor *of* Greek), will be discussed later (p. 220).

2   Non-nuclear stress typically occurs on the word *don't* in a negative imperative:

> /'don't let me `disturb` you/
> /'don't be such an `idiot`/

Positive imperatives with *do* can also take non-nuclear stress, but equally, a nuclear stress with fall + rise is found. Both of the following are acceptable:

> /'do help `yourself`/
> /`do` help `yourself`/

Exercise 4

Tape-record a short piece of spoken English, transcribe it in normal orthography, and mark the intonation by dividing the utterances into tone groups and identifying nucleus, tone and non-nuclear stress. Remember that each tone group normally has only one nucleus.

Exercise 5

Tape-record and transcribe a short passage of conversation or dialogue, as above. Give the passage to one or more speakers familiar with this system of intonation, and ask them to mark in a *possible* intonation pattern. Then compare their version(s) with the original. In cases of disagreement, listen to the tape.

Exercise 6

The football results, when read aloud over the radio, have a characteristic intonation pattern. The pattern, however, when the match was drawn is different from the pattern when the scores were unequal. Compare:

1   Liverpool 4   Arsenal 2
2   Liverpool 2   Arsenal 2

a What are the differences in intonation?
b Can you suggest reasons for these differences?
c Why would the following intonation pattern sound extremely odd?

/Liverpool ˇ*three* / ˋ*Arsenal* one/

For a discussion of the intonation patterns of football results, cf. Bonnet 1980.

Exercise 7

The notice on top of a pile of leaflets says: 'take one'.

1   What would be the normal intonation for this phrase?
2   When I help myself to a handful, the attendant looks at me reprovingly and says: 'it says "take one"'. What intonation would he use in this case? Why does it differ from the original?

We have now distinguished the major components of a system of intonation which will account for at least the grammatical distinctions of meaning which intonation is capable of conveying. These components are:

1   The *tone group*, which divides an utterance into manageable 'chunks' of information for processing by the listener.
2   The *nucleus*, which enables the speaker to distinguish between given (or retrievable) and new information, and to highlight or give emphasis to the latter.
3   The *tone*, which distinguishes a number of major speech functions.
4   The *non-nuclear stress*, which gives prominence to a lexical item in the tone group, without however assigning a nucleus to it.

In the next section we shall consider whether the system of tones we have proposed is adequate, and then we shall see ways in which the other two major components of the description (tone group and nucleus), can distinguish between various types of meaning.

The system of tones

We have proposed a system of three (four, if we include the compound tone) contrasting pitch contours: the fall, the rise, the fall-rise, and the fall + rise. This is a larger set of distinctions than the smallest system has (Daniel Jones contrasts only *fall* with *rise*) but considerably simpler than the majority of systems. Halliday, for example, whose system is one of the less complex and most carefully argued, includes five simple and two compound tones.

A distinction between a *fall* and a *rise* can be made without difficulty. A *fall* can indicate a statement or a command while a *rise* can indicate a question. Almost any of the examples of falls and rises, given earlier, can be taken at random to show the difference:

/book it `now/   (command)
/book it ´now/   (question)

The contrast between a *fall* and a *fall-rise* is also quite straight-forward; the distinction is one of completeness or finality, a fall-rise implying that there is more to follow, or that certain reservations are being made. Compare:

/I'd `like to/   (the offer is accepted)
/I'd ˇlike to/   ('but. . .' – the offer is declined)

More difficult is the problem of establishing the difference between the *rise* and the *fall-rise*. We have seen already (p. 206) that these tones may differ only minimally in pitch pattern. And in many circumstances, the two tones are not in contrast with each other but are in what would elsewhere be called *complementary distribution*, since the rise is used mainly for questions and the fall-rise in utterances *not* intended as questions. So when the grammar marks an utterance as a question, for example by the presence of a WH- word or by subject-auxiliary verb inversion (for example, 'are you listening' vs 'you are listening'), a fall-rise is not likely to occur. Likewise, a sentence modifier like *presumably*, *obviously*, etc. is most unlikely to take on the meaning of a question, and hence will not occur with a *rise*. In order to contrast these two tones, then, we must choose contexts which are neutral, i.e. in which the function is not determined until the tone is applied.

Some possibilities:

> /he's a pretty lousy ˇ*player*/ (statement, but 'reserved')
> /he's a pretty lousy ´*player*/ ('echo' question, meaning 'is that what you said?')
> /it's a good ˇ*offer*/ ('reserved' statement)
> /it's a good ´*offer*)/ (question – equivalent to 'is it a good offer?')
> /got your ´*fare* ready/ ('have you got your fare ready?')
> /got your ˇ*fare* ready/ ('I can see you've got your fare ready')

Exercise 8

The pitch-pattern of a *rise* may not always be distinct from the pitch-pattern of a *fall-rise*. Choose a sentence which can be interpreted with either meaning, i.e. as a question or as a (reserved) statement, such as

> his partner was ill

and pronounce it to a listener (or preferably listeners) with *one* of these meanings in mind. Ask the listeners to indicate which meaning they heard. Repeat the test a number of times, varying the meaning and the sentences. If the listeners disagree about an interpretation, what conclusion could you draw?

We should be able to distinguish the *fall-rise* from the *fall + rise* (compound tone) by the number of nuclei in the tone group: one main nucleus for the fall-rise, but two nuclei, one major, one minor, for the compound tone. Again, this is not always easy, because the pitch-patterns can be very similar. However, the *meanings* are usually quite distinct. For example:

> /I've ˋ*posted* your ´*letters*/ ('unreserved' statement – this pattern is very frequent when initiating a conversation, or when initiating a new topic in a conversation)
> /I've ˇ*posted* your letters/ ('reserved' statement – may be followed by, or implies, something like 'but they won't go for ages')

Similarly:

> /they don't `approve of ´children/
> /they don't ˇapprove of children/ (*but*. . . they're willing to
> take them in this case)

Other tones

We can account for attitudinal meanings by recognizing variants or
sub-types of our three main tones, so that, for example, the rise-fall,
which many authors treat as a separate tone but which leads to no
grammatical distinctions, should be treated as a sub-type of the
falling tone, since this tone always replaces it without changing the
(grammatical) meaning. Similarly, the *level* tone which a number of
authors have included, can be regarded as a variant of the fall or
rise – depending on the context, but mostly a variant of the rise.

In this section we have seen the grammatical distinctions conveyed
by the system of tones, and some of the problems it creates. In the
next two sections we shall look in turn at the other two major
variables of intonation, the tone group and the nucleus.

The tone group and grammatical meaning

It will have become apparent, if the reader completed Exercises 4 or 5
above, that there is often considerable freedom of choice in the matter
of assigning tone group boundaries, and that boundaries are flexible
without greatly affecting the meaning. For example, in the following
extract from the tape, boundaries and nuclei occurred as marked:

> /you make me quite `jealous/ 'cos we've had some very cold
> `weather/ ˇlately/ very ˇblowy/ and ˇraining/ and quite a lot of
> `snow we've had/ this last ˇmonth/

But there are several alternatives, all of which would make small
differences to the presentation of information, but no substantial
difference to the grammatical meaning. For example, *weather* and
lately could be given a fall + rise compound tone, removing the
boundary after *weather*; *we've* could be given a nucleus, making an
extra boundary after *had*; *this last month* could be part of a fall + rise
instead of a separate tone group; the nucleus of this phrase could have
occurred on *last* rather than *month*; and so on.

We see that there are many possible patterns for the same utterance. On the other hand, there are times when the speaker's choice is constrained by the grammar; and sometimes the location of boundaries can affect the grammatical meaning. For an example of the former, compare:

> Arsenal lost easily

This sentence can be spoken as one tone group, or two:

> /Arsenal `lost/ `easily/

But the sentence

> Arsenal lost presumably

must be divided into two tone groups. The presence of a sentence modifier in final position requires a separate tone group.

For examples of boundary placement creating differences of meaning, we look for potentially ambiguous sentences. Ambiguous sentences, here as elsewhere, serve the useful purpose of highlighting distinctions which we might otherwise not be aware of. Here are some examples:

1   In the sentence:

> the houses which were destroyed were of great historic interest

the clause 'which were destroyed' can either tell us *which* houses were of historical interest (the ones which were destroyed), or it can simply add a bit more information to what we know about the houses already. The clue to the distinction is given by punctuation, because with the latter meaning a comma would normally be written after *houses* and *destroyed*:

> the houses, which were destroyed, were of great historic interest

Punctuation is in fact one way of showing tone group boundaries in writing.

2   The sentence

> I didn't see the doctor because I was sick

can mean either:

> I didn't see the doctor (because I was sick and therefore couldn't go)

or:

> it wasn't because I was sick that I saw the doctor (but for some other reason, for example, to get my health card signed)

Thus in one meaning I did not see the doctor and in the other, I did. The difference lies in the *scope* of the negative. In the former meaning the scope is '[not] see the doctor' and in the latter it is '[not] because I was sick'.

The two meanings can be potentially distinguished by assigning different tone group boundaries:

1   /I didn't `see the ´doctor/ because I was `sick/
2   /I didn't see the doctor because I was ˇsick/

These examples show how grammatically ambiguous sentences can be distinguished by placement of tone group boundaries. The distinction is, it must be emphasized, a *potential* one: i.e. the speaker would not necessarily use those particular patterns on every occasion, since the ambiguity could be resolved by other factors such as the preceding utterances, or the listener's knowledge of the situation.

The nucleus and grammatical meaning

Just as tone group boundaries can be assigned according to the way the speaker wishes to structure his information, so can nuclei – indeed, the two are closely related, since a boundary will normally follow immediately after a nucleus. While the speaker will usually assign nuclei on the lexical items he desires to make prominent, there are a number of constructions in which nuclear placement can determine a difference in grammatical meaning. In a sentence like

> he teaches French

the choice of nucleus depends only on what the speaker wishes to emphasize, and there would be no grammatical differences. But in:

> he's a French teacher

we see a potential distinction between:

> he's a teacher of French (he teaches French)

and

> he's a teacher who is French (comes from France)

For the first meaning the nucleus would be on *French*, for the second, on *teacher* (with non-nuclear stress on *French*).

There are many examples of this kind, all involving a noun-phrase consisting of head-noun modified by an adjective or classifier. Similar to *French teacher* would be examples like *German student*, *Greek professor* and *Russian translator*. In these instances the head-noun is derived from a verb (*teach*, *study*, *profess*, *translate*, etc.). In other cases it may be the modifier which is derived from a verb:

> /a `rocking chair/

is a type of chair (a chair for rocking), whereas

> /a 'rocking `chair/

is a chair which is rocking. Similarly, /a `sleeping partner/ is a partner *for sleeping with*, while /a 'sleeping `partner/ is a partner, in a business, who 'sleeps', i.e. who is not actively engaged in running the business. In the Antipodes, /a `freezing worker/ is employed in /the `freezing works/ but /a 'freezing `worker/ is merely very cold.

Exercise 9

1   In the following noun phrases, which lexical item would normally take the nuclear stress? Which noun phrases are ambiguous in meaning?

a poisonous plants	*f* boiling fowl
b jigsaw puzzle	*g* black bird
c coffee grinder	*h* lightning conductor
d plastic bucket	*i* Chinese expert
e German speaker	*j* heavy weight

2   Compare the nuclear placement in the following pairs. Can you

suggest why they differ? Be careful to use a normal, unmarked, non-contrastive pronunciation for each phrase.

paper dart	–	paper boy
geographical survey	–	geographical society
musical ear	–	musical box
rolling stone	–	rolling pin
toy ship	–	toy shop
Oxford Road	–	Oxford Street

A different sort of ambiguity related to nuclear placement can be illustrated by the following sentence:

the historic houses were all destroyed

Historic here either defines *which* houses were destroyed, or it simply gives us more information about the houses ('which incidentally were historic'). For the latter meaning we would expect a nucleus on *houses*:

/the historic ˇ*houses*/ were all ˋ*destroyed*/

For the former meaning, a nucleus on *historic* would be necessary:

/the ˇ*historic* houses/ were all ˋ*destroyed*/

Exercise 10

The following sentences have the potential of being grammatically ambiguous: they have more than one meaning, and the difference is attributable to grammatical structure and not merely to differences of emphasis or presentation of information. First, describe, by paraphrase, the difference of meaning, and then show how each meaning could correspond to a different intonation pattern. Finally, decide whether the intonation differences are due to differences of *tone group boundary*, of *nuclear placement*, or of *tone*. Example:

it's an entertaining problem

Paraphrased meaning:

1   it's a problem which is entertaining (interesting)
2   it's a problem of entertaining

Intonation for 1   /it's an 'entertaining `problem/
Intonation for 2   /it's an `entertaining problem/
The difference is one of *nuclear placement* (nucleus on *problem* vs nucleus on *entertaining*).

1   they're eating apples
2   she speaks French naturally
3   it's too hot to eat
4   they gave her dog biscuits
5   she couldn't bear children
6   I'd like nothing better
7   are you more or less satisfied now
8   the theatre will be open to members only on Monday
9   if you don't help yourself you'll never get anywhere
10   there's a statue of Queen Victoria
11   I've called to see the milkman, Mr Jones
12   health also depends on a change of climate
13   to achieve this correct positioning is vital
14   Dad said he couldn't see anyone driving without it
15   I thought it was going to rain

Exercise 11

When we read silently, we usually supply, subvocally, an appropriate stress and intonation pattern to the material. Sometimes we find we have supplied the wrong pattern, and have to retrace our steps (this is usually a sign of careless writing, because the reader is inconvenienced). Try the following example:

'Some Universities,' he said, 'will have to get used again to lack of growth and occasional declines in real income, and to all the problems that will bring in maintaining staff morale, in making openings for able young scholars, and in providing opportunities for new subjects.'   (*from a University Newsletter*)

1   What is the *intended* intonation pattern in line 2?
2   What pattern is the reader *likely* to supply?
3   What simple change could make the passage unambiguous?

Intonation and discourse

The preceding sections have been concerned with the relationship between intonation and grammatical patterns. To conclude this chapter, we shall consider briefly the role of intonation from a different point of view.

In recent years some promising attempts have been made to describe intonation with reference to structures of discourse, rather than to grammatical categories. By discourse is meant a sequence of utterances, usually involving exchanges between two or more participants. Brazil (1975) suggests that the intonation patterns of a tone group, particularly the choice of tone, is partly determined by the relationships of meaning to what precedes and follows, or to the context of situation. One example he gives is the following:

1   /when I've finished `Middlemarch/I shall read Adam `Bede/

vs

2   /when I've finished `Middlemarch/I shall read Adam ˅Bede/

In 1, the listener is expected to know already that the speaker is reading Middlemarch, and we assume that the reading of Adam Bede is 'news'. In 2, however, 'the question of the speaker's reading Adam Bede has already arisen in some way. He is offering as news information about *when* he will do it' (1975: 6). What is interesting is that the same assumptions hold, even if the order of the clauses is reversed, for example:

1a   /I shall read Adam `Bede/when I've finished ˅Middlemarch/

In 1a, as in 1, 'read Adam Bede' is news, but the hearer is expected to know already about the reading of Middlemarch. Brazil therefore suggests that the *fall-rise* tone 'marks the matter of the tone group as part of the shared, already negotiated common ground occupied by the participants; . . . choice of *falling* tone, by contrast, marks the matter as new' (Brazil 1975). He thus distinguishes between the fall-rise tone as *referring* (symbol *r*) and the falling tone as *proclaiming* (symbol *p*), following a similar distinction made by Jassem (1952).

The advantage of this proposal is that it seems to explain sentences 2 and 1a, above, where other explanations fail. If the fall-rise tone is supposed, as has generally been assumed, to denote 'incompletion', we would expect the first clause always to have the fall-rise (since another clause follows it), and the second clause to have the falling tone, since it is final.

Brazil's proposals, however, immediately land him in difficulties, as is evident from his next example, taken from a doctor–patient interview. I will give the example without marking the tone groups as *referring* or *proclaiming*, and invite the reader to decide, on the basis of the meaning, which tone groups one would expect to be *referring* and which to be *proclaiming* (for example: *with the rash* is probably new information for the doctor: the patient will therefore choose the *proclaiming* tone (a fall)). The reader might also like to decide, independently, whether one would expect a *fall-rise* or a *fall* in each tone group.

3   /I've come to *see* you/with the *rash*/I've got on my *chin*/and *underneath*/which has *developed*/in the past three *days*/well it's *irritating*/and at *work*/with the *dust*/us being a *clothing* factory/well I find it's *irritating*/makes me want to *scratch* it/

Discussing this example, Brazil suggests that the facts that the patient has come to *see* the doctor, that the rash . . . is on his *chin*, and that it has *developed*, are all 'visibly evident', therefore the patient has chosen the *referring* tone for these tone groups. The choice of *referring* for *dust* and *clothing factory*, however, is less easy to explain on this basis. Brazil therefore proposes that these represent a common use of the *referring* tone to present matter *as if* it was already 'shared'. But this would enable us to 'explain' *any* referring tone: its material either *is* shared, or it is presented *as if* shared. One could also argue that on the basis of meaning, *all* the tone groups in this example, except the first, could qualify as new information and therefore should all have proclaiming tone. In the text itself, however, only *rash*, *underneath*, *days* and *scratch* have the falling tone. The rest have 'referring' (fall-rise).

The data thus fails to confirm the hypothesis proposed. The reader is invited to check this distribution of tones against his own expectations. It is worth noting that the assignment of tones according to the more traditional hypothesis of sentence boundaries ('use falling tone if sentence-final; otherwise use fall-rise for incom-pletion') accounts for the data better, since it predicts the falls on *underneath*, *days*, and *scratch*. It fails, however, with *rash*, for which one expects the fall-rise in view of the qualifying clause immediately following, and it fails with the second occurrence of *irritating*, for which one expects the falling tone (in sentence-final position).

Thus neither Brazil's proposals, nor the more generally-accepted grammatical basis, can completely account for the distribution of falls and fall-rises in this particular example. Both, it seems, offer us partial explanations: it is clear that much remains to be done before we have a fuller understanding of the intonation choices through which discourses are structured and maintained.

8 Dialect, accent

In this and the following two chapters we shall be considering some of the major areas which provide data for the study of phonology: variation (i.e. dialects and style); historical change; and language acquisition. This chapter is concerned with dialects – varieties of speech within a single language; and to some extent with *style*: varieties of speech within a single speaker. In the main part of the chapter, we shall discuss methods for *comparing* differences of pronunciation.

Social dialects

The *OED* defines dialect as 'one of the subordinate forms or varieties of a language arising from local peculiarities of vocabulary, pronunciation and idiom'.Traditionally, dialects were considered to be mainly regional, as implied by the term 'local' in this definition. More recently, however, it has been recognized that social variation, i.e. differences between speakers which can be attributed to factors such as social status and education, is as extensive as, and perhaps even more significant for its speakers than, any purely regional variation. The differences are greatest in those societies with the greatest social stratification, particularly in highly-urbanized communities in which education, technology and literacy rank high in importance. In these societies, one variety usually establishes itself as the *standard* (see below, p. 227) – and this is often based on the speech of the most educated, or otherwise most prestigious, group within the community. The other varieties then enjoy greater or lesser prestige, depending on a number of factors. Wilkinson (1977: 51), for example, distinguishes for British English what he calls 'first-class' accents (RP, and certain Scottish and Irish pronunciations), 'second-class' accents (the British regional accents) and 'third-class' accents (those of the large industrial cities, such as Leeds and Birmingham). This hierarchy has been broadly confirmed by experiments, such as those carried out by Giles and his colleagues (Giles and Powesland 1975), which have investigated speakers' attitudes to different varieties of pronunciation.

Social dialects are, in theory, independent of regional variation, but the two interact quite considerably, as is implied by Wilkinson's classification of accents above. Often, the standard is based on the dialect of the capital city, since this is the centre of commerce, government and culture. Parisian, for example, is the standard form ('the form which foreigners are taught') of modern French, as is Athenian of Greek.

Standard vs non-standard

The dictionary defines dialect as 'one of the *subordinate* . . . varieties of a language'. The term 'subordinate' suggests that there exists a normal or 'standard' variety of a language, from which the dialects 'diverge' in some way. This distinction is now usually referred to by the terms *standard* and *non-standard* (varieties). The black English vernacular (BEV) described by Labov and others (Labov 1972b; Wolfram and Fasold 1974) is one example of a non-standard variety. It includes such utterances as:

it ain't nothin' happenin'

(equals standard English 'there's nothing happening', or 'there isn't anything happening') and:

she done already cut it up

(equals she's (she has) already cut it up). *Non-standard* often refers to particular grammatical patterns, such as the use of double negatives, as in (American) white non-standard:

nothin' ain't happenin'

or the use of direct-question forms in indirect questions, as in BEV:

I aks Alvin do he know how to play baseball

(equals standard 'I asked Alvin if he knows . . .')

Non-standard forms may also be phonological, as in the case of 'h-dropping' – a widespread feature of British dialects – and the so-called 'g-dropping', i.e. the replacement of /–ıŋ/ by /–ın/ as in *visitin'*, *watchin'*, *happenin'*, etc.

Non-standard is intended as a purely descriptive term, without the pejorative connotations of labels like 'subordinate' or 'sub-standard'. Contemporary linguists of whatever persuasion always insist that equal status be given to non-standard varieties, such as BEV.

In pre-generative linguistics, this meant describing each non-standard dialect independently, on its own terms, without reference to a 'standard' from which it 'deviated' in some way. More recently, however, linguists have realized that independent descriptions are incomplete, for the speakers themselves recognize the existence of more and less standard forms, and vary their speech according to the situation (see below, on 'style'). We can hardly pretend that standard and non-standard have equal status, when the speakers themselves assign different values to them. When a linguist says that all varieties are equal, then, what he means is that all varieties are potentially capable of performing all the functions demanded of them: there are no dialects which are 'inferior' by virtue of the fact that they 'lack' certain words or meanings, or because they can only be used for certain limited purposes.

Style

Social dialects not only distinguish between different groups of speakers; they also have an influence on the speech of individuals at all levels of society. A speaker may adopt a more or a less prestigious variety, depending on the situation or the occasion. In more formal situations we tend to use a pronunciation (as well as a vocabulary and grammar) which approximates more closely to the standard, and in less formal situations one which is less 'prestigious'.

One example of this is the phenomenon known as 'telephone voice', in which a speaker, in answering the telephone, 'puts on' an accent quite different from the one he (or she) has just been using in casual conversation. Similarly, if we are asking the bank manager for a loan, or trying to make a good impression at an interview, we tend to use a more standard form of pronunciation than when, say, having a drink with friends, where less standard forms are more appropriate and acceptable.

Speakers respond to the actual situation (the important factors being *who* they are speaking to, *what* they are speaking about, and *where* the conversation is taking place) by making quite sensitive adjustments of pronunciation, as has been shown in a number of recent major studies (for example, Labov 1972; Trudgill 1974; Milroy 1980). This 'within speaker' variation is commonly referred to as 'stylistic'.

In New York, for example, Labov (1972) distinguishes 'careful' from 'casual' styles. 'Careful' styles occurred in more 'formal' contexts, which were defined as contexts in which 'more than the minimum attention is paid to speech'. A casual style – what Labov calls 'the vernacular' – is, conversely, the style in which 'the minimum attention is given to the monitoring of speech'. This – the style in which a speaker 'jokes with his friends and argues with his wife' – is the most difficult for the linguist to observe systematically, because the presence of an observer itself makes the situation more 'formal'. An interview, for example, normally comprises a formal context, unless the speaker can be made to 'relax'. Even more formal are those contexts, beloved of linguists, in which speakers are asked to read sentences aloud, or pronounce lists of words. Labov and his fellow researchers took great trouble to obtain recordings of speech which they could confidently label 'casual'.

In describing the pronunciation of a community we must therefore look for variation of two kinds: first, differences *between* speakers of different backgrounds, particularly from different social classes (though other variables such as sex, level of education, and age may be equally important, and may interact with social class); second, differences *within* a speaker's style, depending on situational factors and related to the degree of 'monitoring'. For purposes of description, however, these two kinds of variation can be incorporated into a single scale, for both of them rely on a continuum from a prestigious or standard pronunciation at one end to a 'broad' or non-standard pronunciation at the other. Expressed diagrammatically, the variation can be shown as in Figure 10 (p. 230).

On to the vertical scale goes a suitable phonological variable such as the presence or absence of [r] in words like *card, bar*. The horizontal scale represents the variation in style from casual to careful, and we take, for simplicity, an 'upper-class' and a 'lower-class' group of speakers. Notice that for both groups the presence of [r] increases as the style becomes more careful, but that the increase of [r] for lower-class subjects is greater (their slope is steeper) than the increase among the upper-class, which indicates that the latter are

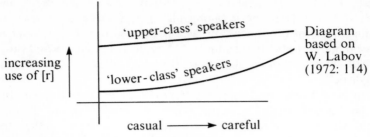

Figure 10   Based on W. Labov (1972: 114)

more consistent in their use of the prestigious [r] pronunciation across a range of styles.

The concept of prestige forms, and the norms acknowledged by the speech community are thus important elements in our description of language behaviour. As far as pronunciation is concerned, a great deal of the observed variation can be accounted for by *comparing* a broad or non-standard form with the standard towards which it is modified. In other words, the whole range of variation can be encompassed by comparing the two extremes. In the latter part of this chapter, methods for making such comparisons will be described.

Urban vs rural dialects

The traditional dialect surveys concentrated mainly on rural areas, recording pronunciations (and items of grammar and vocabulary) which may be of considerable historical interest because of the isolation, and hitherto slow rate of change, of rural communities. Since rural isolation is now being rapidly eroded, these surveys have the additional value of recording the linguistic information before it disappears entirely.

Rural dialects are thus accounted for, and at the other end of the social scale, *standard* dialects have also received adequate description (accounts of the phonetics of English, for example, are usually based either on RP or on standard general American).

Paradoxically, these descriptions encompass the speech of only a minority of the whole community; the urban accents, the accents of, say, Liverpool and Manchester, or Boston and Detroit, which are spoken by the majority of the population, have been until recently largely ignored. It is true that the character of these accents often derives from the local rural accents which exist (or existed) in that area; but the amalgamation of rural accents in an urban environment usually produces something different, a pronunciation which differs less extremely from the standard and is more widely intelligible (cf. Trudgill 1974: 6). Recently, therefore, attention has been focused on urban speech patterns, but there is still much to be done in this area (cf. Wolfram and Fasold 1974; Macaulay 1977; Knowles 1978; and the references mentioned above, p. 229).

Dialect vs accent

The terms *dialect* and *accent* have so far been used interchangeably, in a rather loose manner. Linguists prefer to distinguish the two: *dialect* is generally used to refer to differences at all (or any) linguistic levels, whereas *accent* refers more specifically to differences of *pronunciation* only. Dialect differences thus include, in addition to pronunciation variants, differences of *grammar*, such as:

did you not see them?	vs	didn't you see them?
we was playing	vs	we were playing

They also include differences of *vocabulary*, such as American English *subway*, *elevator* and *freeway* for British English *underground*, *lift* and *motorway* respectively, or words used only locally, such as *mardy*, a Midlands word with no exact equivalent in standard English meaning approximately 'babyish'.

Wells (1982), however, points out that the distinction between dialect and accent is not quite so simple. He prefers to distinguish between what he calls 'traditional-dialect' on the one hand, and 'local pronunciations of General English' (*local accent*) on the other. The difference can be illustrated by the following example: a Scottish teenager, cycling at speed down a hill, shouted out [ne breks] 'nae brakes!'. Had he used merely a local pronunciation of general English, the form would have been: [no breks], [no] being the local pronunciation of 'no', corresponding to RP [nəʊ]. Wells gives, as examples of traditional-dialect, the Westmoreland villager's [t rɪadz əz mɒkɪ] 'the roads is mucky' and the North of England [ða mɒŋ gɛr ɪt ɛtn̩] 'you must get it eaten' (equals 'you must eat it up'). Traditional-dialect often involves differences (from standard English) of grammar and vocabulary, but the differences may involve phonology, which is why 'accent' alone cannot account for all phonological differences. For example, *brig*, *rig* and *kirk* as Northern

England/Scottish words for *bridge*, *ridge* and *church* are *not* just local pronunciations of standard English /ʧ, ʤ/, because *chair* is not pronounced [keə] by these speakers nor is *John* [gɒn]. *Brig*, etc. are traditional-dialect words, coexisting, for their speakers, with the standard English words *bridge*, etc. It is important, then, to distinguish between dialect words and words which are merely standard English with a local pronunciation, though in particular instances this may not be easy. For instance, a Nottinghamshire boy, asked by his teacher why so-and-so was absent that morning, replied,

[pleɪs sʌ eɪ kɔdnə gerɒnʔ bɔs]
'please sir, he couldn't get on the bus'

We can accept [bɔs] as the *local pronunciation* of *bus*, but what about [eɪ] for *he*? Is this a traditional-dialect form, or a local pronunciation, derived by dropping /h/ and shifting the vowel from /i/ to [eɪ]? To answer that question, we would need to know whether standard English /i/ is *regularly* (i.e. in all or most other /i/ words) pronounced [eɪ] in that accent; if so, then [eɪ] is just a local pronunciation of standard 'he'. If not – if [eɪ] is used, say, only for the pronouns *he*, *she*, *we*, but not in *green*, *tree* – then [eɪ], [ʃeɪ], [weɪ] would be regarded as *traditional-dialect* forms. (In fact, however, [eɪ] *is* the usual realization of RP /i/, as suggested by [pleɪs] for *please* in the example.) The term 'accent', then, in what follows, refers to 'local pronunciations of general English'.

Accents may differ from each other at more than one phonological level. There may be *segmental* differences, that is, differences involving the pronunciation of single segments (phonemes), or there may be suprasegmental (prosodic) differences – that is, differences of stress, rhythm, or intonation. Both kinds raise problems of measurement and description, but since relatively few descriptions of suprasegmental differences are available (though cf., for example, Currie 1979; Pellowe and Jones 1978) we shall focus here on *segmental* variation.

The chief source of segmental variation among accents is in vowel quality. Consonants may also show differences, but their role is generally much smaller and less important. The consonants which do have some part to play are usually those which are most vowel-like, namely, the approximants, particularly l, r and h. But there are many consonants, like m, n, ʃ, s, etc. which rarely, if ever, carry accentual differences: it would be difficult, for example, to think of two accents which differ in their pronunciation of the m's of *mummy* or the /ʃ/ of *wash*. One pair of consonants which do show variation are the initial sounds of *thing*, *thought* and *this*, *that*, which in standard English have /θ, ð/, but in other accents may have /f, v/ or /t, d/. /h/ is somewhat unusual in that its variation is confined to presence or absence; it is present in standard English but absent in many non-standard accents.

Four types of accent difference

There are four generally recognized ways in which accents can differ from each other. They have been given different labels by different linguists, but we shall use the terms *realizational, systemic, selectional* and *distributional*, following Wells (1982).[1]

Realizational differences

The simplest and commonest type of variation between accents lies in the way particular vowels are pronounced. Take for example the vowel in the words *bet*, *head*, *ten*, etc. In RP this vowel has a quality about midway between cardinal 2 and 3 and can therefore be symbolized as either an open C2, [ẹ], or as a raised C3, [ɛ̣].[2] In Australian English (Aus E) (and in South African Zimbabwean and New Zealand English) the vowel in these words is closer than in RP; it is near C2 but somewhat centralized, [ë]. In many Northern English (North E) accents this vowel is more *open* than RP, with a quality approaching C3, [ɛ]. (See Figure 11.)

The one vowel /e/ can thus be pronounced (realized) in a variety of ways: as [ẹ], [ë] or [ɛ], depending on the accent. Notice that we are

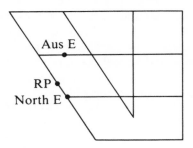

Figure 11 Positions of /e/ in different accents

concerned here with relatively precise phonetic values: the aim is to describe these sounds as accurately as possible, and this is done by referring to the set of cardinal vowels (cf. Chapter 1, p. 38), whose values are relatively stable. Since we are concerned with phonetic values, the descriptions are given square brackets.

The point about accent differences of this kind is that they leave the phoneme system as a whole unchanged. In all the accents just mentioned, there is still a contrast between sets like *bit, bet, bat* or *pin, pen, pan* even though the pronunciation of *bet, pen*, etc. differs from one accent to another. Hence, all the accents have three phonemes, /ɪ, e, æ/, but, as we have seen, the realization of the /e/ phoneme varies. We express this variation by a realization rule similar to those described in Chapter 1, for example:

/e/ → RP [ẹ]
    Aus E [ë]
    North E [ɛ]

The realizations here are not positional variants (allophones) like the ones considered in Chapter 1: they are a kind of dialectal allophone – an allophone which varies according to regional and social factors, rather than according to position in the word. Daniel Jones called them *diaphones* (cf. *dia*lectal allo*phone*), but the term has not caught on and we shall simply call them realizational differences. Others call variants of this kind *non-systemic* (O'Connor 1973), *allophonic, phonetic* (Abercrombie 1979) or simply *phonic* (Kurath 1972), all in recognition of the fact that the variant lies 'below' the level of the phoneme.

We can predict that, if there are accent differences in the realization of /e/ in *bet, pen*, etc., there will be parallel differences in the realization of the neighbouring phonemes /ɪ/ and /æ/, for otherwise these phonemes might not remain distinct. For example, we have seen that Aus /e/ is pronounced [ë]; this puts it very close to the RP pronunciation of /ɪ/ (the vowel of *bit*), so that if Aus /ɪ/ had the same value as RP /ɪ/, it would scarcely be distinct from Aus /e/ and an important contrast would be lost (see Figure 12). Hence we find that the Aus realization of /ɪ/ is some distance away from the RP pronunciation of the same phoneme, so that the distinction between /ɪ/ and /e/ is preserved: they are separated by an adequate amount of 'auditory space'.

In a similar manner, the realization of /æ/ in Aus is a closer vowel

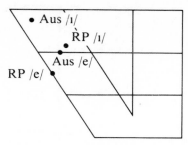

Figure 12 Relative positions of RP and Aus /ɪ/ and /e/, showing preservation of auditory distance

than in RP, which makes the relationship between all three front vowels in the two accents a symmetrical one: the vowels of Aus E can be obtained by, as it were, raising their RP values: all the Aus E vowels are closer (higher) than the RP equivalents (see Figure 13). Symmetrical relationships like this preserve the auditory distance between vowels and thus keep phonemic contrasts distinct, and are frequently met whenever accents are compared. To put this another way, we can say that realizational differences in one phoneme will normally engender parallel, and symmetrical, realizational differences in neighbouring phonemes.

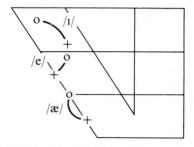

Figure 13 Symmetrical patterns of the front vowels /ɪ, e, æ/ in RP (+) and Aus E (o)

Another example of neighbouring phonemes which can vary in this way are the front-gliding diphthongs (those with a glide towards [ɪ]), namely, /i, eɪ, aɪ/ as in *beat, bait, bite* (we will ignore /ɔɪ/ because of an additional complication). In London E, as well as in large parts of South-East England, the Birmingham area, Aus E, and NZ E, the starting points of these diphthongs are all more open and retracted

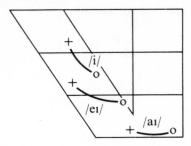

Figure 14 The diphthongs /i, eɪ, aɪ/ in RP (+) and in London E, etc. (o). To simplify the diagram, only the starting points are shown

than their RP counterparts, yielding a symmetrical relationship (Figure 14).

Notice that the starting point for RP /aɪ/ is close to that of London E /eɪ/. It would be quite possible for these points to be identical, without any loss of phonemic contrast, but there would of course be a likelihood of misunderstanding between an RP speaker and a speaker of London E or Aus E. There is the well-known story of the Australian who asked the recent arrival from Britain, 'Did you come here [tədaɪ]?' and the Englishman replied (in his best RP) 'I certainly hope not!'

Similarly, since Aus /e/ is so close, auditorily, to RP /ɪ/, the Australian who asks an RP speaker for a *pen* is likely to be given a *pin*, but of course speakers and listeners usually adjust to one another's accents very quickly and are able to make allowances for overlap like this, quite apart from the fact that the context normally makes clear which meaning is intended. Proper names can often be the source of confusion, for here there is usually no context to provide a clue and the listener thus relies heavily on phonetic (auditory) information. A New Zealander once introduced his wife to me as 'Ellis': this seemed an odd first name for a woman, until I realized that what he meant was 'Alice' and I had interpreted his /æ/ (realized [ɛ]) as my /e/ (realized [ɛ]). The surname *Kemble*, spoken with an English accent, is invariably interpreted by New Zealanders as *Campbell*; the only way to compensate for this is to pronounce it as if it were *Kimble*.

Exercise 1

An Australian named *Drayton* introduces himself. 1 How might this name be interpreted by an RP speaker, and 2 What adjustment could the Australian make in order to ensure that his name is interpreted correctly?

One feature of realizational differences is that they permit a continuum of variation according to the non-linguistic factors we mentioned earlier, namely, social class, etc. and *style* of speech. To illustrate this, let us take another example. In the North of England and in several other accents, the vowel /ɑ/ in *bar*, *smart*, has the quality of an òpen front vowel in the region of C4, [aː] (the dots denote length) – while in RP this vowel has a rather back quality, near C5, [ɑː]. This back vowel is the prestigious version and we may therefore expect speakers of other accents to modify their [aː] in this direction. We shall expect to find differences among speakers of different social class, and we may also find individual speakers using a more back version in 'careful' or formal styles and a more fronted version in 'casual' speech. The gradation of this vowel is, in theory, infinite, for any realization of it may fall at any point along a continuous line from [aː] to [ɑː] (see Figure 15). The same is true, of course, of the starting points of the [ɪ]-gliding diphthongs (Figure 14), and the short front vowels (Figure 13), which can also be continuously modified towards or away from the standard.

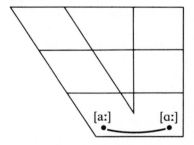

Figure 15   Realizations of /ɑ/, varying continuously from [aː] to [ɑː]

Continuous variation of this kind presents difficulties of description for the phonetician, partly because of the problem of judging whereabouts on the scale a particular instance falls, and partly because there is a limited notation available. The description of realizational differences between accents thus calls for a fine ear and fairly precise techniques of measurement.

Realizational differences are very common in occurrence and it is probably true to claim that any two accents which are distinguishable will involve realizational variation to some extent; usually, these differences pervade the whole vowel system, and make up the distinguishing characteristics of a particular accent. A New Zealander, for example, can be identified quite accurately by his pronunciation of the two phonemes /ɑ/ (for which he has a very fronted version, [a:]), and /ɜ/, which is realized as [ö], a half-close, fronted central vowel with lip rounding.

To summarize: realizational differences between two accents concern the precise pronunciation of a particular phoneme or set of phonemes. They do not entail any difference in the overall phoneme system: each accent has the same set of contrasts.

The realizations may correlate very precisely with factors such as social class and style of speech, and because their variation can be finely shaded they may be difficult for the trained observer to describe and quantify accurately. Realizational differences account for most of the distinction between one accent and another, and hence provide most of the identifying characteristics of each accent.

Systemic differences

A systemic difference arises when two accents have a different number of phonemes in their system, or rather in some part of their system, i.e. a phonemic contrast which is made in one accent is not made in the other. One well-known example of this is the distinction between /ʌ/ and /ʊ/, which is made by RP speakers and by many accents of Southern England, but is lacking in the 'vernacular speech' (using 'vernacular' in the sense given to it by Labov, cf. p. 227) of the Midlands and most parts of the North. In RP the vowel of *cut, run* is different from that of *put, book*, and one can find numerous minimal pairs like *cud–could, putt–put, luck–look*. In the Midlands and North, all these words are pronounced with the same vowel: there is no phonemic contrast of /ʌ/ vs /ʊ/. The actual pronunciation of this one vowel varies: some speakers have [ʊ], others have the unrounded equivalent [ɤ], and others an unrounded vowel of more central quality, [ə]. At this point in the vowel system, then, the Midlands and North has one fewer phoneme than RP, and the accents are thus said to differ systemically.

Another example, found in certain Irish accents (Wells 1982: 443), is a distinction between words like *eye, die, tide*, which are pronounced [əɪ], and words like *I, dye, tied* which are pronounced [aɪ]. There is thus a phonemic contrast here (notice the existence of minimal pairs *eye–I*, etc.) which is not found in RP or in most English accents: at this point in the system, therefore, RP has one fewer phoneme. A similar distinction is found in Scotland, though there are further complicating factors (Aitken and McArthur 1979: 101).

Major systemic differences separate the vowels of Scottish English (Abercrombie 1979) from those of English-English (or Anglo-English as it is sometimes usefully called). Scottish speakers do not distinguish /ɷ/ and /u/ (as in *pull* and *pool*, *good* and *food*), nor /ɒ/ and /ɔ/ (as in *cot* and *caught*). There is also no distinction between /æ/ and /ɑ/, but the situation here is more complicated since many RP words with /ɑ/ have a postvocalic r in Scottish, which preserves the distinction between pairs like *cat* and *cart*, *had* and *hard*. A pair like *cam* and *calm*, however, would not be distinguished in Scots English. Table 3 compares the vowel system of Scottish English with that of RP (after Abercrombie 1979: 72).

Table 3 *The vowel systems of Scottish English compared with RP*

	Scottish	RP
bead	i	i
bid	ɪ	ɪ
bay	e	eɪ
bed	ɛ	ɛ
bad	a	æ
balm	a	ɑ
not	ɔ	ɒ
nought	ɔ	ɔ
no	o	oɷ
pull	u	ɷ
pool	u	u
bud	ʌ	ʌ
side	ʌi	aɪ
sighed	ae	aɪ
now	ʌu	aɷ
boy	ɔe	ɒɪ

In parts of North America, a systemic difference arises between those accents which distinguish *balm* from *bomb* and have different vowels in *father* and *bother*, and those which do not make the distinction. For the former, *balm* and *father* have a long vowel, [ɑː], similar in quality but not in length to the [ɑ] in *bomb, bother*.

Systemic differences are relatively easy to identify and describe, compared with realizational differences, and are less common than the latter. One characteristic of systemic differences is that they seem to affect only part of the phoneme system, and do not usually have repercussions elsewhere. Thus, it is possible for the phoneme inventory of RP and the Midlands to be identical except for the ʌ/ʊ contrast, and it could quite easily be the case that the Midlands accents have an extra phoneme somewhere else in their system, so that the number of phonemes in the inventory would be the same as for RP, but there would be two systemic differences among them.

Selectional differences

A selectional difference arises where two accents have the same set of phonemes, but particular words *select* different phonemes. Cockney, for example, has a phonemic contrast between /ɒ/ and /ɔ/ in words like *cot* vs *caught*, *pot* vs *port*, just as RP does. But there is a small group of words which take /ɒ/ in RP as against /ɔ/ in Cockney: words like *off, cloth, lost, often*.[3] The point about selectional differences is that there is usually no way of predicting which words will be affected – and the number of words may be quite small. Many of the differences between British and American accents can be classed as selectional, such as the American preference for /e/ rather than /i/ in *ecological, amenable*; for /eɪ/ rather than /ɑ/ in *tomato*; and for /ɒ/ rather than /oʊ/ in *progress*. The phonemes /e/ and /i/, /eɪ/ and /ɑ/, /ɒ/ and /oʊ/ are found in the accents on both sides of the Atlantic, so there is no difference in the phoneme system: it is just a different choice of phoneme in certain words.

Distributional differences

A distributional difference arises where two accents have the same set of phonemes, but there is a difference in the *distribution* of one (or several) phonemes. The *distribution* of a phoneme refers to the environments in which it may typically occur, for example word-initially, intervocalically, as initial element of a consonant cluster, etc.

The biggest single distributional difference between accents of English involves /r/; in RP, /r/ occurs only initially in a word or syllable, but in most American, West, and North-West England, Scottish and Irish accents /r/ is also found finally (*car, pour*) and pre-consonantally (*cart, ford*). This is a difference in the *distribution* of /r/. Accents which have this /r/ in final and pre-consonantal positions are said to be *rhotic*, or r-pronouncing. The term *postvocalic r* is normally used as a more convenient label than the awkward 'final and pre-consonantal', though strictly speaking it is less accurate, since the non-rhotic accents also have a 'postvocalic' r in *very, era, sharing*, etc., where the r both follows and precedes a vowel.

Another example of a distributional difference involves /j/. In many American accents /j/ is not found after an alveolar consonant (/n, t, d, s/), so that the sequences /nj–, tj–, dj–, sj–/, which occur in other accents, are simply replaced by /n–, t–, d–/, /s–/, as in *new* (/nju/ vs /nu/), *Tuesday, produce, sue*. The distribution of /j/ in these American accents is thus more limited than in the other accents, though it does of course occur in other positions, for example initially, as in *yes, year*, etc., and after non-alveolar consonants, as in *pure, few, queue*.

The point about a distributional difference is that, by contrast with a selectional difference, its occurrence can be generalized: a rule can be formulated to describe it. So, for example, we can say that in certain accents /r/ is found postvocalically, or that /j/ is not found after alveolars, etc. The possibility of a general statement like this distinguishes distributional from selectional differences, for otherwise it could be argued that they are the same thing: it could be claimed that accent A has, for *new*, /nu/, accent B has /nju/, just as accent A has /e/, accent B /i/ in *ecological*. The selectional differences, however, cannot be predicted by the phonetic environment: a statement to the effect that American accents have /e/ *word-initially*, while British accents have /i/ is impossible, otherwise the Americans would have to pronounce *easy* as /ezi/. Nor could the rule be limited to 'word-initially before /k/', otherwise in addition to /ek–/ vs /ik–/ in *ecological, economic*, etc., we would require *eccentric* with /ik–/ in Britain. The e/i alternation across accents is thus found in only a few words; it cannot be explained on the basis of distribution, and will therefore be classified as selectional.

The Cockney example, quoted above as a selectional difference, is potentially a distributional one, for the ɒ/ɔ choice seems to occur only before a following /f/, /θ/ or /s/, i.e. before a *voiceless fricative*. If this were in fact the case and all the rest of the data was analogous, it could be claimed that the difference was generalizable, and hence involved the *distribution* of /ɒ/ and /ɔ/ before voiceless fricatives. But there are counter-examples on both sides: Cockney has /ɒ/ before voiceless fricatives in *moss* and *hospital* and RP has /ɔ/ in *dwarf*, *sauce*, etc. It is therefore preferable to take the /ɒ/ vs /ɔ/ choice as a selectional one.

Summary

The four categories of accentual difference can now be summarized in Table 4. Take note of the form in which the data is presented, for this will be used again in Exercise 2 below.

Table 4   *Categories of accentual differences*

1 *Realizational*			
/oʊ/ (as in *home*, *road*, *low*, etc.)	*Yorks* [oː]	*RP* [əʊ]	*Birmingham* [aʊ]

2 *Systemic*					
a More phonemes than RP:			b Fewer phonemes than RP:		
	RP	*Ireland*		*RP*	*North*
eye	[aɪ]	[əɪ]	cut	[ʌ]	[ʊ]
die	[aɪ]	[əɪ]	run	[ʌ]	[ʊ]
tide	[aɪ]	[əɪ]	cud	[ʌ]	[ʊ]
I	[aɪ]	[aɪ]	put	[ʊ]	[ʊ]
dye	[aɪ]	[aɪ]	could	[ʊ]	[ʊ]
tied	[aɪ]	[aɪ]			

3 *Selectional*		
	RP	*Cockney*
cot	[ɒ]	[ɒ]
bomb	[ɒ]	[ɒ]
rock	[ɒ]	[ɒ]
caught	[ɔː]	[ɔː]
law	[ɔː]	[ɔː]
off	[ɒ]	[ɔː]

cloth	[ɒ]	[ɔː]
loss	[ɒ]	[ɔː]

---

4 *Distributional*

	RP	*US*
yes	[j]	[j]
yard	[j]	[j]
pure	[pj]	[pj]
cute	ˈ[kj]	[kj]
tune	[tj]	[t]
due	[dj]	[d]
new	[nj]	[n]
suit	[sj]	[s]
lewd	[lj]	[l]

Exercise 2

For the following sets of data, work out whether the differences are realizational, systemic, selectional or distributional. The amount of data is small but should be adequate to give an unambiguous answer. (Notice that the data is given in square brackets, i.e. it is *phonetic*: ascertaining the *phonemic* contrasts is part of the exercise.) Number 5 is rather more difficult than the others.

		RP	*Scottish*			*RP*	*Cockney*	*Yorks.*
1	cot	[ɒ]	[ɔ]	2	late	[ẹɪ]	[ʌɪ]	[eː]
	saw	[ɔː]	[ɔ]		make	[ẹɪ]	[ʌɪ]	[eː]
	long	[ɒ]	[ɔ]		they	[ẹɪ]	[ʌɪ]	[eː]
	sorry	[ɒ]	[ɔ]		frame	[ẹɪ]	[ʌɪ]	[eː]
	thought	[ɔː]	[ɔ]		wave	[ẹɪ]	[ʌɪ]	[eː]
	caught	[ɔː]	[ɔ]

[ʌ] is a central open vowel midway between C4 and C5

		RP	*East Anglia*			*RP*	*Aus E*
3	by	[aɪ]	[ɔɪ]	4	bean	[i]	[i]
	rye	[aɪ]	[ɔɪ]		feed	[i]	[i]
	fight	[aɪ]	[ɔɪ]		lip	[ɪ]	[ɪ]
	boy	[ɔɪ]	[oɪ]		fit	[ɪ]	[ɪ]
	Roy	[ɔɪ]	[oɪ]		happy	[–ɪ]	[–i]
	coin	[ɔɪ]	[oɪ]		study	[–ɪ]	[–i]
					worry	[–ɪ]	[–i]

		RP	Midlands
5	bomb	[ɒ]	[ɒ]
	gone	[ɒ]	[ɒ]
	gun	[ʌ]	[ə]
	rub	[ʌ]	[ə]
	love	[ʌ]	[ə]
	one	[ʌ]	[ɒ]
	none	[ʌ]	[ɒ]

Here is one more problem of the same type, but in this case the reader is invited to contribute additional data to arrive at the best solution:

		RP	North E
6	car	[ɑː]	[aː]
	part	[ɑː]	[aː]
	heart	[ɑː]	[aː]
	man	[æ]	[a]
	cap	[æ]	[a]
	bag	[æ]	[a]
	laugh	[ɑː]	[a]
	bath	[ɑː]	[a]
	pass	[ɑː]	[a]
	basket	[ɑː]	[a]
	dance	[ɑː]	[a]

Discussion of 6

Both accents have two phonemes: RP has /ɑː, æ/, North E has /aː, a/. In both accents, there is a contrast between a *long* vowel ([ɑː] or [aː]) and a *short* vowel ([æ] or [a]). Excluding, for the moment, the *laugh* group of words, the 'realization criterion' is fulfilled.[4] The major difference between the accents now resides in the words *laugh*, etc., which take /ɑ/ in RP but /æ/ in North E. The question is whether the difference is predictable by a general environment (hence, *distributional*) or whether it applies only to these words and a few others (in which case it would be *selectional*). In the examples given, the vowel is always followed by a voiceless fricative (/f, θ, s/), or a nasal plus voiceless fricative (*dance*). We must now look for further data to see whether RP always has /ɑ/, corresponding to North E /æ/, in these environments. If it does, the 'voiceless fricative' generalization holds good, and the difference is distributional; otherwise it is selectional.

There do seem to be a large number of words where the 'voiceless fricative' rule applies: think of *path, after, fast, castle, ask, chance, sample*, etc., all of which take /ɑ/ in RP and /æ/ in North E. But alongside each type of consonant or consonant cluster which behaves 'regularly' in this way, we can put counter-examples which take /æ/, not /ɑ/, in RP. Minimal pairs are given where possible. Thus:

environment	'regular'	exception
/–f/	laugh	gaff, Africa, traffic
/–ft/	after	kaftan
/–θ/	path	maths, hath
/–s/	pass	gas, ass, passage
/–sp/	clasp	asp˙
/–st/	mast	massed, gymnastic
/–sk/	basket	gasket
/–sl/	castle	tassel
/–mp/	sample	ample
/–nt/	plant	rant, ant, Atlantic
/–ns/	chance	romance, finance
/–nd/	demand	grand, expand
/–nsl/	chancel	cancel

Two alternative conclusions are possible: first, the difference is selectional, and the words affected (the 'regular' words above) must be listed individually; second, the difference is really distributional (and can be stated according to a '(nasal plus) voiceless fricative' rule) but has certain exceptions. The answer to this depends partly on how many 'regular' words there are. If they heavily outweigh the exceptions, the 'distributional' solution is preferable. In this case the exceptions are so numerous that the difference is probably best described as selectional.

The problem is that 'selectional' implies that the differences are entirely random, while 'distributional' implies that they are regular (or 'rule-governed'). The truth seems to lie somewhere in between. The example is a good illustration of the way in which linguistic behaviour can sometimes be neither entirely random, nor entirely regular. For further details and an historical explanation, cf. Wells (1982: 100, 134, 232–3).

What we have done so far is to establish a framework for comparing one accent with another, and to suggest the usefulness of contrasting a non-standard accent with the standard accent which is valid for that region. Readers are encouraged to carry out such comparisons for the accents with which they themselves are familiar. We shall go on now to look at some consequences of the accentual differences presented above.

Structural vs non-structural differences

The three categories, systemic, selectional and distributional, differ from realizational in one important respect; they have some effect on the *structure* of the two accents concerned. A systemic difference affects the *phonemic* structure (one accent has fewer phonemes than the other) and a distributional or selectional difference affects the *lexico-phonological* structure (i.e. some words have different phonemes). Realizational differences, on the other hand, leave the structure intact, for the differences are at a sub-phonemic ('allophonic') level. The former three categories are more important (because of their structural effects) than realizational differences both for us, as linguists seeking to describe the language, and for the native speaker, for reasons to be given below.

Structural differences and continuous variation

It was pointed out earlier that when a realizational difference arises between a non-standard and a standard accent, the speaker of the non-standard variety can modify his pronunciation towards or away from the standard along a finely graded continuum, giving a theoretically infinite number of possible pronunciations (see Figure 15), which can be correlated with non-linguistic factors such as social class, education, etc. But when *structural* differences are involved, such a continuum seems impossible: a sound belongs either to one phoneme or to another, and the 'psychological distance' between phonemes makes it unlikely that there could be any intermediate stages. Thus, in the selectional difference from Cockney, quoted above, the vowel of *off*, *cloth* can be either /ɒ/ or /ɔ/, but not something between the two; for the Northern speaker, *bath* has either

/æ/ or /ɑ/, but not an intermediate sound; and so on. We must acknowledge, however, that phonetically it *is* possible to pronounce something midway between two phonemes, particularly where we are dealing with vowels. For instance, midway between /ɒ/ and /ɔ/ (remember that /ɔ/ is a long vowel, [ɔː]) we could have [ɒː] (i.e. a lengthened [ɒ]) or [ɔ] (a shortened [ɔː]). Fine gradations of *quality* (between [ɒ] and [ɔ]), and of *length* are phonetically possible here.

In such cases, do speakers preserve the psychological spacing between phonemes? Or do they treat structural differences as if they were realizational, by making the variation continuous? The evidence available suggests the latter. In New York, for example, Labov found continuous variation not only for realizational items but also for structural ones such as /æ, iə/ and /t, θ/. Most structural differences involve adjacent vowels, which are particularly amenable to continuous variation. Consonants may be less so – /h/, for example, is either present or absent.

Structural differences and hyper-correction

Structural differences, but not realizational ones, give rise to the phenomenon of hyper-correction. A good example to illustrate this is the incidence of /æ/ and /ɑ/ in problem 6. The North E speaker who wants to exchange his non-standard for a standard pronunciation is faced with the difficulty of knowing *which* words should take /ɑ/ and which remain as /æ/. He may have heard standard speakers pronounce *dance*, *after* and *path* with /ɑ/, but he may not know whether *plant* and *clasp* should change or not. If he works out the '(nasal plus) f, θ, s' rule he will tend to over-generalize by applying the rule in all cases, resulting in pronunciations like *gas*, *mass* and *maths* with /ɑ/ instead of the RP /æ/.[5] This over-generalization is known as hyper-correction: the speaker corrects over and beyond what is requisite.

A systemic difference poses similar problems for the speaker. Again we can take the case of North E /ʊ/ which corresponds to both /ʊ/ and /ʌ/ in RP. The speaker has no way of knowing which words should be changed to /ʌ/, and which remain with /ʊ/. *Cut*, *bun* and *rush* require /ʌ/, but *could*, *pudding*, *cushion* and *butcher* have /ʊ/. The problem is more difficult than for a distributional difference, since for the latter, the speaker can at least work out the rule and apply it, whereas for systemic (and for selectional) differences, it is simply a case of knowing which words are affected. Hyper-correction and its opposite, under-generalization, are therefore both likely to occur. The Northerner whose speech has in other respects been modified towards RP may retain /ʊ/ in *bun* and *rush* (a case of under-generalization: the requisite change has not taken place in all instances), or he may substitute /ʌ/ in *butcher* and *sugar* where RP still requires /ʊ/ (hyper-correction). What often happens is that the North E speaker modifies *all* instances of his /ʊ/ along the continuum in the direction of /ʌ/. [ʊ] is distinguished from [ʌ] along a number of phonetic dimensions; [ʊ] is rounded, half-close and has a backish quality, while [ʌ] is unrounded, half-open and central. Intermediate stages between the two are thus [ɤ̈] (unrounded [ʊ]), [ə] (unrounded and central), and [ə] (unrounded, central, and more open). It is common to find North E speakers pronouncing both *cut* and *butcher* with one of these three sounds.

Structural differences between accents thus have important consequences for speakers' behaviour. There is, first, the theoretical question as to whether gradation *between distinct (and otherwise contrasting) phonemes* is really possible (and the evidence suggests that it is), and, second, the imperfect match between the phonemes and the lexical items (the words), which causes speakers either to under-generalize or to hyper-correct, and is doubtless the source of much anxiety, for those who are sensitive to language as a marker of social status.

Exercise 3

Here are two more sets of data describing differences between accents. To which category (realizational, etc.) do they belong?

		RP	Parts of North E			RP	Cockney
1	rain	[eɪ]	[eː]	2	thing	[θ]	[f]
	ate	[eɪ]	[eː]		thought	[θ]	[f]
	way	[eɪ]	[eː]		thin	[θ]	[f]
	reign	[eɪ]	[ɛɪ]		fine	[f]	[f]
	eight	[eɪ]	[ɛɪ]		weather	[ð]	[v]
	weigh	[eɪ]	[ɛɪ]		feather	[ð]	[v]
					heaven	[v]	[v]

Accents and phonology

Accentual differences have wider implications for the study of phonology generally: they may highlight phonological patterns, and provide valuable raw material for phonological theory. We can illustrate some of the possibilities very briefly, by considering some vowel patterns, and certain vowel–consonant relationships.

To take a simple example, accents often show that the distinction between a (long) monophthong and a diphthong is often false: the two form a continuum, which can be extended to include narrower and wider diphthongal glides. This can be illustrated by the various realizations of English /aʊ/. A broad Scots pronunciation of words like *about, house, down*, is monophthongal, [uː]; less broad pronunciations (in Scotland) include a range of values intermediate between [uː] and [aʊ], such as a narrow diphthong, [ʊu], and gradually wider ones [əʊ, ʌʊ]. It is thus possible to have a continuous link between such 'distant' sounds as a close (high) monophthong and an open diphthong. The chain may even continue further: in some dialects (for example, broad Australian) the wide diphthong /aʊ/ has lost its glide, leaving a long open vowel, [aː]. Again, such a process may take place gradually, with 'intermediate' stages, for example [aʊ] → [aə] → [aː]

Other patterns to emerge include *vowel symmetry*: front-vowel values are mirrored by back-vowel values, and vice versa. For instance, RP has two mid diphthongs, one front, /eɪ/, the other back, /oʊ/. In Northern England and many other dialects, these vowels are realized as long monophthongs, [eː] and [oː], or [ɛː] and [ɔː]. The symmetry is shown by the fact that, if one of them is a monophthong, the other one is also. There are no dialects which have, say, [eɪ] for one and [oː] for the other, or [eː] for one and [əʊ] for the other. Furthermore, the dialects that have a half-close value for one (for example, [eː]) have a half-close value ([oː]) for the other; we do not find [eː] with [ɔː], nor [ɛː] with [oː]. The high vowels /i, u/ generally show a similar symmetrical pattern, as do the open diphthongs, /aɪ, aʊ/.

Accents may also reveal connections between vowels, and the vowel-like consonants, /j, w, l, r/. It has already been noted that English accents are divided between those which are *rhotic* (a postvocalic [r] is pronounced) and those which are non-rhotic. In the latter, the sound which corresponds to postvocalic r is often a vowel, [ə], as in:

	rhotic	non-rhotic
beer	[biɹ]	[biə]
cure	[kjuɹ]	[kjuə]
fair	[fɛɹ]	[fɛə]

A similar relationship holds between postvocalic [l] and a back vowel, [ö] or [ɷ]. In some accents, particularly London, the [ł] of *milk*, *fill*, *feel*, etc., has been replaced by this back vowel, which is a very similar sound both acoustically and on articulatory grounds ([ł] has an additional tongue-tip contact, which the back vowel lacks). There are *phonetic* similarities, likewise, between [ɹ] and [ə]; [ɹ] has tongue-tip retroflexion, which [ə] lacks, and the two sounds strongly resemble each other acoustically. Accent differences thus draw attention to the connection between two postvocalic liquids, [ł, ɹ], and two corresponding vowels, [ö, ə].

The significance of the phonological patterns revealed by dialect differences cannot be fully appreciated, however, without seeing the relationships in their historical dimension. It is to this that we turn in the next chapter.

9 Sound change

A thousand years ago, our ancestors spoke a language which was the direct ancestor of the English we speak today. Yet this language, which we call Old English or Anglo-Saxon, is not intelligible to present-day speakers in the written forms in which it has been handed down to us; nor would it be intelligible, if it were spoken: it has to be learnt as if it were a foreign language. There are many reasons for this: there have been changes in vocabulary, and changes in the grammar; but the primary reason for the differences between Old and Modern English is the sound changes which have gradually taken place over the intervening period. To give a simple example: the Old English (OE) word for *night* was *niht*, pronounced (we assume) very like the modern German word for 'not', *nicht*, i.e. [nɪxt]. Because of sound changes, only initial /n/ and final /t/ remain unaltered; the 'h' was lost, though not entirely – its loss was compensated for by a lengthening of the vowel, to [iː] – and the long vowel [iː] became [aɪ], as part of what is called the Great English Vowel Shift, which took place about four to five hundred years ago.

Why such sound changes take place, and how, are not fully understood. Many different factors are at work, and they can interact with each other, with complex results. But the *kind* of sound changes which occur, and the paths which a sequence of changes might follow, are better understood: the same patterns are noted over and over again, in different languages and at different times. In this chapter, then, we shall be concerned with typical, well-documented sound changes, and, more importantly, the phonetic and phonological processes which can bring them about.

We can begin with a more extensive example from English. Compare the following versions of translations of the Bible (*Matthew* 9, 1–2) into the English of three different historical periods:

1   *Old English* (tenth century)   ða astah hēon scyp, and oferseg-

lode, and cōm on his ceastre. Ða brohton hig hym ǣnne laman, on bedde licgende.

2   *Early Modern English* (Tyndale 1526)   And he entered into the shippe: and passed over and cam into his awne cite. And lo they brought unto him a man sicke off the palsey lyinge in his bed.

3   *Modern English* (New English Bible 1970)   So he got into the boat and crossed over, and came to his own town. And now some men brought a paralysed man lying on a bed.

Present-day English seems very different from its Old English ancestor; yet evidence of the continuity is plentiful, if we know where (and how) to look for it.

In spite of the apparent differences, many of the Old English words have recognizable modern counterparts: notice *cōm* (came), *hē* (he), *brohton* (brought), *on*, *hym* (him), *and*, *bedde*.[1] *Scyp* was almost certainly pronounced nearly as at present ([ʃɪp]), with perhaps minor differences in the pronunciation of the vowel; *oferseglode* looks unrecognizable until seen as a compound of *ofer* (*over*) ('f' medially was pronounced [v]), and *segl* (*sail*, via loss of [g]). *Ceastre* (pronounced [tʃɛəstr̩]) appears in modern place-names such as Chester, Winchester.

Gradual change

Sound changes are gradual: the time scale for significant changes is usually measured in hundreds of years, rather than decades. The English spoken in the 1930s, which we can still listen to from newsreels of the period, sounds 'old-fashioned', but the changes are in details only, such as the quality of particular vowels. For two stages of 'the same' language to resemble different languages requires a much longer period: Greeks today study the Classical Greek of the fifth century BC as if it were a foreign language, just as English speakers need assistance in reading Chaucer (fourteenth century) and Old English. But a period of two or even three hundred years may produce only relatively minor changes in a language, given a reasonable climate of social and cultural stability.

Predictable change

Sound changes, then, occur gradually. And they are predictable; not in the sense that we can predict what changes will take place in the future, and when, but in the sense that from our experience of many changes in many different languages, the same *types* of changes, and the same general *direction* of change, recur constantly, in different places and at different times. The change whereby [s] is replaced by [h], for example, and [h] is lost (notation, [s] → [h], [h] → ø) are well-known changes: they happened in the Indo-European languages (cf. Latin *septem*, *super*, Ancient Greek *hepta*, *hyper*, Modern Greek *efta*, *iper* 'seven', 'above'); they happened in the Polynesian languages (cf. Exercise 4, below); they are happening in some modern dialects of Spanish, for example Andalusian (Hooper 1976: 32; cf. also Lass 1976: 157ff.).

A change in the opposite direction, however, namely ø → [h], or [h] → [s] is quite unknown, and if it ever did occur, would be considered most unusual. Similarly, experience tells us that [k] frequently changes to [tʃ], while the reverse ([tʃ] → [k]) does not occur. Sound changes thus conform to certain expectations; we cannot always explain *why* they take the direction they do take, but we know approximately what those directions are. It is in this sense that sound change is 'predictable'.

Principles of sound change

Some of the principles governing sound change can be derived from the discussions of *markedness* and *language universals* (cf. especially Chapter 4, pp. 114ff.: also Chapter 3, p. 91 and Chapter 2, p. 59). Before discussing sound changes in detail, a summary of the predictable or expected patterns will be given, based on the conclusions reached earlier. For convenience, these processes can be classified according to the domains in which they operate, namely word structure; syllable structure; consonant clusters; consonantal segments; and vowel segments.

Word structure

Words are the largest unit within which sound changes are usually considered. Polysyllabic words consist of sequences of stressed and unstressed syllables, often in alternation. When changes occur, *unstressed* syllables of a word are more likely to be lost, or shortened, than stressed syllables. Hence:

> Principle 1   Unstressed syllables are more vulnerable than stressed syllables.

Syllable structure

Syllables have a structure consisting minimally of a vowel (or a syllabic consonant) preceded or followed (optionally) by one or more consonants. The universal syllable-types, found in all languages, are V and CV (cf. Chapter 4, p. 123). VC and CVC patterns, with a consonant *following* the vowel, are common but not universal, and are generally not as frequent (as V and CV) in any particular language (in some languages, such as Italian, Greek, Thai and Korean, the *range* of final consonants is much more restricted than the range of initial consonants). Consonants *before* a vowel are thus in a 'stronger' position than final consonants; the latter are more readily lost or changed in some way. Hence:

Principle 2   Final consonants in a syllable are more vulnerable than initial consonants.

Consonant clusters

Consonant clusters have been discussed in detail in Chapter 2. The consonants most likely to be changed, or lost, are those which are located *furthest from the peak of the syllable* (i.e. furthest from the vowel). Thus the *first* consonant of an initial cluster and the *last* C of a final cluster are most vulnerable. However, if the consonant next to the vowel is an approximant, it is the approximant which is most vulnerable.

Principle 3   In consonant clusters, approximants yield to an adjacent 'strong' consonant. But otherwise, *outer* consonants are more vulnerable than *inner*.

Consonant segments

Consonants are classified along three dimensions; voicing, place of articulation, and manner of articulation.

Voicing may be affected by the position of a consonant in the word or syllable. Voiceless sounds tend to be preferred in final position, while voiced sounds are preferred between vowels. Sound changes in which an intervocalic voiceless sound becomes voiced, and a final voiced sound becomes voiceless, are thus to be expected; the converse (for example, intervocalic voiced becoming voiceless) is much less probable.

In initial position, the preferred combination of features, for plosives at least, is [−voice] and [−aspirated], i.e. a sound midway between voiced and voiceless (cf. Chapter 4, pp. 120ff.). This is the sound normally acquired first by children. Hence:

Principle 4   *a* In final position, voiced sounds are more vulnerable than voiceless sounds;

           b intervocalically, voiceless sounds yield to voiced;

           c in initial position, voiceless unaspirated sounds take priority.

The voicing value of a consonant may also change through assimilation: a voiced consonant becomes voiceless when preceding another voiceless consonant, and vice versa. The assimilation is usually *regressive*, i.e. it is the second of the two sounds which influences (or dominates) the first.

Principle 5   In assimilations, the voicing value is determined by the second of the two consonants.

Place of articulation may likewise be affected by assimilation: a consonant can change its position under the influence of a neighbouring consonant. Again, regressive assimilation is the norm.

Principle 6   In assimilations of *place*, the first consonant yields to the second.

Changes may take place in small steps along the 'place' continuum, for example velars become palatal, or dentals become alveolar. But *labial* and *velar* sounds often behave as if related: a velar consonant may, for example, become a labial without passing through the intervening palatal, alveolar, etc. steps. The reasons for such a development, which seems unusual in articulatory terms, are primarily acoustic: labials and velars divide the oral cavity in ways which produce similar resonance properties. Jakobson's feature *grave*, and the *SPE* feature *coronal* which derives from it, provide a valuable means of describing the labial-velar link (cf. Chapter 3, p. 94).

Manner of articulation can be arranged into a hierarchy from strong (most consonant-like, sharpest constriction of the airstream) to weak (most vowel-like, least obstruction of the airstream) (cf. Chapter 2, pp. 65ff.). If a consonant is vulnerable to change, it often 'weakens' by one position along the hierarchy; thus plosives weaken to fricatives, fricatives weaken to glides; glides may become vowels. The opposite process, strengthening, is also found, and in this case the hierarchy operates in reverse. *Strengthening* usually occurs when a consonant is in syllable-initial position, and *weakening* when it is in medial or final position (see syllable-structure, above).

Principle 7   Manner-of-articulation changes are determined by the 'strength' hierarchy.

Vowel segments

Unstressed vowels, as mentioned, may reduce to [ə], losing their distinctive properties. Vowels with distinctive properties are some-times said to be *chromatic*, in contrast with the colourless, achromatic [ə] (Stampe 1972; Miller 1973). Vowel reduction is thus a loss of 'colour'.

Stressed vowels are distinguished in terms of five major properties, *height* (the 'vertical' dimension on the vowel chart), *length, rounding, advancement* (the 'horizontal', front-central-back dimension on the chart), and *glide* (monophthong vs diphthong). There are certain universal associations between these categories, namely, first, *front* vowels are more usually *unrounded*, and back vowels rounded. Second, rounding is normally associated with high and mid vowels, but to a much lesser extent with open vowels, which are generally unrounded (though open *back* vowels can be distinguished by rounding). Third, long vowels (but not short) are associated with *gliding*: a long vowel may acquire a glide and become a diphthong (this is a process known as 'breaking'), and a diphthong may lose its glide and become a long vowel ('smoothing'). The change can thus go in either direction. Similarly, narrow diphthongs may become wider, and wider ones narrower, but these are not contradictory changes: widening is usually achieved by making the first element more open, while *narrowing* results from lessening the glide of the second element. These contrary tendencies are difficult to formulate as principles, but the following principles can be based on *rounding*:

Principle 8   *a*   A vowel which becomes *front* will tend also to become [−round].
b   A vowel which becomes *back* will tend also to become [+round].

Sound changes and dialect

There is a straightforward relationship between sound changes and the dialect or accent differences of the sort discussed in the previous chapter. A sound change does not take place for all speakers of a language, simultaneously, in all possible words. It spreads gradually and by degrees; some speakers may adopt it fully, others may never adopt it at all. Dialect differences arise because of the uneven spread of a sound change. For example, in about the seventeenth century, Southern England speakers 'dropped' the [g] after a nasal, in words like *sing*, *thing*, *hang*, *long*, etc. This change did not spread to the Midlands, where [g] is still retained. The result is an accentual difference: the Midlands has [sɪŋg], etc., where RP and the South has [sɪŋ].

Sound changes and language acquisition

There is also a connection between sound changes, and the stages of development through which children pass as they acquire the sounds of their language. In this case the relationship is less direct. Phonologists have noted that the same types of process which occur in sound change, occur also in language acquisition. For example, it was noted earlier that a common sound change is

[s] → [h] and [h] → ø

It is also fairly common for language-delayed, and even normal children at a certain stage, to replace adult /s/ with [h], as in [hʌn, hi, hɪli] for 'sun', 'see', 'silly', [maʊh] 'mouse', [mehi] 'messy', etc. And 'h-dropping' (i.e. [h] → ø) is also a common developmental process, as well as being a common sound change.

There may, in some cases, be a causative relationship between a sound change and developmental processes, if, for instance, a delay in acquisition becomes permanent. If h-dropping, for example, persists into adulthood, and is adopted by a whole community, then a sound change has taken place, and an accent difference may have emerged (if a neighbouring community does not adopt the change). But this is only one way in which a sound change may originate. When similarities are noted between sound changes and acquisition processes, we may not want to say that one is the *cause* of the other, but simply, that both are illustrating certain general, perhaps universal, phonological processes, and thus contributing to our understanding of the way phonology 'works'. We assume, in other words, that it is not accidental that the changes which take place historically are the same as, or very similar to, the changes made by children as part of their learning.

Attrition and expansion

Many – perhaps most – sound changes bring about the 'wearing away' (attrition) of phonic substance: the *loss* of either features, or segments, or even of entire syllables. Unstressed syllables are deleted; vowels reduce to [ə] and may then be lost; long vowels are shortened; consonant clusters are simplified; plosives weaken to glides, which then become unstressed vowels, which are then lost; sequences of vowel plus nasal merge into nasalized vowel; and so on. All these processes 'reduce' the phonetic substance in a variety of ways: the history of a word is largely a history of its attrition. The Modern English words, for example, whose origins can be traced back to Old English, are almost invariably shorter, in terms of segments, than their OE equivalents:

OE word	OE segments[2]	Mod E word		Mod E segments[2]
sunnandæg	9	/sʌndɪ/	(Sunday)	5
hlāfordes	10	/lɔdz/	(lord's)	4
frogga	6	/frɒg/	(frog)	4
siŋgan	6	/sɪŋ/	(sing)	3
brōhte	7	/brɔt/	(brought)	5
eal swā	7	/æz/	(as)	2
hlāfdige	9	/leɪdɪ/	(lady)	5

Examples of the opposite trend (for example, OE gǣt, four segments; Mod E *goats*, five) are difficult to find, and do not involve a difference greater than one segment.

The same process of attrition is evident in other languages too. Comparing modern French words with their Latin sources, there are many examples such as (number of segments in brackets):

French			Latin		
vie	(2)	<	vita	(4)	('life')
cousin [kuzɛ̃]	(4)	<	consobrinum	(11)	'cousin'

temoin	[temwɛ̃]	(5)	<	testimonium	(11)	'witness'
ont	[ɔ̃]	(1)	<	habent	(6)	'(they) have'
froid	[frwa]	(4)	<	frigidum	(8)	'cold'
aout	[u]	(1)	<	augustum	(8)	'August'
cent	[sɑ̃]	(2)	<	centum	(6)	'hundred'
vingt	[vɛ̃]	(2)	<	viginti	(7)	'twenty'

Again, examples of the opposite tendency are infrequent, and the attrition which is so remarkable in French is not confined to that language, but found also (though not always so devastatingly) in the other Romance languages.

How is it then that, in spite of sound change consisting typically of attrition, the lexical items of Modern English are on average no shorter (taking the language as a whole, rather than just the words derived from OE) than the lexical items of OE? And how is it that all languages have not been reduced to a vocabulary of short monosyllables, given the inevitability of attrition and the length of time man has been speaking? The latter, more general question can perhaps be answered by the general principle that efficient communication depends, first, on the distinctiveness (from each other) of individual lexical items and, second, on the listener's ability to perceive the message despite 'noise' of various sorts. If words become too short, too many homophones (one form, two meanings, as in *list* 'to catalogue'; 'to incline (of ships)') arise; or there may be too little material for the hearer's needs, as in the following barely comprehensible (to the observer – in this case myself) exchange:

> A tɪnˈtin
> B tɪz

(A 'it isn't in'.   B 'it is')

Particular languages use various devices to maintain stability in the overall average length of words. The commonest processes contributing greater length to words are the so-called word-formation processes, of compounding, prefixation and suffixation. Many lexical items are formed by adding a prefix to an already-existing item:

> anti-nuclear
> sub-atomic
> de-register

Others are formed by adding suffixes:

> nation-al-ity
> migrat-ion
> terror-ist

Compounds are formed from two already-existing words, put together to give a new meaning: the true compound is a single unit, from a semantic point of view, i.e. in its meaning it is on a par with single-stem items:

> workshop   (cf. factory)
> shop steward   (cf. supervisor)
> closed shop   (cf. cartel)
> shoplifting   (cf. robbery)

Longer words may also be introduced into a language through borrowing from other languages. The scientific, technical and learned vocabulary of English (and of many other European languages) is based on a special kind of borrowing, namely the formation of words based on Latin and Greek roots:

> individual
> education
> economy
> productivity

Many short OE words were replaced, after the Norman conquest, by longer words 'borrowed' from French ('borrowed' in inverted commas, since the outcome of the process was more in the nature of a fusion of the two languages than of English 'borrowing' a few French words):

OE	*Anglo-French*
dōm (cf. 'doom')	judgement
gisl	hostage
hǣse (cf. 'behest')	command
wræc (cf. 'wrack')	avenge
fēond (cf. 'fiend')	enemy

Once a word has come into a language through borrowing, it then, of course, becomes subject to the same processes of sound change as any other word. These will include processes that 'wear away' the phonic substance (such as loss of unstressed syllables, as in *secretary*, *medicine*; or coalescence, as in [neɪʃn̩] from earlier [neɪsɪən], 'nation'). In the translations from Matthew quoted earlier, *paralysis* replaces *palsy*. But *palsy* and *paralysis* are the 'same' word: *palsy*, having been in the language longer, was 'worn away' by sound changes. *Paralysis* was re-formed, from the Ancient Greek stems *para-lysis*, in the sixteenth century. Once borrowed, a word is subject to the same changes as any other item in the language.

Splits and mergers

Sound changes can be divided into those which affect the phonemic system of the language and those which do not. Of the changes which affect the system, some lead to the creation of new phonemes, and others to the loss of old ones. The former is known as phonemic *splitting* (one phoneme splits into two), the latter as a *merger* of two (or more) previously separate phonemes.

Phoneme splitting has occurred many times during the history of English. Some examples will be given first, and then we consider the various stages which bring about the change.

1 /k/ and /tʃ/. The OE /k/ phoneme split into two separate phonemes, modern /k/ and /tʃ/. Thus alongside *cat*, *cool* and *cow* from the OE *catt*, *cōl* and *cū*, we have *choose*, *chin* and *chide* from OE *cēosan*, *cinn* and *cīdan*. Minimal pairs such as *kin–chin*, *kip–chip* and *care–chair* establish that Modern English has the two sounds as separate phonemes. In some of the Northern dialects the split did not always take place, as we can see from pairs of related words such as *church–kirk*, *birch–birk*, *beseech–seek*.
2 /n/ and /ŋ/. Until about the seventeenth century, [ŋ] was an allophone of /n/. In modern RP and many other dialects [ŋ] is now a phoneme, /ŋ/, as illustrated by minimal pairs like *sin–sing*, *run–rung* and *ban–bang*. But in some Midlands and Northern accents [ŋ] is still an allophone of /n/ because *sin–sing*, etc. are distinguished as [sɪn] vs [sɪŋg] – in the latter, final /g/ is still pronounced. In these dialects, [ŋ] is a pre-velar allophone of /n/, and the phonemic representation is thus /sɪn, sɪng/. (Our spelling of /ŋ/ reflects this.)

3 The centre-gliding diphthongs /iə, eə/ and /uə/ were originally allophones of /i, eɪ/ and /u/. That they are now separate phonemes is shown by minimal pairs such as *bee–beer*, *pay–pair* and *too–tour*. But in many accents in which postvocalic [r] is still pronounced (the rhotic accents), no phonemic split has occurred: the vowels of *beer* and *pair* are still allophones of /i, eɪ/.

4 /ʊ/ and /ʌ/. The vowels /ʊ/ and /ʌ/ were originally a single phoneme, /ʊ/. Minimal pairs such as *look–luck*, *book–buck* and *could–cud* establish their status as phonemes in many modern accents including RP, though in Northern accents they remain as a single phoneme for many speakers.

Phonemic splitting typically involves a number of separate stages: it does not occur suddenly. In the first stage, the single phoneme acquires allophones distinguished according to the phonetic environment. In the case of /k/, we have seen that it is quite normal for the velar to have a fronted, somewhat palatal variant when it precedes a front vowel such as /i, ɪ, e, eɪ/. This allophone, [k̟], may gradually become more fronted, until it becomes a palatal plosive, [c]. At that point it begins to sound rather like [tʃ], particularly because palatal plosives usually acquire a fricative off-glide, [ç], by way of transition as the closure is released (i.e. the plosive becomes an affricate, [cç]). The stages so far, then, are phonetically [k] → [k̟] → [c] → [cç]. Notice that [cç] and [tʃ] are very similar acoustically; and the articulatory step from [cç] to [tʃ] is a small one, involving the spreading of the tongue-contact.

By this stage, the /k/ phoneme has diverged into two rather distinct allophones but the relationship between them is still that of allophones of a single phoneme. The change in phonemic status is not brought about until we also have words in which front vowels are preceded by an ordinary, unfronted [k]. This comes about because of changes elsewhere. In Old English, /k/ was followed by the front rounded vowels [y, ȳ, ø and ø̄], which originally derived from the corresponding back vowels [u, ū, o and ō]. While the change from [k̟] to [cç] was taking place, these front *rounded* vowels were still treated as back vowels and therefore did not affect the quality of [k]. But afterwards, the front rounded vowels became unrounded, to [i, ī, e and ē]. This was the critical stage which introduced words with [k] before a front vowel. These vowel changes can be illustrated as follows:

	OE	*cyning* ('king')	*cēlan* ('to cool')	*cȳ* ('cows' – cf. kine)
Back vowel origin		kuning	koljan	kū
Fronting		kyning	køl(j)an	kȳ
Unrounding		kining	kēl(j)an	kī

By the last stage, [k] is now followed by a front vowel, and this becomes phonemically distinct from the [cç] which had resulted from earlier [k] before front vowels. It is likely indeed that the unrounding of [y, ø], etc. 'encouraged' the final step from [cç] to [ʧ], since languages often tend to maximize the 'distance' between two phonemes in order to emphasize their distinctiveness (Martinet 1952; Strang 1970). This process is known as polarization (Samuels 1972: 39).

Later changes have resulted in the k/ʧ split becoming even more firmly established. Originally the new phoneme /ʧ/ occurred only before front vowels, but it is now found before back vowels too, as in *choose, choice* and *chore*. Extension of the distribution of a phoneme can come about through further vowel changes, or from borrowings from other languages, such as *chocolate* (from Aztec *chocolatl*) which provides English with an instance of /ʧ/ before a back vowel.

The splitting of /n/ into /n/ and /ŋ/ also took place in stages. In the first place, [ŋ] was the allophone of /n/ which preceded velars, and since words like *sing, ring* and *hang* were pronounced with a final [g] as [siŋg], etc., [ŋ] was at this stage only an allophone. Phonemic status was achieved when speakers 'dropped' the final [g], a step which had a precedent in loss of final [b] in words like *comb* and *lamb*. Dropping of [g] was made easier by the fact that words like *sing* and *rung* were doubly distinct from *sin* and *run*: through the presence of [g], and the distinctive allophone [ŋ]. Loss of [g] therefore did not result in any new homophones: *sing* remained (and remains) distinct from *sin*.

This phenomenon whereby a change is *facilitated* by a double signalling of a distinction can also be seen in the origin of the phonemes /iə, eə, uə/. These phonemes arose through the deletion of postvocalic r, but the deletion itself was facilitated because the preceding vowels /i, eı, u/ already had quite distinct pre-r allophones. The changes proceeded in the following way:

1   At first, words like *beer, beard* and *pair* were distinguished from *bee, bead* and *pay* only by the presence of /r/: thus

[biːr, biːrd, peır]
vs [biː, biːd, peı]

2   The vowels /i, eɪ/ developed centring allophones, [iə, eə], before /r/. This was a natural development, since [r] has many of the properties of a central vowel: the allophones thus arose as an instance of co-articulation.

3   *beer*, etc. are now distinct from *bee*, etc. in two ways; the presence of [r], and the allophones [iə], etc. Loss of [r] is thus possible without *beer*, etc. becoming homophonous with *bee*, etc.

To summarize, we can see that the process of phonemic splitting proceeds in stages. First, allophones of the phoneme arise: second, their presence may in turn trigger a further change, as in the case of *a* the recent postvocalic [r] loss; and *b* g-dropping; alternatively, a change occurs somewhere else, bringing new contrasts along, as in the case of k/ʧ. The result, in both cases, is that the allophonic difference changes its status and becomes phonemic. As a third stage, the distinction between the two sounds may be enhanced by further (polarizing) changes, such as [cç] → [ʧ], which serve to maximize the distance between the two phonemes.

Phonemic mergers can be seen as the opposite of phonemic splitting. Where splitting creates two phonemes out of one, merging makes one phoneme out of two. Mergers are mainly confined to vowel phonemes, and in the history of English they are quite common, perhaps because English has so many vowel phonemes that some rationalization is always desirable.

Two mergers can be seen in the recent history of English: the loss of a contrast between /ɔ/ and /ɔə/; and the similar falling together of /uə/ and /ɔ/. /ɔ, ɔə/ used to distinguish pairs such as *war–wore*, *law–lore* and *paw–pour*. Over the past century /ɔə/ has gradually monophthongized to /ɔː/ , a very 'natural' change since the movement of the diphthong, from mid back to mid central, with slight loss of rounding, was minimal. The merging of /uə/ with /ɔ/ (*poor–pour*), is a similar process; [uə] has been 'smoothed' to [ʊə], and the glide of the diphthong is then minimal, allowing it to fall in with a monophthong, [ɔː], whose vowel quality is very similar to it. The merger is one which is still not complete; some speakers still distinguish *boor* from *bore*, *dour* from *door* and *tour* from *tore*, though for many, these words are homophones. (The less common words, like *boor* and *dour*, seem to be the most resistant to change, while the commoner words, like *poor*, *moor*, have accepted it.)

An even more remarkable merger took place about 300 years ago; the words now spelt '-ea-', and pronounced with /i/ (*meat, bead, sea*, *read*, etc.) as well as many others, fell in with the words now spelt '-ee-', as in *keep, meet, been, see, reed*, etc. As part of the earlier Great Vowel Shift, the '-ee-' words had undergone a vowel raising, from [eː] to [iː], and '-ea-' words likewise were raised from [ɛː] to [eː]. The merger then was of /eː/ (the '-ea-' words) and /iː/ (the '-ee-' words). It is an unusual merger for two reasons: first, because it merged two vowels, high front /iː/ and mid front /eː/, which normally succeed in remaining clearly distinct (other mergers, for example of the mid vowels /eː/ with /ɛː/, or of /oː/ with /ɔː/, are much more common); and second, because of the large number of homophones (*read–reed, seam–seem*, etc.) which resulted. It is often argued that the reason certain changes are 'allowed' to happen in a language is because few homophones are created; and conversely, that avoidance of homophones 'prevents' certain changes from taking place: languages maintain an optimum level of 'efficiency' (cf. Martinet 1955; Bynon 1977: 87ff.). The -ee-/-ea- merger constitutes a major exception to this principle. A possible explanation is that the merger occurred at a time when the whole vowel system of English was in a state of flux, following the Great Vowel Shift; and at a time when social conditions in England produced a mixing of different dialects on a scale previously unknown (cf. Samuels 1972: 92ff.).

The sound changes discussed so far involve a change in the phonemic system: new phonemes arise, old ones disappear. Many sound changes do not change the system as such, but alter the composition of the words affected. In what follows, we shall summarize the changes according to the classification suggested earlier in the chapter, namely in terms of *word-structure, syllable structure, consonant clusters, consonant segments*, etc. Some changes are not always easy to classify, since they could well be described under more than one heading.

Word-structure

Syllable loss

As a general principle of sound change, unstressed syllables tend to weaken or be lost. The weakest position is that of an unstressed vowel which either immediately follows a primary stress, or immediately precedes one. Syllable loss is evident in present-day English: words of three syllables, like *family, slackening, dangerous* frequently lose their medial, unstressed syllable in fast speech (on the 'rules' governing this behaviour, cf. Chapter 6). Many words which historically had three syllables, such as *every*, *Wednesday*, *business* (cf. *busy-ness*, from which it derives) now have only two syllables, even in careful speech. Similar changes are noted in other languages; French *table* derives from Latin *tabula*, and Italian *caldo* from *calidum*.

Syllable loss also occurs when the unstressed syllable is in initial position. Children's pronunciations such as *'nana* (banana), *'tend* (pretend), etc. are well known. Historically, we find examples such as *tawdry* (< *St Audrey*), *bishop* (cf. Greek *episkopos*) and *story* (ultimately from Greek *historia*, cf. *history*). Similar examples are found prolifically in Greek:

Modern Greek		Ancient Greek	
ðondi	<	odont-	'tooth'
mati	<	ommation	'eye'
roloï	<	horologion	'watch'
θelo	<	ethelo	'I want'
vjeno	<	ekbaino	'I go out'
ðo	<	eido	'I (shall) see'

In the history of English, however, the greatest effect of syllable loss was the disappearance of unstressed *final* syllables:

Mod E		OE
sun	<	sunne
soon	<	sōna
days	<	dæges
stones	<	stānas
head	<	hēafod
hide	<	hȳdan

Loss of unstressed syllables may lead to further changes. *Ant* and *hemp* derive from OE *'æmete* and *'henep* respectively. Once the unstressed syllables were lost, the pressure for the nasal to assimilate to the following consonant was irresistible: so *æmete > æmət > æmt > ænt*, and *henep > henp > hemp*.

Epenthesis

Unstressed syllable loss is relatively common; the opposite process, in which a vowel is *added* is, however, known to occur, though rather infrequently. A vowel may be *inserted* (the process is called *epenthesis*) to break up an otherwise awkward cluster. In popular speech an [ə] vowel is inserted into the words *film*, *kiln* and *athletic*, to break up the unfamiliar sequences /–lm, –ln/, and /–θl–/. *Sclerosis* likewise becomes /skeləroʊsɪs/, and *Henry*, /henəri/. Historically, *thorough* and *borough* acquired their second syllables by epenthesis (< OE *θurh, burh*); they are related to *through* and *-burgh* (cf. German *burg*) respectively.

Syllable structure

The existence of a universal syllable-type, CV, means that iṅ sound change syllable-*initial* consonants are favoured (i.e. preserved or even strengthened) whereas syllable-final consonants may be subject to loss or weakening. It is remarkable how well-preserved initial consonants can be, sometimes over thousands of years, and particularly if they occur in stressed syllables. Many Old English words come into Modern English with their initial consonants unchanged: *ribb > rib*, *pott > pot*, *seofon > seven*, *fæst > fast*, *dæg > day*, etc. The only exceptions are /h/, which is lost in most modern dialects, though not in RP, and some allophones of /g/ (see below, p. 268). Initial consonants, indeed, are often preserved across many Indo-European languages, and help to establish the relationship between these languages: for a single example, compare English *brother* with German *Bruder*, Latin *frater*, Greek *pʰrater*, Russian *brat*, Irish *brathir* and Sanskrit *bhrātar*.

In syllable-final position it is a different story. Once again, it is the sonorant consonants which are the most vulnerable, particularly the approximants. In the recent history of English we see the loss of postvocalic r in the non-rhotic accents, yielding pronunciations such as /fɔ/ (*four*) and /stɑ/ (*star*). This development brought about widespread changes in the vowel system (see below, p. 268). Syllable-final /l/ is developing in the same direction, though the changes have not yet been so far-reaching: under a process known as *vocalization*, [ɫ] has become, in some dialects such as London, a back vowel, similar in quality to [ɒ], and is thus being incorporated into the vowel system (cf. Chapter 8, p. 250). The glides /j, w/ occurred finally in Middle English (as in *grow, day*), but they too vocalized (to [ɒ] and [i]) and became part of the vowel system (cf. [groɒ, deɪ]).

When *nasals* follow a vowel, the tendency is for the sequence vowel plus nasal to coalesce into a single segment, namely a nasal vowel.

This has not happened to a great extent in English, but is responsible for all the nasal vowels in French, as in *cent* [sã] < Latin *centum*, *quand* [kã]<Latin *quando*, etc. Where the nasal was not syllable-final, it was protected; compare masculine *bon*, [bɔ̃], with feminine *bonne* [bɔnə] ('good'); in the feminine form, the nasal has been protected by the [ə] vowel which, until recently, followed it. Notice that the nasal consonant does not disappear without trace; it transfers its critical feature, nasality, to the preceding vowel, so that the chief features are now carried in one segment instead of two (cf. Chapter 5, p. 146).

Compensatory lengthening

Another way in which nasals leave traces of themselves, before 'disappearing', is in vowel length. *Tooth* and *goose* derive, via OE *tōð* and *gōs*, from earlier forms [tonð] and [gans]; related words in other languages (Latin *dent-, anser*, German *zahn*, *gans*, cf. also English *gander*) still retain the nasal, but the vowels are short. When the /n/ of [tonð] and [gans] was lost, the vowels lengthened in compensation. Try pronouncing [tonð] with heavy nasalization of the vowel; you will hear that it resembles [toːð].

Compensatory vowel lengthening also accompanied (or rather it usually preceded, and perhaps facilitated) loss of English postvocalic r. The vowels of *bird*, *stir*, *word*, *star*, *born*, etc. are all long vowels, though originally they were short.

One way in which syllable-final consonants disappear, then, is by leaving traces of themselves in the preceding vowel, either by *lengthening* a short vowel or by adding the feature [nasal] to it.

Syllable-final obstruents are more resistant to loss, as the general consonant hierarchy (Principle 7, above) would suggest. Even so, losses do occur, as for instance with English /g/ and the velar fricative /x/. /g/ became a fricative, which was velar after back vowels, as in *plōg* 'plough' and *burg* 'city, borough', and palatal after front vowels, as in *bodig* 'body', *dæg* 'day' and *sægde* 'said'. The velar fricative later weakened further to the back glide [w], while the palatal fricative weakened to [j]. These glides then became part of a diphthong, as reflected in our spellings of *day*, *said*, etc. In unstressed syllables, /g/ disappeared altogether (*body* < bodig, *holy* < hālig).

Old English also had a voiceless fricative /h/, which we assume was velar after back vowels and palatal after front vowels.[3] Being spelt 'h', it was probably an allophone of initial [h]. From Middle English times onwards, it has been spelt -gh-. It occurred finally, and before /t/, as in:

| (velar) | rūh | 'rough' | brōhte | 'brought' |
| (palatal) | hēh | 'high' | riht | 'right' |

In Middle English, the palatal fricative weakened, and disappeared in words like *high* and *thigh*; where a /–t/ followed, as in *right*, *night*, *light*, its loss was compensated by vowel lengthening. The velar fricative also weakened and became a diphthongal glide (just as happened to /g/), as in *taught*, *bought*, *drought*, *dough*. But in some words it underwent a most unusual development: it became [f], and caused a preceding long vowel to shorten, giving present-day *rough*, *enough*, *cough*, *trough*, etc. with /f/ and a short vowel.[4] The change of [x] to [f] is very difficult to explain in articulatory terms, since it involves a leap from velar to labial without an intervening alveolar stage. In perceptual terms, however, it is but a short step, since acoustically the two 'grave' (non-coronal) fricatives [x, f] have very similar properties. The feature grave, which links labials with velars, proves its usefulness in being able to describe a change of this sort (cf. Chapter 3, p. 94).

Consonant clusters

Clusters in Modern English have the shapes (C)CCV and VCC(C) (C). Since the preferred syllable structure is CV we can expect sound changes to proceed in the direction of *simplification* (reduction) of clusters, and as we have seen, the reduction will predictably follow certain principles. If the C adjacent to the V (on either side) is an approximant, it will be more vulnerable than the outer C; but in all other cases, it is the outer C (further from the vowel) which is more vulnerable than the inner C.

The history of English affords many examples of cluster reduction. One well-known type is the loss of a consonant from clusters which arise through compounding. Since English permits both initial and final clusters, and favours compounding as a word-formation process, we can expect the formation of some rather dense clusters, which will then be subject to reduction. Well-known examples of this are *gospel* from *godspell* (the compound god+spell), *gossip* from *godsibb*, *answer* from *and+swarien*, and /hæŋkə(r)tʃif/ from *hand+kerchief*.

Initial clusters have also undergone reduction in certain cases. Look at the following data:

Mod E		OE
laugh	<	hlæhhan
leap	<	hlēapan
loaf	<	hlāf
raven	<	hræfn
ring	<	hring
ridge	<	hrycg
wheel	<	hwēol
which	<	hwilc
whisper	<	hwisprian
nut	<	hnutu
nit	<	hnitu
neigh	<	hnǣgan

The OE clusters /hl–, hr–/ and /hn–/ have been reduced to /l, r/ and /n/ respectively. /hw–/ is now /w–/ for many speakers, though some, particularly in Scotland, retain /hw–/. The inherent weakness of /h/ is again demonstrated by its loss from syllable-initial position, in most non-standard dialects of English, which is a unique event for a syllable-initial single consonant.

Loss of /j/ (Wells (1982: 206) calls it *Yod-dropping*) from a cluster has occurred in quite a large number of words, and the process is still in evidence in the present century: in British English /j/ has all but disappeared from /lj–/ clusters, as in *lute, lurid,* and is rapidly being lost after other alveolars, for example *suit, assume, presume*. In American English, /j/ is lost after *all* alveolars, including /t, d, n/ as in *tune, duke, new*.

Final consonant clusters have suffered heavier casualties than initial clusters, as might be expected from their post-peak position (Principle 2, above). Many of the losses have already been mentioned, and are clearly evident in English from the spelling, which usually reflects the older pronunciation. Note the loss of /r/ in *word, heard, farm*, etc., and the loss of the other liquid, /l/, in *calm, half, talk, should*, etc.

When the final cluster contains a nasal, we expect the outer consonant to be lost rather than the inner. The losses which have occurred are again indicated in the spelling:

> comb, climb, dumb
> king, long, stung

These losses confirm a number of expectations: first, it is only the *non-coronal* sounds which have disappeared (we still preserve the clusters in *pint, want, find, pound, inch, plunge*); second, the *voiced* sounds have fared worse than the voiceless (we still have the clusters in *bump, hemp, sink* and *bank*); and third, as mentioned, the *inner* consonant (the nasal) is retained and the outer is lost.

Loss of outer consonants in present-day casual speech can be readily observed, as in:

> [lɑs wik]   'last week'
> [neks deɪ] 'next day', etc. (cf. Chapter 6, p. 171)

Consonant segments

Changes in consonant segments, other than syllable-final consonants which have already been discussed under 'syllable structure', can be conveniently divided into changes of *voicing*, *place* (locus) and *manner*.

Voicing

Voicing changes have not affected English in any significant way, as they have, for example, German, where all syllable-final voiced sounds have now become voiceless (at least in standard German). It is, however, possible that there may be significant changes in the future, since the voicing contrast is now being realized not so much by properties of the consonants themselves, but by their effect on neighbouring vowels. In final position, the voicing contrast is achieved largely by vowel length; vowels are shorter before voiceless sounds, and longer before voiced ones. Thus in *bad* and *leave*, [d] and [v] may have little or no voicing (i.e. the vocal cords are not vibrating); the consonantal segments themselves resemble the [t] and [f] of *bat* and *leaf*. So far, this is only a *phonetic* change, not a phonological one, because the distinction between *bat–bad, leaf–leave*, etc., is maintained by the vowel length.

A voicing change known as (intervocalic) *t-flapping* is current in many accents of English. Between vowels, /t/ comes to be pronounced as a voiced alveolar tap, [ɾ]. The change is particularly favoured when the preceding vowel is stressed and the following vowel unstressed, and it may cross a word boundary, for example:

putting	university
getting	political
get it	British
put 'em	what'll (happen)
let 'er	bitter

Place
Place of articulation usually changes as a result of an *assimilation*. Velar sounds become palatalized (and may eventually become palatal or palato-alveolar, as with [k → ʧ]) before front vowels: examples of [k] and the fricative [x] being affected in this way have already been mentioned. Nasals are particularly prone to assimilate to a following consonant: an *umpire* was originally a *non-per* and *comfort* derives from *con-fort*. The Latin prefix 'in-' had assimilated even before it was borrowed into English, giving us *im-possible*, *im-moral*, *il-legal*. Today we assimilate nasals, in casual speech, both within and across word boundaries, as with *incorrect* and *in case* ([ɪŋk–] for both).

A different type of assimilation is found when two sounds coalesce into a single sound, while still preserving features of both. The best-known are the sequences /tj–/ and /dj–/, which coalesce to [ʧ–] and [ʤ–], and /sj–/ and /zj–/ which merge into [ʃ–] and [ʒ–]. These changes have been discussed in detail in Chapter 6 (p. 187ff.). In all cases the changes are in line with the general principle whereby approximants are more vulnerable than an adjacent 'stronger' consonant.

While discussing assimilation we should mention that vowels, too, may change their quality by assimilation, either 1 towards other vowels as in the case of OE *mutation* (or *umlaut* as it is often known), where the back vowels, [ū, ō] were fronted to [ȳ, ø̄] when a front vowel followed, as in mūsi → mȳs(i), 'mice', and fōti → fø̄t(i), 'feet', or 2 towards consonants: in OE, mutation was also triggered by a following [j], as in fōdjan 'to feed', which became fø̄d(j)an (later fēdan). Another prominent example of vowel assimilation is in words like *want*, *was*, *watch* and *wander* which originally, as the spelling suggests, had [ɑ], which was then rounded to [ɒ] because of the roundedness of the preceding [w]. A contemporary manifestation of the same change is evident in New Zealand English, where *women* is homophonous with *woman*: both are pronounced ['womən]. This comes about because the /ɪ/ of 'women' is normally realized as a central vowel, [ɨ], in that accent, and the preceding [w] then rounds this to [o].

Exercise 1

Compare the following Modern English words with their OE equivalents:

1   What changes have taken place in each word?
2   Does each change follow the expected pattern?

Mod E	OE
ladder	hlǣdre
nail	nægel
heart	heorte
light	lēoht
eye	ēage
each	ælc
head	hēafod

Exercise 2

The following Spanish words are derived from their Latin equivalents. What sound changes do they illustrate?

Spanish	Latin	
caer	cadere	'fall'
mudar	mutare	'change'
diestro	dexterum	'skilful'
pan	panem	'bread'
siete	septem	'seven'
agua	aqua	'water'
voz	vox	'voice'
veo	video	'I see'

Exercise 3

The following Spanish words are given in 1 their modern pronunciation, 2 their usual spelling (reflecting an earlier pronunciation), 3 their Latin origin. What happened to Latin /f/ in Spanish?

Sp. pron.	Sp. spelling	Latin	
[iho]	hijo	filium	'son'
[asienda]	hacienda	faciendum	'property' lit. 'makings'
[ermosa]	hermosa	formosa	'beautiful'
[arina]	harina	farina	'flour'
[umo]	humo	fumus	'smoke'
[erir]	herir	ferire	'strike'

Exercise 4

The following are related words in various different (but related) Polynesian languages. What typical phonological relationships (including sound changes) do they exemplify? For example:

1   *fili : firi*   shows the interchange of the liquids [l, r].
2   *hala : ala*   shows h-dropping (a typical sound change).

	Ton.	Sam.	Mao.	Eas.	Haw.	Fij.
'spirit'	mana	mana	mana	mana	mana	mana
'yam'	ʔufi	ufi	ufi	uhi	uhi	uvi
'plait'	fii	fili	firi	hiri	hili	viri
'seven'	fitu	fitu	fitu	hitu	hiku	vitu
'tooth'	nifo	nifo	niho	niho	niho	–
'nipple'	huhu	susu	uu	uʔu	uu	suθu
'road'	hala	ala	ara	ara	ala	sala
'sandalwood'	ahi	asi	–	–	ahi	yasi
'food'	kai	ʔai	kai	kai	ʔai	–
'fish'	ika	iʔa	ika	ika	iʔa	ika
'bitter'	kava	ʔava	kawa	kava	ʔawa	–
'bat'	peka	peʔa	pekapeka	–	peʔa	beka
'canoe'	vaka	vaʔa	waka	vaka	waʔa	waŋga
'laugh'	kata	ʔata	kata	kata	ʔaka	–
'mouth'	ŋutu	ŋutu	ŋutu	ŋutu	nuku	ŋusu
'cry'	taŋi	taŋi	taŋi	taŋi	kani	taŋi

Note: Ton. = Tongan; Sam. = Samoan; Mao. = Maori; Eas. = Easter Island; Haw. = Hawaii; Fij. = Fijian.

Exercise 5

The word *discover* derives ultimately from a late-Latin form *dis-cooperire*. In French it is *découvrir*, Italian *scoprire*, Spanish *descubrir*. What typical sound changes do these developments reveal?

Exercise 6

The Italian words below are given alongside their Latin source. Describe the changes which have taken place.
Note: double consonants in Italian are pronounced long, for example -dd-, [dː]. Some other pronunciation details are noted in the data itself.

Italian	*Latin*	*Gloss.*
fare	facere	'make'
pore	ponere	'put'
dire	dicere	'say'
posto	positum	'position'
aprire	aperire	'open'
freddo	frigidum	'cold'
scrissi	scripsi	'I wrote'
scritto	scriptum	'written'
detto	dictum	'word'
io	ego	'I'
e	est	'is'
scindere ([ʃ])	discindere ([–sk–])	'split'
spiacere ([spj–])	displacere	'displease'
fiore ([fj–])	florem	'flower'
chiesa ([kj–])	ecclesia	'church'
piu ([pj–])	plus	'more'

10 Acquisition, normal and delayed

The vast majority of children learn their mother tongue gradually and progressively and unproblematically. By the age of about $4\frac{1}{2}$ the language patterns, including the phonological systems and structures, have become firmly established. Considering the complexity of language, the period of normal acquisition is remarkably short. But for a small minority, language does not develop normally: speech may be delayed or retarded, pronunciations do not approximate the adult norm. As we have seen in previous chapters, patterns of pronunciation may vary greatly according to accent, style, tempo, age of speaker, etc.; nevertheless, we can distinguish 'normal' variation of this kind from 'deviant' pronunciations; even the phonetically-untrained person is often able to recognize the latter as being 'unusual' or 'aberrant'.

Children are not the only ones who may have phonological disorders. Adults, too, may show 'loss' of language, including phonological impairment, for example after a stroke, or on suffering brain damage as the result of an accident. 'Clinical phonology', which is one of the main topics of this chapter, is thus concerned with the 'errors' of both children and adults, though there is usually greater emphasis on children, partly because they constitute the majority of patients, and partly because comparisons with normal patterns of acquisition are possible.

Clinical phonology has made important contributions to the study of phonology as a whole; as with many disciplines concerned with human mental functioning, our understanding is increased by observing what happens when things 'go wrong'; the normal can only be fully understood by including a study of the abnormal. But the benefits are two-way: the insights gained from studying general phonology have proved valuable in application for speech therapists, whose job it is to assess, diagnose and treat the patients for whom language has 'gone wrong'. During the past fifteen years in particular, clinical methods have benefited from phonological studies: from the realization that errors of pronunciation cannot be treated as isolated single sounds to be corrected one by one, but that sounds are structured, patterned and systematic, and that treatment has to be based on the *system*.

Adult targets and developmental norms

The patterns of phonological disorder in children lend themselves to two kinds of comparison: we may compare first, the child's pronunciation with the adult norm, the 'target' pronunciation. Suppose, for example, that a child aged 5 years 6 months pronounces *glove* as [gʌf] and *spoon* as [bun], a comparison of the child's with the target pronunciation reveals that the initial clusters /gl–/ and /sp–/ have been simplified to [g–] and [b–], and final /v/ has been devoiced to [f]. Further data may confirm that /gl–/ → [g], /sp–/ → [b] and /–v/ → [–f] are typical substitutions for this child.

But this comparison is not in itself sufficient; what we also require is a comparison with the developmental stages of normal children. The questions we ask are: is it *normal* for children, during the stages of language acquisition, to simplify initial clusters and devoice final consonants? And if it is, up to what age does this usually happen? The answer to the latter would then give us some indication of how far our child's development lags behind the norm. Since most children's phonological disorders involve 'delay' of this kind, there is a very strong link between clinical phonology and normal language development. The same types of process which characterize language acquisition, such as cluster simplification and final devoicing, are typical also of phonological disorders.

Articulation tests

A child's phonological abilities (and disabilities) are usually assessed by means of an articulation test, such as Fisher and Logemann (1971), Goldman and Fristoe (1969), or, best known in Britain, the Edinburgh Articulation Test (EAT) (Anthony *et al* 1971). Articulation tests elicit the pronunciation of a list of words by means of pictures (with younger children up to $3\frac{1}{2}$ years, objects may be used rather than pictures). The pictures are chosen so as to represent as comprehensive a range of sounds as possible. Ideally, one would like a test which included every phoneme of the language in every possible position of structure (initial, final, etc.) and (for consonants) in every possible combination. In practice, this would make the test impossibly large, so a sampling must be made. The authors of the EAT found that, generally speaking, similar structures pass through similar stages of development, and therefore one or two examples can serve as representatives of the whole range. For example, of the six English clusters consisting of plosive + r(/pr–, br–, tr–, dr–, kr–, gr–/) it was considered sufficient to include one at each place of articulation, and at least one voiced and one voiceless. /br–, tr– and kr–/ were thus chosen to represent the complete pattern.

By sampling the total range of sound-patterns in this way, the EAT succeeds in being comprehensive yet has only forty-one test items (in comparison with over 100 for some of the other tests).[1] More than one sound may be tested in each item; *milk*, for example, tests both initial /m/ and the final cluster /–lk/. There are sixty-eight phonological items in the test; for a quantitative result, the items are scored right or wrong, and the child's percentage of errors can then be compared with standardized norms. Most articulation tests work on this basis; usually the child is given an 'articulation age' on the basis of his standardized score, and the scores are also used to select the children to be referred for therapy.[2]

One major problem which arises with articulation tests is the question of scoring. If items are scored only 'right' or 'wrong', 'right' can only be the achievement of the target and anything else is 'wrong'. There are two problems here; one is that the adult target may itself be subject to variation, and the other is that a 'wrong' response may be only marginally different from the target, or it may be vastly different and untypical, with all possible degrees between these extremes. There are many kinds of 'wrongness' and some kind of *qualitative* assessment is thus essential. Most articulation tests thus aim to provide qualitative, as well as quantitative, measurement.

Target variation

With regard to the first problem (variability of the target), consider the following:

Which of these responses to the /–ns–/ sequence in *pencil* would be judged 'wrong'?

1	[penʔsl̩]	4	[penʔtsl̩]
2	[pensl̩]	5	[penθl̩]
3	[pentl̩]	6	[pẽhl̩]

The authors of the EAT agreed that on the basis of their observations, [penʔsl] and [penʔtsl] (as well as [pensl], of course) should be counted as 'correct' responses while the rest are 'wrong'. All the variant 'correct' forms fall within the adult norms of variability. The important thing is, however, that a test must *state* what variation is permissible and what is not, so that there can be some reliability when the test is administered by others.

Qualitative assessment

The second problem, that of degrees of 'wrongness', can also be illustrated from the above example. From our knowledge of the typical development of sounds in language acquisition, we can classify errors on a scale from 'almost mature', via 'immature' and 'very immature', to 'atypical'. On this scale, the pronunciations [–nʂ̩–, –nʂ–] and [–nʂ–] in *pencil* are regarded as 'almost mature': we know that these constitute the last stage before the child's pronunciation reaches the adult target. At an earlier stage, pronunciations such as [–nθ–] and [–nç–] are encountered, and earlier still, [–nɬ–]; these are categorized as 'immature'. [–nt–] and [–nh–] are 'very immature', while [–θ–] and [–h–] are 'atypical'. This latter category includes pronunciations which are not 'normally' found at any stage of development, but which may occur exceptionally. With these categories, the EAT succeeds in providing a qualitative analysis based on a comparison with normal development, in addition to a purely quantitative (right/wrong) assessment. The errors are not just errors but are classified on the basis of development (from 'very immature' to 'almost mature'). The success of such a classification depends, clearly, on the extent of our knowledge of what pronunciations are to be found at each stage, and of the 'developmental history' of particular sounds, such as the /–ns–/ sequence above.

In the EAT format, the qualitative scale is set out on a left-to-right basis; the target pronunciation appears on the left, followed by separate columns for the categories 'minor variations', 'almost mature', etc., through to 'atypical substitutions' on the extreme right. The left-to-right axis can then be used *within* each column for further refinements. As a second example (cf. *pencil* above), the substitutions for the /j/ of *yellow* are arranged as follows:

Adult form	Minor variations	Almost mature	Immature	Very immature	Atypical
j	zj		l ð h	ç ʤ d	p
	dj		r ʔ	ɣ	
			w		

On this basis, the substitutions [l, r, w] are regarded as 'immature', but are not as immature as [h, ʔ], which are in turn more advanced than [ç, ɣ].

Normal development

The qualitative information for each sound or sound-combination was compiled from the analysis of errors found in a sample of 510 normal children from Edinburgh, aged between 3.0 and 6.0, who were given the test. Broadly, it confirms what has been found in other studies of phonological acquisition, though the overall picture is by no means clear. A useful summary of phonological acquisition is given in Crystal (1981: ch. 2). We are not in a position to establish, for any particular language, a unique, fixed order in which sounds are acquired, in spite of Jakobson's claims about the universal nature of phonological development and the associated 'implicational hierarchy' of speech sounds.

There is, first, much variation between individuals in the order in which sounds appear. Second, the position in the word or syllable has to be taken into account, since a sound which appears in one position may not appear in other positions until some time later. At what stage, then, can we say that such a sound has been 'acquired'? Third, a target sound may appear sporadically and inconsistently, perhaps in one or two words or on one or two occasions, before it is achieved on a regular basis. This again makes it difficult to say exactly what stage constitutes 'acquisition'.

All statements about the order of acquisition of sounds must thus be treated with caution. Nevertheless, there does seem to be substantial agreement in certain areas, particularly when sounds are compared like with like. For example, it seems generally accepted that among the (English) approximants, /w/ is acquired first and /r/ last, and that in the transitional period, several different approximants may be substituted for the target, for example *red* may be pronounced [wed], [led] or [jed] before [ɹ] is finally achieved.

It seems to be generally agreed also that *plosives* and *nasals* are among the earliest language sounds to be mastered; fricatives come later, though it is common for children to have at least one fricative at quite early stages. The preferred places of articulation are *labial* and *alveolar*; putting together these 'place' and 'manner' preferences, we can establish that the earliest sounds are [p/b, t/d], and [m, n], i.e. labial and alveolar plosives and nasals. In the early stages, *voicing* is not distinguished: it is usual for plosives to be unaspirated and voiceless both initially and finally, namely, [b̥, d̥] – sounds which are intermediate between p/b and t/d (cf. Chapter 1, p. 44). In addition, [ʔ], the plosive which requires no *oral* occlusion, is also very common at the earliest stages: it may indeed claim to be the most 'basic', i.e. least 'marked', of all plosives (cf. Lass 1976: 151).

The earliest *fricatives* follow a similar pattern: labial /f/ and alveolar /s/ are the first to appear, preceded (or accompanied) only by the 'archetype' fricative which requires no oral occlusion, namely /h/. /s/ may develop towards its 'target' in stages, via [ç], then [ş] or [ʂ]. /f/, similarly, may pass through a bilabial ([ɸ]) stage. The fricatives /θ, ð/ are acquired late: they are among the last sounds to be achieved.

The preferred syllable structures in the early stages are CV and CVCV; this means that syllable-final consonants are at first omitted, though this stage is usually passed quite quickly, giving the child access to CVC structures, as well as to two-syllable structures of the shape CV(C) CV(C). The next stage is the acquisition of clusters such as CCV(C) and CVCC, but the latter is not reached until relatively late.

This necessarily brief survey of the order of acquisition of sounds and structures is a preliminary to the study of the processes which characterize phonological disorder. In most cases the processes involve, as we shall see (p. 286ff.), a *reversion* to an earlier stage in the normal developmental sequence.

Adult's system vs child's system

In recent years, the importance of the child's own developing phonological system (as against the adult or 'target' system) has been increasingly recognized. It often happens that a child may *seem* to have achieved the target system, but on further investigation we find that the sounds do not correspond to the normal system at all. The following data offers an example:

Carolyn, aged 3.6. *Question*: Has Carolyn acquired /p, b, t, d/?

top	[dɒp]	time	[daɪm]
bed	[bet]	knob	[nɒp]
pin	[bɪn]	hide	[haɪt]
bat	[bat]	sleep	[ɬip]

A cursory glance at this data suggests that Carolyn has acquired all the labial and alveolar plosives, i.e. /p, b/ and /t, d/. [p] occurs in *top* and *sleep*, [b] in *bed* and *bat*, etc. But a closer inspection shows us that this is not the case at all; the voiced sounds [b, d] occur only in *initial* position, and the voiceless ones only in *final* position. Instead of being phonemes, the voiced–voiceless pairs are, for Carolyn, allophones of a single phoneme; their distribution is complementary.

We are not justified, then, in assuming that just because a child can produce the sounds, his system is in one-to-one correspondence with the adult system. The first step in an assessment must always be to investigate the child's own system, looking to see how far it corresponds to the adult norm. This is done by making an inventory of the child's sounds for each position (initial, final) separately. This usually reveals what gaps occur, and gives some indication of possible cases of complementary distribution; we may then test these assumptions by looking for further data. The emphasis clinically, in both assessment and treatment, is on establishing the phonological *patterns* in the child's speech, rather than on teaching correct articulation of *individual* sounds.

Mismatch between the child's and the adult's systems may reveal itself in a further, rather unusual way. There are several cases quoted in the literature in which the following type of substitutions take place:

seat	[θit]	think	[fɪŋk]
sing	[θɪŋ]	through	[fru]
sorry	[θɒwi]	thank you	[faŋkju]
soon	[θun]	thin	[fɪn]

The child here is pronouncing /s/ as [θ], but /θ/ as [f]. Thus he shows that he is capable of pronouncing [θ], but only in words in which this sound corresponds to /s/. Smith's well-known example of A, who pronounced *puzzle* as [pʌdəl] but *puddle* as [pʌgəl], is similar; although A can pronounce [pʌdəl], he chooses not to use this as his realization of *puddle*, even though to do so would achieve the adult norm. Such phenomena can be seen as evidence of the importance of the child's own system, which in these instances is able to *maintain* a phonemic contrast (for example, between /s/ and /θ/) but does so in a way peculiar to the individual.

Production vs perception

A further important distinction, in developmental phonology, is between *production* (or *expression*) and *perception* (or *comprehension*). Some language-delayed children have deficits in both, but others have a deficit in one but not the other: production may be impaired more or less independently of perception, i.e. production problems are not necessarily accompanied by perception difficulties – though the converse is much less likely. Consider the following data, noting especially the production of the fricatives /f, s, θ, h/:

Catriona, aged 3.11

fish	[hɪʔ]	spoon	[b̥un]
stamps	[d̥amp]	horse	[hɔrʔ]
Christmas	[krɪʔməʔ]	feather	[hebr̩]
flower	[hlɑɔr̩]	elephant	[eləhənʔ]
finger	[hɪŋgr̩]	thumb	[hʌm]
three	[hri]	pencil	[penhl̩]

In production, Catriona is unable to distinguish between /f, θ, h/ and sometimes /s/; she pronounces them all as [h]. But it becomes clear from tests and observations that she has no difficulty in *perceiving* the differences between these sounds: she is simply unable to produce them herself. This typical mismatch between perception and production is sometimes referred to as the *fis* phenomenon, so named from a child studied by Berko and Brown (1960) who rejected an adult's pronunciation of *fish* as [fɪs], even though the child himself pronounced it that way: in correcting the adult, the child said something like: 'not [fɪs], [fɪs]!' The problem, as in Catriona's case, is not in the child's *knowledge* of the phonemic system of the language (she is well aware of the difference between /f, θ, s, h/), but in the adequate *production* of it.

Error analysis

Traditionally, clinical data has been analysed by comparing the child's production with the 'target' adult forms. The major categories of articulatory error included *omissions*, *distortions* and *substitutions* (with *insertion* and *transposition* as additional minor categories). While many clinicians have abandoned this method of error analysis in favour of a process-oriented approach (see below), others continue to use it (cf., for example, Van Riper and Irwin 1958: 77). An example will therefore be given to illustrate this method, with a discussion of some of its advantages and disadvantages. Look at the following data:

John (age 4.11)

[bɪk]	'big'	[gin]	'green'
[bɒp]	'Bob'	[maʊ́ʔ]	'mouth'
[boʊk]	'broke'	[ɒdi]	'noddy'
[geɪk]	'cake'	[beɪn]	'plane'
[du]	'chew'	[weʔ]	'red'
[gɒʔ]	'cross'	[dɜʔ]	'shirt'
[daʊn]	'down'	[dɒk]	'sock'
[dægə]	'dragon'	[bun]	'spoon'
[beɪt]	'face'	[deəʔ]	'stairs'
		[dɪt]	'this'
		[dɒwi]	'trolley'

This data shows that John is making the following types of error:

Omissions

A number of 'target' consonants are omitted, as follows:

/s/ in *spoon*, *stairs*
/r/ in *broke*, *green*
/l/ in *plane*
/n/ in *dragon*, *noddy* (but not in *green*, *spoon*)

Substitutions

Substitution of one consonant for another is one of the commonest types of error. John's data reveals the following substitutions: (the table also includes, for comparison, any *correct* pronunciations of target phonemes which are subject to substitution):

Target		Child	
/b/	→	[b]	(*big, Bob*)
		[p]	(*Bob*)
/s/	→	[t]	(*face*)
		[d]	(*sock*)
		[ʔ]	(*cross*)
/k/	→	[k]	(*sock*)
		[g]	(*cake*)
/g/	→	[k]	(*big*)
		[g]	(*green*)

The advantage of this type of error analysis is that it provides a comprehensive list of errors, and a classification into their respective categories (*omission*, etc.). The disadvantage, however, is that the essential patterns underlying the data fail to be revealed, and the categories themselves (*omission*, etc.) are too general to be of much use, either for assessment or as a guide to remediation. There is nothing to show, for example, that the *omissions* of /s, r, l/ in the data are all instances of *initial consonant cluster reduction*, whereas omission of /n/ in *dragon* is an instance of *final-consonant deletion* (in an unstressed syllable). Furthermore, the cluster reductions all follow the pattern we have come to expect on the basis of the general phonological principles outlined in earlier chapters, namely, the loss of *approximants* in favour of an adjacent 'stronger' consonant, and the loss of 'outer' consonants (in favour of 'inner' ones) otherwise. It is also important to note that John's cluster reductions follow the pattern expected of normal children during language development, but at an earlier age: persistence of these processes up to John's age (4.11) indicates language delay. The omission of /n/ in *dragon* is similarly part of an 'expected' pattern, but the omission of /n/ in *noddy* is not, involving, as it does, loss of an *initial* consonant in a *stressed* syllable. Such an omission (apart from /h/) is quite unusual and atypical, and would call for further investigation. Here again, an analysis simply in terms of 'omission' fails to reveal the important patterns underlying the data.

The *substitutions* in the data above can also benefit from a process-type of analysis. Before making it, however, the processes themselves will be outlined. These phonological processes follow much the same patterns as we have already come to expect, on the basis of language universals (Chapter 4), connected speech (Chapter 6), and historical change (Chapter 9). There are, however, some additional processes, and some new terminology. The same format of presentation as before (cf. Chapter 9: pp. 265ff.) will be adopted.

Word-structure

There are two major word-structure processes in clinical/developmental phonology. The first, unstressed-syllable deletion, is already familiar:

'tato	<	potato
'pellor	<	propellor
'morrow	<	tomorrow
[ɒbļ]	<	horrible

The second, *reduplication*, is a feature of both normal and clinical child language, particularly at the *early* stages. Reduplication typically produces a two-syllable structure, of the pattern:

'CVCV

with stress on the first syllable. The second vowel is usually identical to the first, though it may 'weaken' to [ɪ] or [ə]. The consonants are often, but not always, identical. Examples:

[dada]	'daddy'	[sɒsɷ]	'sugar'
[mama]	'mummy'	[nɔni]	'naughty'
[wawa]	'flower'	[bɪkbɪk]	'biscuit'

Reduplication may extend across word-boundaries: one child observed by the writer regularly pronounced 'tummy-button' as ['ʌʔi bʌʔi].

A third word-structure process, less significant than the other two, is *vowel-insertion*: an [ə]-vowel is inserted, usually to break up a consonant cluster. It occurs, typically, at the stage of development when clusters are just beginning to appear. Examples:

[gəlʌv]	'glove'	[θəɹi]	'three'
[səpun]	'spoon'	[pəleɪt]	'plate'
[stərɪŋ]	'string'	[dəwʌm]	'drum'

Syllable-structure

The major syllable-structure process is *final-consonant deletion*. This process is already familiar: final position in a syllable is more vulnerable than initial position, because loss of a final C changes CVC to the 'optimum' unmarked syllable form, CV. Children typically pronounce *cake*, *bus* as [keɪ, bʌ], rather than as [eɪk, ʌs].

Consonant clusters

Consonant clusters are subject to *cluster reduction*, *coalescence*, and *lengthening*.

Cluster reduction
This operates, as we have seen, in regular and predictable ways. Examples:

[fawə]	'flower'	[peɪd]	'spade'
[bɪʤ]	'bridge'	[mæk]	'smack'
[gʌv]	'glove'	[poʊs]	'post'

Coalescence
This is a process in which two segments in sequence are 'collapsed' into one, which may carry features from both of the originals. It affects particularly clusters with /s–/, such as /sl–/, which may coalesce to [ɬ], a voiceless lateral fricative. [ɬ] preserves the features 'lateral' from /l/, 'fricative' from /s/, and 'voicelessness' from both. Similarly, /sm–/ and /sn–/ may be coalesced into voiceless nasal fricatives, [m̥, n̥].

Coalescence may also result in a vowel + nasal sequence being pronounced as a nasal vowel (a change which also affects the syllable structure by converting CVC to CV – see above).

Lengthening
A process not previously mentioned, lengthening is characteristic of emerging consonant clusters. It affects approximants in initial clusters, and nasals in /s–/ clusters. Examples:

[brrɪʤ]	'bridge'	[snnoʊ]	'snow'
[pllein]	'plane'	[smmoʊk]	'smoke'
[kllaʊd]	'cloud'		

Lengthening is thus a stage in the development of clusters; it is often an alternative to [ə]-insertion, mentioned above.

Consonant segments

There are a number of major processes affecting consonent segments:

Voicing (*context-sensitive* voicing is a more accurate, if less concise title)

This is a process whereby the obstruents (i.e. those sounds in which voicing can be distinctive) are *voiced* in syllable-initial position and *voiceless* syllable-finally. When this process operates, voicing ceases to be distinctive, since voiced and voiceless are in complementary distribution.

Grunwell observes that the voicing contrast is normally established for initial and medial position first (by the age of about 3.0), but that final -C devoicing may persist until a later age (1981: 181).

Place of articulation

These processes include *fronting*, *glottalling* and *consonant-harmony* (the latter a type of *assimilation*).

Fronting describes the replacement of *velar* and *palato-alveolar* consonants by *alveolars*. At early stages of development, /k, g, ŋ/ are regularly realized as [t, d, n]. It is also normal to find [s, z] for /ʃ, ʒ/, and for /tʃ, dʒ/ to become [ts, dz], as in [wɒts] 'watch', [pɒwɪdz] 'porridge'. The process is thus one in which back consonants are replaced by alveolars. We have already mentioned that labials and alveolars are the earliest sounds acquired, and the velar-alveolar link is familiar from language typology (note the many languages in which [ŋ] is a pre-velar allophone of /n/), accentual differences (cf. English 'g-dropping') and language change (with examples like Ital. *detto* < Lat. *dictum*). The term *fronting* for this process is not entirely suitable, since alveolars themselves do not 'front', i.e. there is no trend for alveolars (or any other sounds) to become labial. A term which recognized that *alveolar* is the 'basic' or unmarked place of articulation among tongue-contact sounds (so that replacement by alveolars is an 'optimization' – cf. p. 289 below) would also be preferable.

Glottalling means that plosives and fricatives may be replaced by [ʔ] (plosives) and [h] (fricatives). [ʔ] and [h] are the most 'basic' or 'unmarked' of all consonants, since they involve no oral occlusion but only a glottal closure or, in the case of [h], general cavity friction (they are therefore 'simpler' from an articulatory point of view). These sounds are among the earliest acquired. Glottalling is one instance of *optimization* – a general term for the replacement of any sound by an 'optimum' or less marked sound, which would include, for example substitution of alveolars for velars. Examples are:

[kɒhi]	coffee	[hu]	shoe	[wɒʔ]	watch
[ʔʌmi]	tummy	[mɪh]	miss	[ṇeɪʔ]	snake

Consonant-harmony (Grunwell 1981) is the process by which two (or more) consonants in the same word or syllable are given the same place of articulation, for example [gɒg] 'dog'. Other examples are:

[mʌmpi] or [ŋʌŋki]	'monkey'
[kaɪgə]	'tiger'
[lelədɪn]	'elephant'
[bum]	'spoon'

Consonant harmony is a kind of assimilation, but whereas assimilation usually involves adjacent sounds (for example, [–mp–] in *tenpence*), harmony involves non-adjacent sounds, usually separated by a vowel. The assimilation often favours velars (surprisingly, in view of the usual dominance of alveolars),[3] hence the terms *back assimilation* (Ingram 1974a) and *velar harmony* (Smith 1973) for this process. However, consonant harmony may also favour labials and alveolars, as in:

[ʧɪmmi]	'chimney'
[bum]	'spoon'
[dedə]	'feather'
[leloʊ]	'yellow'

It may even favour palato-alveolars, as in [ʃɒlʤə] 'soldier'. Consonant harmony is sometimes progressive (antecedent sound influences subsequent sound), as in [ʧɪmmi] 'chimney', [geɪŋ] 'game', but it is usually, like assimilation generally, regressive, as in most of the examples above. It may also be both at once, as in [lelədɪn] 'elephant', where the /f/ has been 'swamped' by the surrounding alveolars. It is common for the /s/ of /s–/ clusters to assimilate, when these clusters are emerging. Examples:

[l̥lip]	'sleep'	[m̥muv]	'smooth'
[ṇneɪk]	'snake'	[ʍwetɪn]	'sweating'

Manner of articulation

These processes include *stopping*, *gliding* and *vocalization*.

Stopping is the process whereby fricatives and affricates are replaced by plosives at the corresponding point of articulation: /s/ becomes [t], /f/ becomes [p], /z/ becomes [d], etc. The affricates /ʧ, ʤ/ normally become alveolar ([t, d]) rather than palatal ([c, ɟ]), and likewise stopping converts /ʃ, ʒ/ to [t, d]. Examples:

[ti]	'see'	[dɒn]	'John'
[paɪb]	'five'	[tu]	'shoe'
[weɪdən]	'raisin'	[pɪt]	'fish'

This process is an 'expected' one, in view of the fact that plosives are generally acquired earlier than either fricatives or affricates.

Gliding means the replacement of a sound, usually the liquids /l, r/, by the glides /j, w/, which are the earliest acquired approximants. Examples:

[jet]	'let'	[tɒji] or [tɒwi]	'trolley'
[wed]	'red'	[sɒji] or [sɒwi]	'sorry'

Vocalization affects liquids in syllable-final position, where they become vowels. Examples:

[mɪʊk]	'milk'	[æpu]	'apple'
[bɒtʊ]	'bottle'		

Final /r/ (for 'rhotic' speakers only, of course) becomes [ə], as in:

[peɪpə]	'paper'	[fɔə]	'four'
[bʌtə]	'butter'	[faɪə]	'fire'

Summary

The major phonological processes of language development are:

Syllable-loss	Cluster reduction	Voicing
Reduplication	Coalescence	Fronting
Insertion		Consonant harmony
Final-C deletion		Stopping
		Gliding
		Vocalization
		Glottalling

'Processes' vs 'substitution errors'

These phonological processes offer a more revealing analysis of both normal and delayed acquisition, since they are based on, or related to, many of the general phonological properties noted in other domains, such as language typology and historical change. To illustrate use of the processes, the data from John (above, p. 284) can be re-submitted for analysis. The processes responsible for the error-category *omissions* have already been mentioned (namely, *cluster-reduction* and *final-C deletion*); we can now look at the *substitution* errors.

A mere list of the substitution errors (see p. 285) presents a mass of unrevealing data. The same target phonemes appear to be pronounced (realized) differently in different words: for example, John pronounces /g/ correctly in *green*, but as [k] in *big*. Sometimes, two sounds have overlapping realizations; for instance, target /k, g/ are both realized sometimes as [k] and sometimes as [g]. If we approach the data from the child's pronunciations, we find the same sound realizing a wide range of target phonemes, for example:

[d] realizes	/t/	(*trolley*)
	/d/	(*down*)
	/tʃ/	(*chew*)
	/(s)t/	(*stairs*)
	/ð/	(*this*)
	/s/	(*sock*)
	/ʃ/	(*shirt*)

Most of the data can be explained quite straightforwardly on the basis of only two phonological processes, which operate together. They are *stopping* (fricatives and affricates are pronounced as stops) and (context-sensitive) *voicing*: John has only voiced sounds initially, and only voiceless finally (i.e. the distribution is complementary). *Stopping* accounts for, for example, [dɪt] 'this' (/ð/ → [d], /s/ → [t]); *voicing* accounts for [bɪk] 'big' (/g/ → [k] finally) and [geɪk] 'cake' (/k/ → [g] initially). The two processes operate in conjunction: thus /tʃ/ in *chew* is first 'stopped' to [t] and then 'voiced' to [d], giving [du]. The /s/ of *sock* is likewise stopped (/s/ → [t]) and then voiced ([t] → [d]). The [g] of *cross* results from the operation of two processes: *cluster reduction*, which reduces /kr–/ to [k], and *voicing* ([k] → [g]). Similarly, the /sp–/ of *spoon* is first *reduced* to [p], and then *voiced* to [b].

John's data contains, in addition, many instances of [ʔ]. This can be accounted for by the process of *glottalling*, in which oral sounds are replaced by 'simpler' glottals. For example, the /t/ of *shirt* is replaced, via the glottalling process, by [ʔ]. In conjunction with other processes, the [ʔ] of *cross* results from *stopping* (/s/ → [t]) and *glottalling* ([t] → [ʔ]); the [ʔ] of *stairs* is derived via *stopping* (/z/ → [d]), *voicing* ([d] → [t]) and *glottalling* ([t] → [ʔ]).

Exercise 1

1   Work through the whole of the data from John, describing each pronunciation in terms of the process(es) which are responsible for it.
2   What processes are responsible for each of the seven target phonemes (see data, p. 291) being realized as [d]?

Conclusion

A number of phonological processes have been established on the basis of normal language development. These processes are 'natural' because they are based on our knowledge of the ways in which normal children fail to pronounce the adult 'target' phonemes, and on our knowledge of the order of acquisition of sounds (*stopping*, for example, is a process by which 'later' sounds (for example, fricatives) are replaced by 'earlier' ones (plosives)). The developmental processes are also in accord with the highly general principles established in other areas of phonology, such as (accentual) variation and language change. Further, they have the advantage of enabling clinical cases, in which language is delayed, to be compared with normal development. In clinical analysis, the data can be accounted for quite simply and economically, whereas, by contrast, a list of 'omissions' and 'substitutions' fails to reveal the underlying patterns. The processes may operate singly, or in conjunction with each other. Finally, atypical or unusual omissions/substitutions, such as John's deletion of initial /n/ in *noddy*, can be immediately identified, since they do not conform to the expected patterns.

The processes: psychological reality, or descriptive convenience?

There is no doubt that an understanding of phonological processes contributes greatly to clinical practice, and to our knowledge of 'what to expect' both in the clinic, and in normal development. There is, however, some controversy about the 'psychological' status of these processes. Are they rules, *internalized* by the child and governing his speech production? Or are they simply *descriptions* of events, based on our observations and experience of normal and disordered children? Smith (1973) takes the former view: he worked out, on the basis of detailed observation of his son A, a set of *realization rules*, similar to the processes outlined above, which convert the adult (target) pronunciation into the child's actual realizations. The child's competence, Smith claims, 'is a close reflection of the adult form he hears and . . . his deviant output is the result of the operation of a set of psychologically valid realization rules' (1973: 133). The rules have to be 'gradually unlearned as the child approximates more closely to the adult language'. Stampe (1969) bases his own 'natural phonology' on a similar basis: he claims that the child possesses an innate phonological system, which is universal; phonological development then consists in revising the universal system in the direction of a particular language: and the revision involves either *suppression* of the phonological processes (for example, fronting) or *limitation* on their application (for example, context-sensitive voicing becomes limited to syllable-final position only).

This view requires that the child *perceives* words in terms of the adult surface forms. The evidence in favour of this is of several kinds: first, children show that they understand and perceive differences they cannot make; for instance, Smith's child made no distinction (in production) between *mouth* and *mouse* ([maɑs] for both), yet he responded correctly when asked to bring a picture of a *mouth* vs a picture of a *mouse*. He also, at one stage, had complete free variation between [l] and [r] for adult words beginning with /r/, but invariably had [l] for adult /l/ – showing that he perceived the l/r distinction, even though he did not always make it. Second, children sometimes show an ability to make a particular sound, but not in the adult words that require it: the *puzzle/puddle* case, and the example of /s/ → [θ] but /θ/ → [f], have previously been mentioned. If a child perceived words on a purely phonetic rather than a phonological basis, these 'mismatches' could not arise; if the child can say [pʌdəl], the word *puddle* would *have* to be pronounced correctly. Third, the 'psychologically-real' view requires that new developments, when they occur, will apply 'across-the-board' – for example, once the child learns to pronounce initial /s/ with a version of [s] rather than [θ], he will do this for all words that have initial /s/; the change will not be a gradual or spasmodic one, since the *perception* (of adult /s/) has always been correct. And, fourth, the operation of the realization rules causes the child to produce forms which he has never heard; an impossibility, if perception were entirely phonetic. An example is the operation of velar harmony in A's system: not only does it produce [gɒg] 'dog' and [ga:k] for 'dark', but also [ŋek] for 'neck' and [ŋeɪk] for 'snake'. Production of [ŋ] word-initially, which is impossible in the adult system, shows that the rule of velar harmony must be a 'psychologically-real' one for the child.

The opposite opinion is that the rules or processes we establish are nothing more than a convenient descriptive device for classifying and categorizing articulatory errors. Grunwell (1981) inclines towards this view, though only to the extent of stating that all claims of psychological reality must be 'treated with caution'. Among a number of arguments she puts forward is the fact that changes do not, in fact, occur 'across the board', as the hypothesis would predict, but often take place gradually, over a period of days or even weeks. Smith admits this, even from his own data. Edwards (1974), using data collected from twenty-eight children aged 1.8 to 3.11, concluded that children as late as 3.0 do not have complete phonemic perception; and that perception develops gradually, though usually in advance of production.

That the child's perception should match the adult system exactly, seems unlikely on *a priori* grounds. The raw material of speech is, after all, presented to the child phonetically; he cannot know in advance which adult distinctions are going to be phonemic and which are not. For example, the child may hear, in any particular language, a range of bilabial plosive sounds: [p], [b], [pʰ], etc. But languages differ in the way these sounds are distributed phonemically. Some languages make two distinctions, /p, b/ (English, French, etc.); others make only one (Maori); others three, /ph, p, b/ (Thai). In languages with only one phoneme, the variants [p, b] will be allophonic; in languages with two or more, they will be phonemic. It will clearly take the child some time to work out the system for his own particular language; correct perception will be achieved only gradually.

There is also evidence that children continue to perceive on a phonetic rather than a phonological basis even at later stages of acquisition. For instance, there is a persisting confusion between /tr–/ and /ʧ/ in English. Children pronounce [ʧeɪn] for 'train', [trɜʧ] for 'church', [truzdi] for 'Tuesday', etc. This can be readily explained on phonetic grounds, but is difficult to account for on a phonological basis. Phonetically, /tr/ is realized (by adults) as an affricate [ʧ̞], whose properties are similar in phonetic respects (both articulatory and perceptual) to the other affricate [ʧ]. But phonologically, [ʧ̣] realizes a *sequence* of sounds, /t+r/, while [ʧ] realizes a unit phoneme, /ʧ/. If children fully understood the phonological system, confusion between /tr/ and /ʧ/ would be impossible.

The same argument is valid at another linguistic level, namely syntax. Those who make strong claims regarding children's underlying competence, knowledge of 'deep' structures, etc., find it difficult to account for actual occurrences of forms like I *must of* and he *should of*; for how could anyone with underlying knowledge of the grammar of English confuse a preposition (*of*) with an auxiliary verb (*have*)? But if we assume that speakers' knowledge is 'superficial' (in the sense of 'governed by surface forms rather than by "deep" structures') the confusion is readily explained: unstressed *of* and unstressed *have* are both pronounced [əv] 'on the surface', i.e. in actual pronunciation; and [tɹ–ʧ] are similar 'on the surface', no matter how different their 'deep' configurations may be.

In sum, it is difficult to accept in its entirety Smith's (and Stampe's) view that children always correctly perceive adult forms even though they deform them in pronunciation. On the other hand, to attribute only 'descriptive convenience' to the phonological processes we have outlined seems to do them less than justice, since they fit in so well with what we have come to expect from the study of many different areas of phonology: dialectal variation, historical change, acquisition, the typology of languages, and the differences between careful and casual speech.

Phonetic and phonological

The distinction between *phonetic* events and *phonological* (or *phonemic*) events is an important one in language development, just as it is in other areas. It has proved particularly useful in clinical phonology where it is applied in two rather different ways.

Basically, a *phonetic* disability is one in which individual sounds may be articulated incorrectly, but the phonological system of contrasts remains intact. An often-quoted example is the misarticulation of /s/, which may be realized as [s̪], (dental) [ʂ] (palatalized), [ş] (retroflex) or even [ç] (palatal). These are all 's-like' sounds but will be perceived by listeners as 'errors' or 'distortions' of the target (alveolar) production. However, so long as the sounds are 's-like', and provided that neighbouring sounds, namely /θ/ and /ʃ/ remain distinct, the phonological system is intact: no essential contrasts have been lost. Other examples of *phonetic* disability include the substitution of a bilabial fricative [ɸ], for /f/ and substitution of the labio-dental approximant, [ʋ], for /r/.[4]

The important point about *phonetic* disorders is that the system of contrasts remains unaffected. A *phonological* disability is one in which the speaker's system of contrasts fails to match that of the normal adult. The simplest case is one in which misarticulation of a sound results in a confusion between two or more phonemes. For example, if /s/ is pronounced [s̪] and /θ/ is also realized as [s̪], the potential s/θ contrast is not being achieved and the phoneme system is the poorer: *sick* and *sing* will not be distinguished from *thick* and *thing*.

Treatment of a patient will thus depend very much on whether a phonetic or a phonological disorder is diagnosed. If phonetic, then the aim is to improve the articulation of individual sounds; the therapist may work on the production of /s/, or /f/ or /r/, etc. If phonological, then the sounds are not treated individually, but as part of a system. The therapist has to establish first that the patient can *perceive* the distinction between contrasting phonemes; there is no hope of getting someone to produce a distinction they are not aware of. Then, the therapist may wish to treat a group of sounds all at the same time, for example all the voiced and voiceless plosives, not just /t/ or /d/. Third, the techniques of treatment will involve hearing and producing minimal pairs, in order to establish and maintain phonemic contrasts. The sounds will, in other words, be treated as part of a pattern, not as sounds requiring individual correction.

This last point provides a fitting conclusion to the book: treating sounds as part of a pattern is, in a nutshell, what phonology is about.

Exercise 2

Of the following pairs of sounds and sequences, which would be expected to replace which during language acquisition – and why?

Example: [tʃ – ts]; [ts] replaces [tʃ] (fronting)

[l – w]	[h – s]	[n – nj]	[s – ʃ]
[ed – et]	[p – ʔ]	[ʤ – d]	[ŋ – n]
[d – g]	[s – t]	[fu – vu]	[w – v]

Exercise 3

What processes are illustrated in the following pronunciations?

[jemə]	lemon	[gɒk]	sock
[feɪf]	face	[wɒwi]	lorry
[gugɷ]	Dougall	[ɫedz]	sledge
[praɪz]	surprise	[fə'lʌhi]	fluffy
[daɷd]	cows	[tʌʔ]	cup

Exercise 4

Of the following items, which represent typical, and which atypical, developmental pronunciations? Give reasons.

Example: [kæs] 'cat': atypical (fricative has replaced plosive)

[bɒku]	bottle	[hɔti]	horsie
[soɷk]	smoke	[bʌbʌ]	cupboard
[gɪg]	pig	[laɷə]	flower
[fɷsi]	pussy	[rʌʃ]	brush
[deʃ]	desk	[maɷh]	mouse

Glossary of terms used in the description of speech sounds

The glossary is arranged on a 'notional' basis rather than alphabetically.

Consonants

Manner of articulation

stop   a sound involving complete, but brief, blockage of vocal tract. *Stop* is an inclusive term for *plosives* and *affricates* but often used loosely for *plosives*.

plosive   a stop which is released quickly. Three phases are involved: *closure*, *hold* and *release*. Plosives in English are /p, b, t, d, k, g/.

affricate   a stop which is released slowly with accompanying friction. English affricates are /ʧ, ʤ/.

fricative   a sound made by narrowing the aperture sufficiently to cause friction. English fricatives are /f, v, θ, ð, s, z, ʃ, ʒ/.

nasal   complete blockage in the oral cavity directs airstream through nasal cavities. Soft palate in lowered position. English nasals are /m, n, ŋ/.

oral   soft palate is in raised position directing airstream through mouth. All English sounds except *nasals* are *oral*.

lateral   centre of tongue makes complete closure, air escapes round sides. English /l/. Opposite to *central*.

central   air escapes over the centre of the tongue (cf. *lateral*). In English, all vowels plus /r, j, w/ are *central* sounds.

retroflex   tip of tongue curled upwards and back. Centre of tongue hollowed. English /r/.

liquid   inclusive term for *lateral* and *retroflex* sounds.

glide   vowel-like (i.e. *vocoid* – see below) sounds moving rapidly towards or away from a syllable peak. Includes the consonants /j, w/ and the second component of diphthongs, namely, [i, u, ə] as in [aⁱ, aᵘ, iᵊ].

approximant   inclusive term for *liquids* and *glides*. English /l, r, j, w/.

sonorant   sounds made without friction or a total occlusion, and dependent for their characteristics on vocal cord vibration and resonance. Includes *vowels*, *nasals*, and *approximants*. Opposite to *obstruent*.

obstruent   sounds involving a total occlusion, or friction. Includes *plosives*, *fricatives* and *affricates*. Opposite of *sonorant*.

continuant   a sound which can be prolonged. Opposite to *stop*.

vocoid   articulated without interruption to airstream. In English all *central oral continuants* (i.e. the vowels plus /r, j, w/ are *vocoids*). Opposite to *contoid*.

contoid   articulated with interruption to airstream, namely stops, fricatives, nasals, laterals. Opposite to *vocoid*. Terms contoid/vocoid replace the terms consonant/vowel in their *articulatory* definition.

syllabic consonant   a contoid occurring at the peak of a syllable, for example [ḷ, m̩, n̩] as in /'bɒtḷ, kjubɪzm̩, kɒtn̩, steɪʃn̩/.

vowel   a vocoid occurring at syllable-peak.

consonant   a contoid occurring at syllable-margin (cf. *syllabic consonant*).

syllable   an articulatory movement with a single, obligatory peak, optionally preceded or followed by a margin.

voiceless   not accompanied by vocal-cord vibration. English /p, t, k, f, θ, s, ʃ, tʃ, h/. Opposite to *voiced*.

voiced   accompanied by vocal-cord vibration. English /b, d, g, v, ð, z, ʒ, dʒ/, plus all vowels, nasals and approximants. Opposite of *voiceless*.

fortis   with strong articulation involving some muscular tension. In English all *voiceless* consonants have *fortis* articulation. Opposite to *lenis*.

lenis   with relatively weak, lax articulation. In English, all *voiced* consonants have *lenis* articulation.

aspirated   accompanied by a puff of air after plosion. In English, voiceless plosives occurring *initially* in a stressed syllable are *aspirated*, for example the [p] of /pen, pju/, the [k] of /kɪn, klin/.

unaspirated   opposite to *aspirated*.

Place of articulation

(bi)labial   at the lips. English /p, b/.

labio-dental   (usually) lower lip in contact with (or close to) upper teeth. English /f, v/.

dental   tip of tongue in contact with (or close to) teeth.

alveolar   tip/blade of tongue in contact with (or close to) teeth-ridge (alveolum). English /t, d, s, z, l, n/.

palatal   front of tongue in contact with (or close to) hard palate.

palato-alveolar   blade and front of tongue in contact with (or close to) teeth-ridge and hard palate respectively. English /ʃ, ʒ, tʃ, dʒ/.

velar   back of tongue in contact with (or close to) soft palate (velum). English /k, g/.

uvular   back of tongue in contact with (or close to) uvula.

glottal   at the vocal cords (*glottis* = the opening between the vocal cords).

Divisions of tongue

tip   blade   front   back

Environments

initial   occurring at the beginning of a word or syllable, for example the /p/ in /pen/.
medial   occurring in the middle (of a word or syllable).
intervocalic   (consonant) occurring between two vowels.
final   occurring as the final sound (of a word or syllable).

Vowel quadrilateral: *Horizontal dimensions*

front   central   back
Modifiers: *centralized* = 'nearer the centre than', for example [ë] is a (half-close) centralized front vowel.

Vowel quadrilateral: *Vertical dimensions*

close   half-close   mid   half-open   open
Modifiers: *raised* = higher than, for example [ẹ] is a raised half-close vowel (more close than [e]).
lowered = lower than, for example [ẹ] is a vowel more open than [e] (but not as open as [ɛ]).

Lip position

rounded
unrounded (or **spread**)

Notes

Chapter 1 Phonemic and phonetic

1 Native speaker (of a language) is a term we shall use frequently. It is a difficult concept to define precisely; it refers essentially to those who speak the language as their first, or primary language, as opposed to those who learn it as a 'foreign' or second language.

2 There is unfortunately no convention for representing in writing the difference between phone and allophone: square brackets are used for both. The context often makes it clear which is intended. Occasionally phones may be written without any brackets to show their indeterminate status.

3 It would be unfair to imply that phoneticians of 'structuralist' persuasions took no account of native speaker opinions; in practice, they usually did. But, in their anxiety to emphasize the need for proper ('scientific') methods and procedures, some of them came to regard the procedures as ends in themselves, rather than as a means towards understanding linguistic behaviour.

4 They are also known as P (for 'phonetic') rules.

5 A morpheme is a minimal unit of meaning. A word may be composed of one or more morphemes, for example *singers* = *sing*, *-er*, *-s*.

6 Acoustic and auditory phonetics are sometimes regarded as sub-disciplines of a single branch of phonetics (acoustico-auditory phonetics), on the grounds that acoustic phonetics measures what the listener hears (the vibrations of air particles) and is thus closely related to auditory phonetics. In the discussion which follows we shall assume two main branches, articulatory (speaker's point of view) and acoustico-auditory (listener's point of view); the terms acoustic and auditory are to be regarded as interchangeable unless the context distinguishes them.

7 The distribution of /h/ in English is in fact unique: it does not behave quite like any other sound. For further discussion see Chapter 4, p. 109.

8 Slant bracket notations, being relative to the language concerned, must always refer to a specific language. If the context does not make it clear *which* language, then phonemic representations should be prefixed with the name of the language, for example English /t/, German /x/, etc.

9 The term *co-articulation* is used by other phoneticians with a quite different meaning which should not be confused with this one; it refers to

sounds articulated at two points simultaneously, for example the labial-velars [k͡p, g͡b] (O'Connor 1973: 55; Catford 1977). The term *double articulation* can be used instead of co-articulation in this sense.

10 *Fortis* 'refers to a sound made with a relatively strong degree of muscular effort and breath force, compared with some other sound (known as *lenis*)' (Crystal 1980: 151). The voiceless sounds are usually fortis, and the voiced, lenis. However, 'when the voicing distinction is reduced, it is (often) only the degree of articulatory strength which maintains a contrast between sounds' (ibid.).

11 RP stands for 'received pronunciation', i.e. the standard pronunciation of English in England, sometimes known as 'BBC English'.

12 The acoustic properties of labials (like [ɸ]) and high back vowels are very similar, as are those of palatal consonants (like [ç]) and high front vowels. See the discussion of the feature *grave*, in Chapter 3.

13 The IPA meets from time to time to revise, update, and add to the inventory. For a recent version, cf. Wells (1982: 1). Additional diacritics, devised mainly for clinical purposes, are also now available (Grunwell 1981: 212ff.)

14 Alternatively, the symbols [p, t, k] without diacritics may mean 'unaspirated', as compared with aspirated [pʰ, tʰ, kʰ].

15 Examples of final /b/ are scarce, but other voiced plosives follow the same pattern: *rug* [g̊ʌk], *leg* [g̊ɛk], *hard* [aːt].

16 Some of the realization rules can be expressed more economically, and can cover a wider variety of cases, if features like [voice], [plosive], etc. are used instead of individual phonemes like /p/, /n/, etc. For the time being, simple articulatory features like [fricative], [alveolar], etc. will be used.

Chapter 2   Phonemes in sequence

1 This exercise is based on a similar idea in Gleason (1955).

2 Acoustically, [kl–] and [tl–] (likewise [gl–] and [dl–]) are so similar that it takes a keen observer to be aware of the difference.

3 Nasals are 'non-continuant' because they require a complete closure in the *oral* tract. Many phoneticians prefer to define 'continuants' as sounds which can be prolonged – including nasals.

4 In Greek, voiced plosives are pre-nasalized.

5 From Greek root [ksir–], 'dry'.

6 Rhotic accents are those in which an 'r' is pronounced in words such as *car*, *bear*, *card*, firm, etc. Non-rhotic accents have a long vowel or dipthong without 'r', for example /ka, beə, fɜm/, etc. The non-rhotic accents include (in Britain) RP, the south, east and Midlands of England, and most of Wales (cf. Wells 1982: 75–6, 215ff.). The term derives from *rho*, which is the Greek name for 'r'.

7 'Non-alveolar' means 'labial' and 'velar'. The position of the palato-alveolars /tʃ, dʒ/ is not clear; long vowels are permitted with /n/ (*paunch*, *lounge*, *strange*) but not with /l/.

Chapter 3   Distinctive features

1 [ʔ] is widely used to represent /t/ in word-final position (*that*, *bit*, *lot*), and before syllabic consonants (*button*, *written*), and elsewhere.

2 A number of good introductions are available, for example Gimson 1980: ch. 3; Fry 1979; Denes and Pinson 1963.

3 These spectrographic recordings of [e] were made by direct microphone input to a Kaye Sonagraph 6061B. The vowel was spoken by the author at an average pitch (fundamental frequency) of approximately 120 Hz. Figure 1 shows a section of the vowel, on an expanded scale, 80–4000 Hz, using a 6076C Scale Magnifier, with a narrow-band (45 Hz) filter. For Figure 2 a wide-band (300 Hz) filter was used, again with an expanded scale, 80–4000 Hz. The horizontal striations in Figure 1 represent the harmonics; note for example the peak of the first formant at the second harmonic (approximately 375 Hz).

   Direct comparison with Ladefoged's (1967: 88) extensive data on cardinal vowel frequencies is not possible, since his data is given in mels rather than Hz. However, the frequencies for *English* vowels published in Gimson (1980: 101) show that my cardinal [e] is very similar to his RP /ɪ/, for which he gives an F1 of 360 Hz, an F2 of 2220 Hz and an F3 of 2960 Hz. RP /ɪ/ is usually located near to cardinal [e] on the vowel chart. I am indebted to R. Motherwell for technical assistance.

4 The important links are *high* and *back*; *low* has a negative value for all consonants except /h/, whose analysis is doubtful anyway. The vowels are also redundantly specified for *anterior* and *coronal*; since the values are negative throughout, the link appears to serve little purpose.

5 It would be unfair to imply that Jakobson was not concerned with phonological processes; the features in *PSA* are in fact supported by discussions of phonological patterns in a variety of languages. Jakobson's aim was to combine 'naturalness' with economy and this achievement remains unsurpassed by later developments.

Chapter 4   Neutralization, marking and language universals

1 After sonorants, the plural is 'truly' /z/, because a contrast between /s, z/ is possible; compare *pence/pens*, *else/sells*, *place/plays*. cf. Chapter 5, p. 127.

2 In most cases, as we have seen, the 'neutralizing' sound *cannot* be unambiguously assigned to one phoneme or the other.

3 The presence of front rounded vowels thus presupposes, or *implies*, the presence of front unrounded vowels. See section on 'implication'.

4 The fact that the plosives of Maori are written with 'p, t, k' means nothing, since the choice between 'p, b', etc. is arbitrary. Note that the early (English-speaking) settlers in New Zealand frequently interpreted the sounds as voiced, as in *Otago* from 'otakou', *biddy-bid* from 'piripiri'.

Chapter 5   Phonology and morphology

1 Notice that when *knife*, *loaf*, etc. are used as verbs, the third-person singular present form has /f/, not /v/; for example, he *loafs* (around). Thus the allomorph with /v/ is confined to plurals only.

2 The rule is best formulated this way round, because the long version is also found when V is final, as in *sea*, *say*, etc.

3 The lengthening rule is required to overcome the problem of *pot*, *pod* having, in the opinion of native speakers, the 'same' vowel. So *pod* is initially /pɑd/ but the vowel must then be lengthened so as to fall in with the /ɑ/ in *balm*. The whole line of (Chomsky's) argument here is, it must be admitted, suspect (see note 4), though Halle's example from Russian is more convincing.

4 Readers may, however, have noticed a fundamental flaw in Bloch's (and hence Chomsky's) line of argument. If there are two vowels, /ɑ/ and /ɑ·/ as in *bomb*, *balm*, both of these will be subject to the vowel lengthening rule, since this rule applies to *all* vowels. If the pronunciations of *pot*, *pod*, are [pɑt], [pɑ·d], then the vowel of *Pa'd*, which is phonemically /ɑ·/, must be even longer than the vowel of *pod*; we could symbolize it with the full colon, [ɑ:]. *Pod* must therefore contrast with *Pa'd*, as [pɑ·d] vs [pɑ:d]. But Bloch's initial premise, on which his whole argument depends, is that *pod* and *Pa'd* are *identical* in pronunciation. If this premise is false, the argument collapses, and Chomsky's case against traditional phonemics is considerably weakened.

5 For some speakers, perhaps in very careful styles of speaking the coalescence may not take place, preserving /-sj-/, for example in *sensual* /sensjuəl/. Compare, likewise, *issue*, *assume* with /sj/ or /ʃ/.

6 Rule 3 was incorporated into the sequence of Rules 1 and 2 (above, p. 138).

7 If the past tense allomorph is pronounced /əd/, this problem does not in fact arise; but in some accents the pronunciation is /ɪd/.

8 Labov (1963) has traced interesting developments of these two vowels, both historically and contemporaneously, on the island of Martha's Vineyard.

9 In American English, the vowel of *can't* is /æ/ rather than /ɑ/.

10 Generative phonologists seem to have assumed that the spelling is determined by the existence of alternating morphemes, for example that *professor* is spelt 'or' because of *professorial*, while *manager* is spelt 'er' because of *managerial*. This assumption is probably false. In a literate society, it is just as likely that pronunciations *are determined by* the spelling, instead of the other way round. Take for example the name of the composer, *Wagner*. The adjective derived from it is *Wagnerian*. But if the name had been spelt *Wagnor*, the adjective would be *Wagnorian*. Clearly it is the spelling which has determined the pronunciation in this case.

11 Note that the velar softening rule is also needed as the first stage in an OGP derivation of words like *education* from *educate* and *division* from *divide*, namely:

edʒukeɪt → edʒukeɪs-ɪən → edʒukeɪʃən
dɪvaɪd → dɪvɪz-ɪən → dɪvɪʒən

12 As late as 1974, Anderson was able to write: 'our goal is a description in which each morpheme has a single underlying phonemic form ... to which various phonological rules can apply in appropriate environments' (1974: 51).

Chapter 6   Connected speech

1 This is sometimes stated as: 'the listener is interested mainly in *what* is said, not *how* it is said'. As such, it is only partly true, because the listener may be very interested in certain aspects of 'how' something is said; for example, the intonation, pausing, rate of utterance, etc. of the speaker may be an important guide to the speaker's mood, to nuances of his intention, to his social and geographical origins, etc. This applies also to deletions and assimilations: the *absence* of these, and the use of full forms instead, can be very meaningful: compare [sd̪ɪnə taɪm] ('neutral') with [ɪt ʔɪz dɪnə taɪm] ('emphatic' – 'come at once').

2 Since we are giving the actual pronunciation in a phonetic representation, strictly speaking the segment [r] should be represented as [ɹ]. For convenience, however, we shall use [r] in the discussion.

3 On 'lexical' vs 'grammatical', cf. Chapter 5, p. 130. Grammatical items are those whose main function is to outline and convey the grammatical structure of the sentence (and their behaviour is thus described in a *grammar* of the language). Lexical items are more 'meaningful' in themselves and convey greater information: they belong in a *dictionary* of the language. Lexical items generally belong to the 'open' word-classes – nouns, verbs, adjectives and adverbs; grammatical items belong to 'closed systems', each containing a small number of mutually-related items, for example pronouns and articles. The 'lexical-grammatical' distinction is relative, not absolute: they are end-points of a scale.

4 The validity of a division of languages into 'stress-timed' vs 'syllable-timed' hàs recently been questioned (see below, p. 191). This, however, does not affect our discussion of rhythmic patterns.

5 As was pointed out in Chapter 4, [ə] is a 'neutral' or 'colourless' vowel – the sound which occurs when the vocal tract is in its most relaxed position. It is 'colourless' in the sense that it has no distinguishing mark, such as frontness, roundness, openness, etc. Note that the hesitation sounds *um, er* are really lengthened (and/or nasalized) versions of [ə].

6 The similarity between the [ʊ] of [tʊ] and the /ʊ/ of, say, *book* is thus

recognized as being coincidental. Most vowels have no intermediate 'phoneme' between their full forms and [ə]. /i/ and /u/ are the exceptions: when partially reduced, their pronunciation may coincide with /ɪ/ and /ʊ/ respectively.

Chapter 7 Intonation

1 These titles are, needless to say, my own invention, P. H.

2 The terms we use are taken from Crystal and/or Halliday. For *nucleus*, Halliday uses the term *tonic*. *Tone group* is Halliday's term; Crystal's equivalent is *tone unit*.

3 The correlation: nucleus = 'new' information, non-nucleus = 'given', is admittedly an over-simplification. It is intended for examples like 'I don't *like* eating chocolates' or 'did *John* hear you', in which 'eating chocolates' and 'hear you' are given no emphasis (hence are 'given'), whereas *like* and *John* are made the focus of attention by being given the nucleus. cf. further the discussion on *referring* and *proclaiming* (below, p. 223).

4 On lexical vs grammatical, cf. Chapter 5, p. 130 and Chapter 6, p. 177.

5 Notice that a nucleus on *him*, *it* or any of the other grammatical items is very easy for a hearer to identify, while the predictable nuclei on *see* and *need* are less easy to recognize.

6 A simple 'linear' notation is sufficient to show the typical pitch patterns. The open circle marks the nucleus.

7 The advantage in specifying grammatical categories in relation to tones is that beginners, at any rate, particularly those without any musical training, often have difficulty in *recognizing* tone differences, i.e. in *identifying* the different tones. Correlation of a tone with its typical uses may be helpful in such circumstances.

8 Questions are divided into two basic types: WH-, and *polar* (or *yes–no*) questions. A WH-question begins with a word which has WH- as its initial letters (with the exception of *how*): *what, who, which, why* etc. A WH-question cannot be answered by *yes* or *no*. Polar questions do not have a WH- word, and can be answered by *yes* or *no*.

9 Tag-questions consist of an auxiliary verb and a pronoun, and are 'tagged' on to the end of a main sentence, for example, 'it's cold today *isn't it*'. If the main sentence is positive then the tag-question is usually negative, and vice versa. Other examples of tag-questions: *don't they, can't we, has he,* etc.

10 Quirk *et al.* (1973) call these 'disjuncts' and they are also known as 'sentential adverbs'. They include words like *personally, possibly, unfortunately, obviously,* etc. and they are felt to modify the sentence as a whole (hence the name), whereas 'ordinary' adverbs modify only part of the sentence. Compare:

he drove quickly ('ordinary' adverb, modifies *drove*)
he drove presumably (sentence-modifier, belongs with whole sentence)

The grammar of these two sentences is quite different and so is their intonation pattern. The sentence-modifier would normally require its own tone group, with a fall-rise tone. In writing, this would be shown by separating it with a comma:

/he drove `quickly/
/he `drove/ ˇpresumably/(= he drove, presumably)

11 A non-nuclear stress often involves no change of pitch; if there *is* a pitch change, it is of 'high pre-nucleus' type – cf. Pattern A (p. 203).

Chapter 8   Dialect, accent

1 *Selectional* is a term used by O'Connor (1973). Wells (1970) used the term *incidential*, modified subsequently (1982) to *lexical-incidential*.
2 The hook beneath a cardinal vowel denotes a more open (lower) sound; the dot denotes a more close (raised) sound; two dots above the vowel, for example [ë], denote centralization, i.e. *retraction* in the case of a front vowel and *advancement* in the case of a back vowel: a position nearer to the central area, in both cases.
3 The incidence of /ɒ/ and /ɔ/ is actually more complicated than I have implied. There are, for example, some RP speakers, particularly of the older generation, who use /ɔ/ rather /ɒ/ in this group of words.
4 The 'realization criterion' is a test for distinguishing realizational differences, and can be phrased as follows:
   In a realizational difference between accents, all the words with (allo)phone [P] in accent A have (allo)phone [Q] in accent B,

   i.e. there is a one-to-one correspondence of allophones across accents. For an example see the data in Exercise 2 (p. 242).
5 Even in RP there is a certain amount of overlapping between these two vowels. Some words can be pronounced with either /æ/ or /ɑ/, for example *elastic, plastic, lather*; and the sequence *gas mask* is particularly liable to mispronunciation (cf. Wells 1982: 135).

Chapter 9   Sound change

1 The macron over a vowel (for example [ō]) denotes a long vowel; the notation is equivalent to [oː]. Use of the macron to denote length is traditional in historical studies.
2 We shall (arbitrarily) count long vowels (diphthongs) as two segments, to allow vowel shortening to be included in the reckoning.
3 This fricative had already weakened from an earlier plosive, /k/, as shown by related words in other Indo-European languages. Compare, for

example, OE *niht* with Latin *noct-*, Greek *nukt-*, 'night'; OE *eahta*, Latin and Greek *okto*, 'eight'.

4 *Laugh* and *draught* apparently have a long vowel, but they had a short vowel, [a], until relatively recently. In general American they still do.

Chapter 10   Acquisition, normal and delayed

1 The items are presented as coloured pictures in a booklet, mainly of individual pictureable nouns, such as *monkey*, *tent*, *umbrella*, *bridge*, etc.

2 For example, in the EAT, a child aged 4.0 who scores forty-one correct out of the sixty-eight items is performing at the average level for his age, where a child of 5.0 requires a score of fifty-three in order to do so. A child of 5.0 who scores only forty-one, on the other hand, is said to have an 'articulation age' of 4.0, i.e. his phonological development lags by about one year. Children with delays of one year or more are likely candidates for therapy.

3 Ingram (1974b) suggests that in syllable-final position, the unmarked place is velar, not alveolar. In initial position, it is the reverse.

4 [ʋ] is indeed often referred to as 'defective r', though whether it counts as a 'disability' depends on our (i.e. society's) attitude towards it: some regard it more as an affectation; it may even be a feature of a regional or social accent.

Bibliography

Abbreviations

J. Ling.	*Journal of Linguistics*
J. Phon.	*Journal of Phonetics*
J. Ch. Lang.	*Journal of Child Language*
J. Int. Phon. Assoc.	*Journal of the International Phonetic Association*
Lang. and Sp.	*Language and Speech*
Amer. Sp.	*American Speech*

Abercrombie, D. (1965), *Studies in Phonetics and Linguistics*, London: Oxford University Press

Abercrombie, D. (1967), *Elements of General Phonetics*, Edinburgh: Edinburgh University Press

Abercrombie, D. (1979), 'The accents of Standard English in Scotland', in A. J. Aitken and T. McArthur (eds.), *Languages of Scotland*, Edinburgh: Chambers

Aitken, A. J. and McArthur, T. (eds.) (1979), *Languages of Scotland*, Edinburgh: Chambers

Anderson, S. R. (1974), *The Organisation of Phonology*, New York: Seminar Press

Anthony, A. *et al.* (1971), *The Edinburgh Articulation Test*, Edinburgh: Livingstone

Balasubramanian, T. (1980), 'Timing in Tamil', *J. Phon.*, **8**, 449

Berko, J. and Brown, R. (1960), 'Psycholinguistic research methods', in P. Mussen (ed.), *Handbook of Research Methods in Child Development*, New York: Wiley

Biedrzycki, L. (1980), 'Isochronous feet in a reading of Polish verse', *Edinburgh Univ. Wkg. Papers in Linguistics*, **13**, 50

Bloch, B. (1941), 'Phonemic overlapping', *Amer. Sp.*, **16**, 278. Reprinted in V. B. Makkai (ed.) (1972), *Phonological Theory*, New York: Holt Rinehart & Winston

Bloomfield, L. (1933), *Language*, London: George Allen & Unwin

Bolinger, D. (ed.) (1972), *Intonation: selected readings*, London: Penguin Books

Bolinger, D. (1975), *Aspects of Language*, 2nd edn, New York: Harcourt Brace Jovanovich

Bolozky, S. (1977), 'Fast speech as a function of tempo', *J. Ling.*, **13**, 217

Bolozky, S. (1982), 'Remarks on rhythmic stress in Modern Hebrew', *J. Ling.*, **18**, 275

Bonnet, G. (1980), 'A study of intonation in the soccer results', *J. Phon.*, **8**, 21

Brame, M. K. (ed.) (1972), *Contributions to Generative Phonology*, Austin: University of Texas Press

Brazil, D. (1975), *Discourse Intonation*, Eng. Lang. Research Monograph, University of Birmingham

Brown, G. (1977), *Listening to Spoken English*, London: Longman

Bynon, T. (1977), *Historical Linguistics*, Cambridge: Cambridge University Press

Cairns, C. E. (1969), 'Markedness, neutralisation, and universal redundancy rules', *Language*, **45**, 863

Catford, J. C. (1977), *Fundamental Problems in Phonetics*, Edinburgh: Edinburgh University Press

Chao, Y. R. (1968), *Language and Symbolic Systems*, Cambridge: Cambridge University Press

Chen, M. (1970), 'Vowel length variation as a function of the voicing of the consonant', *Phonetica*, **22**, 129

Chomsky, N. (1964), 'The nature of structural descriptions', in *Current Issues in Linguistic Theory*, The Hague: Mouton. Also in V. B. Makkai (ed.) (1972), *Phonological Theory*, New York: Holt Rinehart & Winston

Chomsky N. and Halle M. (1968), *Sound Pattern of English (SPE)*, New York: Harper & Row

Classe, A. (1939), *The Rhythm of English Prose*, Oxford: Basil Blackwell

Courtenay, B. de (1895), *Versuch einer Theorie Phonetischer Alternationen*, Strasbourg: Trübner

Cruttenden, A. (1970), 'On the so-called grammatical function of intonation', *Phonetica*, **21**, 182

Crystal, D. (1969a), 'Review of Halliday 1967', *Language*, **45**, 378

Crystal, D. (1969b), *Prosodic Systems and Intonation in English*, Cambridge: Cambridge University Press

Crystal, D. (1975), *The English Tone of Voice*, London: Edward Arnold

Crystal, D. (1980), *A First•Dictionary of Linguistics and Phonetics*, London: Andre Deutsch

Crystal, D. (1981), *Clinical Linguistics*, Wien: Springer-Verlag

Currie, K. L. (1979), 'Contour systems of one variety of Scottish English', *Lang. & Sp.*, **22**, 1

Daniloff, R. G. and Hammarberg, R. E. (1973), 'On defining co-articulation', *J. Phon.*, **1**, 239

Davidsen-Nielsen, N. (1969), 'English stops after initial /s/', *English Studies*, **4**

Delattre, P. (1965), *Comparing the Phonetic Features of English, French, German and Spanish*, Heidelberg: Groos

Denes, P. B. and Pinson, E. N. (1963), *The Speech Chain*, New York: Anchor Books

Derwing, B. L. (1973), *Transformational Grammar as a Theory of Language Acquisition*, Cambridge: Cambridge University Press

Dinnsen, D. A. (ed.) (1977), *Current Approaches to Phonological Theory*, Bloomington: Indiana University Press

Edwards, M. L. (1974), 'Perception and production in child phonology: the testing of four hypotheses', *J. Ch. Lang.*, **1**, 205

Fischer-Jørgensen, E. (1975), *Trends in Phonological Theory*, Copenhagen: Akademisk Forlag

Fisher, H. B. and Logemann, J. A. (1971), *Test of Articulation Competence*, Boston: Houghton Mifflin

Fries, C. C. (1940), *American English Grammar*, New York: Appleton Century

Fry, D. B. (1979), *The Physics of Speech*, Cambridge: Cambridge University Press

Giles, H. and Powesland, P. F. (1975), *Speech Style and Social Evaluation*, London: Academic Press

Gimson, A. C. (1980), *An Introduction to the Pronunciation of English*, 3rd edn, London: Edward Arnold

Gleason, H. A. (1955a (1961)), *An Introduction to Descriptive Linguistics*, New York: Holt, Rinehart & Winston

Gleason, H. A. (1955b), *Workbook in Descriptive Linguistics*, New York: Holt Rinehart & Winston

Goldman, R. and Fristoe, M. (1969), *Test of Articulation*, Minnesota: American Guidance Service

Greenberg, J. H. (1966a), 'Synchronic and diachronic universals in phonology', *Language*, **42**, 508

Greenberg, J. H. (1966b), *Language Universals*, The Hague: Mouton. Also in T. Sebeok (ed.), *Current Trends in Linguistics*, vol. 3, The Hague: Mouton

Grunwell, P. (1981), *Clinical Phonology*, London: Croom Helm

Hale, K. (1971), 'Deep-surface canonical disparities in relation to analysis and change', in T. Sebeok (ed.), *Current Trends in Linguistics*, vol. 2, The Hague: Mouton

Halle, M. (1959), *The Sound Pattern of Russian*, The Hague: Mouton

Halle, M. and Stevens, K. (1967), 'On the mechanism of glottal vibration for vowels and consonants', MIT QPR, Research Lab. of Electronics

Halle, M. and Stevens, K. (1971), 'A note on laryngeal features', MIT QPR 101, 198

Halliday, M. A. K. (1967), *Intonation and Grammar in British English*, The Hague: Mouton

Halliday, M. A. K. (1970), *A Course in Spoken English: Intonation*, London: Oxford University Press

Harris, J. W. (1969), *Spanish Phonology*, Cambridge, Mass.: MIT Press

Heffner, R.-M. S. (1950), *General Phonetics*, Madison, Wi.: University of Wisconsin Press

Henderson, E. J. A. (ed.) (1971), *The Indispensable Foundation*, London: Oxford University Press

Hewlett, N. (1980), 'Stylistic variation and phonetic realisation in a generative phonology', Ph.D. Thesis, University of Essex

Hogg, R. M. (1979), 'Analogy and phonology', *J. Ling.*, **15**, 55

Hooper, J. B. (1972), 'The syllable in phonological theory', *Language*, **48**, 525

Hooper, J. B. (1976), *An Introduction to Natural Generative Phonology*, New York: Academic Press

Hooper, J. B. (1977), 'Substantive principles in natural generative phonology', in D. A. Dinnsen (ed.), *Current Approaches to Phonological Theory*, Bloomington: Indiana University Press

Hornby, A. S. *et al.* (1974), *The Oxford Advanced Learner's Dictionary*, London: Oxford University Press

Hyman, L. M. (1973a), 'The feature [grave] in phonological theory', *J. Phon.*, **1**, 329

Hyman, L. M. (1975), *Phonology: Theory and Analysis*, New York: Holt, Rinehart & Winston

Ingram, D. (1974a), 'Phonological rules in young children', *J. Ch. Lang*, **1**, 49

Ingram, D. (1974b), 'Fronting in child phonology', *J. Ch. Lang.*, **1**, 233

Jakobson, R. (1941 (1968)), *Child Language, Aphasia and Phonological Universals*, The Hague: Mouton

Jakobson, R., Fant, G. and Halle, M. (1952), *Preliminaries to Speech Analysis*, Cambridge, Mass.: MIT Press

Jakobson, R. and Halle, M. (1956), *Fundamentals of Language*, The Hague: Mouton

Jassem, W. (1952), *Intonation in Conversational English*, Warsaw: Polish Academy of Science

Jespersen, O. (1909 (1965)), *A Modern English Grammar on Historical Principles*, London: George Allen & Unwin

Jones, D. (1950), *The Phoneme*, Cambridge: Cambridge University Press

Jones, D. (1960 (1956)), *An Outline of English Phonetics*, 9th edn, Cambridge: Heffer

Joos, M. (ed.) (1957), *Readings in Linguistics I*, Chicago: University of Chicago Press

Keiler, A. R. (ed.) (1972), *A Reader in Historical and Comparative Linguistics*, New York: Holt, Rinehart & Winston

Kim, C.-W. (1972), 'Two phonological notes: A-sharp and B-flat', in M. K. Brame (ed.), *Contributions to Generative Phonology*, Austin: University of Texas Press

Kingdon, R. (1958), *The Groundwork of English Intonation*, London: Longman

Kiparsky, P. (1971), 'Historical linguistics', in W.O. Dingwall (ed.), *A Survey of Linguistic Science*, University of Maryland Linguistics Program

Kisseberth, C. W. (ed.) (1973), 'Studies in generative phonology', *Papers in Linguistics*, monograph 3

Knowles, G. O. (1978), 'The nature of phonological variables in Scouse', in P. Trudgill (ed.), *Sociolinguistic Patterns in British English*, London: Edward Arnold

Kurath, H. (1972), *Studies in Area Linguistics*, Bloomington: Indiana University Press

Labov, W. (1963), 'The social motivation of a sound change', in Labov (1972a)

Labov, W. (1972a), *Sociolinguistic Patterns*, Philadelphia: University of Pennsylvania Press

Labov, W. (1972b), *Language in the Inner City*, Philadelphia: University of Pennsylvania Press

Ladefoged, P. (1967), *Three Areas of Experimental Phonetics*, London: Oxford University Press

Ladefoged, P. (1971), *Preliminaries to Linguistic Phonetics*, Chicago: University of Chicago Press

Ladefoged, P. (1972a), 'Phonetic prerequisites for a distinctive feature theory', in A. Valdman (ed.), *Papers in Linguistics and Phonetics to the Memory of P. Delattre*, The Hague: Mouton

Ladefoged, P. (1972b), 'Phonological features and their phonetic correlates', *J. Int. Phon. Assoc.*, **2**, 2

Ladefoged, P. (1975), *A Course in Phonetics*, New York: Harcourt Brace Jovanovich

Ladefoged, P. (1980), 'What are linguistic sounds made of?', *Language*, **56**, 485

Lass, R. (1976), *English Phonology and Phonological Theory*, Cambridge: Cambridge University Press

Lehiste, I. (1977), 'Isochrony reconsidered', *J. Phon.*, **5**, 253

Lewis, J. Windsor (1972), *A Concise Pronouncing Dictionary*, London: Oxford University Press

Lieberman, P. (1965), 'On the acoustic basis of the perception of intonation by linguists', *Word*, **21**, 40

Lightner, T. M. (1965), 'Segmental phonology of modern standard Russian', PhD. Thesis, Massachusetts Institute of Technology

Liljencrants, J. and Lindblom, B. (1972), 'Numerical simulation of vowel quality systems', *Language*, **48**, 839

Lindblom, B. (1972), 'Phonetics and the description of language', *Proceedings of VII International Congress of Phonetic Sciences*, The Hague: Mouton

Linnell, P. (1979), *Psychological Reality in Generative Phonology*, Cambridge: Cambridge University Press

Lyons, J. (1968), *Introduction to Theoretical Linguistics*, Cambridge: Cambridge University Press

Macaulay, R. K. S. (1977), *Language, Social Class and Education: a Glasgow study*, Edinburgh: Edinburgh University Press

Makkai, V. B. (1972), *Phonological Theory*, New York: Holt, Rinehart & Winston

Malmberg, B. (ed.) (1968), *Manual of Phonetics*, Amsterdam: North-Holland

Martinet, A. (1952), 'Function, structure and sound change', *Word*, **8**, 1. Also in Keiler (ed.) (1972)

Martinet, A. (1955), *Economie des Changements Phonétiques*, Berne: Francke

Martinet, A. (1964), *Elements of General Linguistics*, trans. E. Palmer, Chicago: University of Chicago Press

Matthews, P. H. (1973), *Morphology*, Cambridge: Cambridge University Press

Miller, P. D. (1973), 'Bleaching and coloring', Papers of 9th Regional Meeting of Chicago Linguistic Society, pp. 386–97

Milroy, J. (1981), *Regional Accents of English: Belfast*, Belfast: Blackstaff Press

Milroy, L. (1980), *Language and Social Networks*, Oxford: Basil Blackwell

O'Connor, J. D. (1967), *Better English Pronunciation*, Cambridge: Cambridge University Press

O'Connor, J. D. (1973), *Phonetics*, Harmondsworth: Penguin Books

O'Connor, J. D. and Arnold, G. F. (1961), *Intonation of Colloquial English*, London: Longman

Orton, H. *et al.* (eds.) (1962), *Survey of English Dialects. Basic Material*, 4 vols., Leeds: Edward Arnold

Pagliuca, W. and Mowrey, R. (1980), 'On certain evidence for the feature [grave]', *Language*, **56**, 503

Pellowe, J. and Jones, V. (1978), 'On intonational variability in Tyneside speech', in P. Trudgill, *Sociolinguistic Patterns in British English*, London: Edward Arnold

Pike, K. L. (1943), *Phonetics*, Ann Arbor: University of Michigan Press

Pike, K. L. (1945), *The Intonation of American English*, Ann Arbor: University of Michigan Press

Pointon G.E. (1980), 'Is Spanish syllable-timed?', *J. Phon.*, **8**, 293

Quirk, R. *et al.* (1973), *A Grammar of Contemporary English*, London: Longman

Roach, P. J. (1974), 'Glottalization of English /p, t, k, ʧ/', *J. Int. Phon. Assoc.*, **3**, 10

Rudes, B. A. (1976), 'Lexical representation and variable rules in Natural Generative Phonology', *Glossa*, **10**, 111

Sampson, G. (1970), 'On the need for a phonological base', *Language*, **46**, 586

Samuels, M. L. (1972), *Linguistic Evolution*, Cambridge: Cambridge University Press

Sanders, G. (1977), 'Equational rules and rule functions in phonology', in Dinnsen (ed.) (1971)

Sapir, E. (1970 (1921)), *Language*, London: Harcourt Brace World

Schane, S. A. (1968), *French Phonology and Morphology*, Cambridge, Mass.: MIT Press

Sebeok, T. (ed.) (1966), *Current Trends in Linguistics*, vol. 3, The Hague: Mouton

Shibatani, M. (1973), 'The role of surface phonetic constraints in generative phonology', *Language*, **49**, 87

Shockey, L. (1973), 'Phonetic and phonological properties of connected speech', PhD. thesis, Ohio State University

Skousen, R. (1973), 'Evidence in phonology', in Kisseberth (ed.) (1973)

Smith, N. V. (1973), *The Acquisition of Phonology*, Cambridge: Cambridge University Press

Sommerstein, A. H. (1977), *Modern Phonology*, London: Edward Arnold

Stampe, D. (1969), 'The acquisition of phonetic representation', Papers from 5th Regional Meeting of Chicago Linguistic Society, pp. 443–54

Stanley, R. (1967), 'Redundancy rules in phonology', *Language*, **43**, 393

Stockwell, R. P. and Macaulay, R. K. S. (eds.) (1972), *Linguistic Change and Generative Theory*, Bloomington: Indiana University Press

Strang, B. M. H. (1970), *A History of English*, London: Methuen

Tatham, M. A. A. (1980), 'Phonology and phonetics as part of the language encoding/decoding system', in N. Lass (ed.), *Speech and Language*, vol. 3, New York: Academic Press

Trager, G. L. and Smith, H. L. (1951), 'An outline of English structure', Norman, Oklahoma: *Studies in Linguistics, Occasional Paper 3*

Trubetskoy, N. S. (1969 (1939)), *Principles of Phonology*, trans. C. A. M. Balthaxe, Berkeley: University of California Press

Trudgill, P. (1974), *The Social Differentiation of English in Norwich*, Cambridge: Cambridge University Press

Trudgill, P. (ed.) (1978), *Sociolinguistic Patterns in British English*, London: Edward Arnold

Twaddell, W. F. (1935), 'On defining the phoneme', in Joos (ed.) (1957)

Umeda, N. and Coker, C. H. (1975), 'Subphonemic details in American English', in G. Fant and M. A. A. Tatham (eds.), *Auditory Analysis and Perception of Speech*, London: Academic Press

Valdman, A. (ed.) (1972), *Papers in Linguistics and Phonetics to the Memory of P. Delattre*, The Hague: Mouton

Van Riper, C. and Irwin, J. (1958), *Voice and Articulation*, Englewood Cliffs, NJ: Prentice Hall.

Wells, J. C. (1970), 'Local accents in English and Wales', *J. Ling.*, **6,** 231

Wells, J. C. (1982), *Accents of English*, 3 vols., Cambridge: Cambridge University Press

Wenk, B. J. and Wioland, F. (1982), 'Is French really syllable-timed?', *J. Phon.*, **10,** 193

Wilkinson, A. *et al.* (1977), *Spoken English*, Amsterdam: Swets and Zeitlinger

Wolfram, W. and Fasold, R. W. (1974), *The Study of Social Dialects in American English*, Englewood Cliffs, NJ: Prentice Hall

Zwicky, A. M. (1972), 'Note on a phonological hierarchy in English', in Stockwell and Macaulay (eds.) (1972)

Index